D0076043

SCHEDULING STRATEGIES FOR MIDDLE SCHOOLS

Michael D. Rettig
Robert Lynn Canady

EYE ON EDUCATION

EYE ON EDUCATION
6 DEPOT WAY WEST, SUITE 106
LARCHMONT, NY 10538
(914) 833–0551
(914) 833–0761 fax
www.eyeoneducation.com

Copyright © 2000 Eye On Education, Inc.
All Rights Reserved.

For information about permission to reproduce selections from this book, write: Eye On Education, Permissions Dept., Suite 106, 6 Depot Way West, Larchmont, NY 10538.

Library of Congress Cataloging-in-Publication Data

Rettig, Michael D., 1950–
    Scheduling Strategies for middle schools / by Michael D. Rettig and Robert Lynn Canady.
       p.   cm.
    Includes bibliographical references.
    ISBN 1-883001-67-6
    1. Block scheduling (Education)—United States. 2. Middle schools—United States.   I. Canady, Robert Lynn. II. Title

    LB3032.2 .R48 2000
    373.12'42—dc21

                                   99-059277

10 9 8 7 6 5 4 3

Editorial and production services provided by
Richard H. Adin Freelance Editorial Services
52 Oakwood Blvd., Poughkeepsie, NY 12603-4112
(914-471-3566)

Also Available from EYE ON EDUCATION

Teaching in the Block:
Strategies for Engaging Active Learners
Edited by Robert Lynn Canady and Michael D. Rettig

Block Scheduling:
A Catalyst for Change in High Schools
by Robert Lynn Canady and Michael D, Rettig

Supervision and Staff Development in the Block
by Sally Zepeda and R. Stewart Mayers

Socratic Seminars in the Block
by Wanda Ball and Pam Brewer

Teaching English in the Block
by Joe Strzepek, Jeffry Newton, and Dan Walker

Teaching Mathematics in the Block
by Susan Gilkey and Carla Hunt

Teaching Foreign Languages in the Block
by Deborah Blaz

Supporting Students with Learning Needs in the Block
by Conti-d'Antonio, Bertrando, and Eisenberger

Collaborative Learning in Middle and Secondary Schools
by Dawn Snodgrass and Mary Bevevino

Questions and Answers about Block Scheduling:
An Implementation Guide
by Donald D. Gainey and John M. Brucato

Encouraging Student Engagement in the Block Period
by David Marshak

Action Research on Block Scheduling
by David Marshak

The 4×4 Block Schedule
by J. Allen Queen and Kimberly Gaskey Isenhour

Best Practices from America's Middle Schools
by Charles R. Watson

The Interdisciplinary Curriculum
by Arthur Ellis and Carol Stuen

Banishing Anonymity:
Middle and High School Advisement Programs
by John Jenkins and Bonnie Daniel

The Paideia Classroom:
Teaching for Understanding
by Terry Roberts with Laura Billings

What Schools Should Do to Help Kids Stop Smoking
by William L. Fibkins

Staff Development:
Practices That Promote Leadership in Learning Communities
by Sally J. Zepeda

Performance Standards and Authentic Learning
by Allan A. Glatthorn

Performance Assessment and Standards-Based Curricula:
The Achievement Cycle
by Glatthorn, Bragaw, Dawkins, and Parker

Writing in the Content Areas
by Amy Benjamin

ABOUT THE AUTHORS

Michael D. Rettig currently is associate professor in the School of Education and Director of the Center for School Leadership at James Madison University in Harrisonburg, Virginia. He taught public school for 10 years in the Syracuse City Schools in New York and has served as an elementary and middle school administrator in two Virginia school districts.

During the past decade Mike has conducted workshops and seminars on the topic of school scheduling at over 50 national and state conferences. In addition, he has served as a consultant on school scheduling and instructional issues with over 300 school districts in 30 states.

Mike earned a Ph.D. in Educational Leadership and Policy Studies from the University of Virginia, a masters degree from SUNY at Cortland, and the bachelors degree from Syracuse University. Mike was named a University Scholar in 1972 by Syracuse University and was the recipient of the Phi Delta Kappa outstanding graduate student award in 1991 at the University of Virginia. In March 1999, Mike was named a Madison Scholar at James Madison University.

Mike and his wife, Sally, have a son, Dan, and a daughter, Anne, who currently are college students. Their daughter Alison attends high school in Albemarle County, Virginia.

Robert Lynn Canady currently is professor emeritus, University of Virginia and Senior Education Consultant, Center for State and National Programs for Educators, Continuing Education, University of Virginia. He received his Ed.D. degree from the University of Tennessee and his M.A. degree from Peabody-Vanderbilt, Nashville. His major publications have been in the areas of grading practices, implementing programs for at-risk students, and restructuring schools through block scheduling. He has served as a consultant in 36 states and with the Dependent Schools in Germany.

Lynn has taught in grades 4 through 12 and served as principal of elementary, middle and junior high schools in Tennessee and Kentucky. He also served in various supervisory positions in the central offices of the Chattanooga and Oak Ridge Schools in Tennessee.

In addition to receiving the Phi Delta Kappa Distinguished Service Award and the Outstanding Professor Award in the Curry School of Education, Lynn has received two university-wide awards for distinguished teaching and service at the University of Virginia. In June, 1997, he was presented the Lamp of Knowledge Award by the Virginia Association of Secondary School Principals (VASSP) and in 1998 he received the Educator of the Year Award by the Virginia Association of Supervision and Curriculum Development (VASCD).

Lynn and his wife, Marjorie, have four children—Carol C. Payne, Donna L. Canady, Robert G. Canady, and Sarah C. Schultz—all of whom completed their K–12 education in the public schools of Virginia.

Mike and Lynn have co-authored the following monograph and journal articles: "Unlocking the Lockstep High School Schedule," December, 1993, *Phi Delta Kappan*; "Restructuring Middle Level Schedules to Promote Equal Access," Summer, 1992, *Schools in the Middle*; "When Can I Have Your Kids? Scheduling Specialist Teachers," December, 1995, published as a National Association of Elementary School Principals (NASSP) "Here's How" monograph; "The Power of Innovative Scheduling," November, 1995, *Educational Leadership*; "High Failure Rates in Required Math Courses: Can a Modified Block Schedule Be Part of the Cure?", March, 1998, *NASSP Bulletin*; and "The Effects of Block Scheduling," March, 1999, *School Administrator*.

Their co-authored and co-edited books include: *Block Scheduling: A Catalyst for Change in High Schools*, 1995, and *Teaching in the Block*, 1996. They served as series editors for the following: *Teaching Mathematics in the Block*, 1998, by Susan N. Gilkey and Carla H. Hunt; *Supporting Students with Learning Needs in the Block*, 1998, by Marcia Conti-D'Antonio, Robert Bertrando and Joanne Eisenberger; *Teaching Foreign Languages in the Block*, 1998, by Deborah Blaz; *Socratic Seminars in the Block*, 2000, by Wanda H. Ball and Pam F. Brewer; and *Teaching English in the Block*, 2000, by Joseph E. Strzepek, Jeffry Newton, and L. Daniel Walker.

ACKNOWLEDGMENTS

We first thank the many teachers, administrators, parents, students and colleagues with whom we have worked and whose ideas and suggestions have helped shape this text. Specifically, we wish to thank Susan G. Smith for her review of literature related to the development of the middle school concept and for her doctoral study of three middle-level schools.

At James Madison University we wish to thank our colleagues Elizabeth D. Morie, Karen E. Santos, and Charles W. Watson for their continued interest, support, and encouragement. We also thank Dana Chmiel and Margaret Parker for their patient assistance.

At the University of Virginia we thank Harold J. Burbach for his friendship through the years and especially for his support while serving as Chair of the Department of Educational Leadership, Foundations and Policy. We also thank Paula Price, Donna Farnum, Peggy Powell and Rebecca (Becky) Burbach for their patience and valuable assistance. And last we express our appreciation to Nancy Iverson, Martha Ann Toms and Barbara E. Bragg from the University of Virginia Continuing Education Center for State and National Programs for Educators, for their many years of loyal support and encouragement. They not only have helped us with technical assistance, but they also have provided us with opportunities for workshops and conferences to help us develop and disseminate many of the ideas set forth in this book.

At Eye On Education we wish to thank Celia Bohannon, our editor, for making us appear to be better writers than we are. We also thank Bob Sickles, president of Eye On Education, for his patient persistence and support.

DEDICATION

We could never have completed this book without the support and encouragement of many people. We express our appreciation to our wives, Sally Rettig and Marjorie Canady, who nudged and cajoled us as wives know best how to do, and to our children—Danny, Anne, and Alison Rettig, and Carol, Donna, Robert, and Sarah Canady.

We also wish to dedicate this book to the thousands of teachers and administrators throughout the country who have permitted us to work in their middle schools during the past 37 years. We have found most middle school personnel to be extremely student-focused and to be caring, dedicated professionals. We wrote this book with them in mind.

TABLE OF CONTENTS

PREFACE

Since its inception during the 1960s, a major design component of the middle school has been flexible scheduling; too often, however, we have found that what many middle school principals and teachers call "flexible scheduling" provides a minimum amount of flexibility for both students and teachers. Instead, we often find a large number of students are rotated each day for a period of instructional time with each of their assigned team teachers and then to a period of time for an elective and some type of rotating exploratory wheel. It is not unusual to find middle school students reporting to 8 to 12 teachers each school year and to see middle school teachers who are assigned 135 to 180 students each school day. Occasionally we find a double period or block for reading and language arts, and in a few schools, a block of time for exploratories. This book will help middle school personnel who want to be more creative in designing their schedules.

Why write about middle school scheduling? As we stated in our 1995 book on high school block scheduling, we continue to believe that school scheduling is far more important to the success of an instructional program than the simple mechanical assignment of students to teachers and classes to spaces. Within the school schedule resides *power*: the power to address problems, the power to facilitate the successful implementation of programs, and the power to institutionalize effective instructional practices. As well, those who design the school schedule also have the power to create confusion, to waste resources, and to cause unnecessary stress for all school client groups.

We believe that too little thought and action have been given to the educational and emotional impact of a school schedule on the lives of students and teachers who must learn to function each day within the confines of the schedule. As we review 30-plus years of literature relative to the implementation of the middle school concept, we find that much was said about the importance of scheduling, but in reality we have found a lack of information on *how* to design the schedule talked about for middle schools. It is to that purpose we have written this book.

During the two and one-half years it has taken us to write this text, we have worked with thousands of middle and high school teachers and administrators in 40 states across the country. With the continued press for accountability and the documented high failure rates of students in grade 9, concerns are being expressed about the traditional philosophy and purpose of middle schools and the achievement levels of many middle school students. We believe middle schools need to question some of their organizational patterns and the amount of time scheduled for certain disciplines. We are not arguing against the original concepts and goals of middle schools; we do question, however, the way some of those concepts have been implemented. For example, we believe that the "balance" that exists among electives, exploratories and core classes such as English, mathematics, social studies and science, must be questioned. Also, we often find little integration of core with what some call "encore" or "non-core" classes.[1] Many exploratories have become mini-courses taught in isolation with little or no relationship to skills and content of other disciplines. We strongly believe that a well-designed middle school schedule, while not a panacea, *can be* a catalyst for several changes needed in middle schools across America.

Finally, we invite your comments and suggested improvements; we, too, are searching for the best schedule for middle school students and teachers. We hope this text will be a valuable contribution to your search.

Mike and Lynn
January, 2000

---

1 We prefer the term "encore" over "non-core," but both terms are used interchangeably in the literature. In this age of high stakes testing "core" typically is defined as language arts (including reading), mathematics, science, social studies, and sometimes foreign language. The terms *encore* and *non-core* refer to all other subjects.

1

THE CRITICAL ROLE OF SCHEDULING IN FULLY IMPLEMENTING MIDDLE SCHOOL PRACTICES

Schools designed specifically for middle-level students were implemented beginning in the mid-1960s. Since that time there has been a continuous trend away from the traditional junior high school that serves grades 7–9 toward middle school configurations, typically involving grades 6–8 (Viadero, 1996). In 1973, there were nearly four junior highs for every middle school; by 1993, there were approximately three middle schools for every remaining junior high (9,573 vs. 3,970) (National Center for Education Statistics, 1995). While there has been widespread adoption of the general concept of the "middle school," not all aspects of its philosophy have been implemented equally.

Despite the progress made during the past three decades toward the implementation of middle school philosophies and practices, such as interdisciplinary teaching teams, exploratory courses, and teacher-based guidance programs, the dominant form of scheduling continues to be daily periods of uniform duration rather than the more flexible scheduling patterns that middle school advocates endorse (Viadero, 1996). In this book, we advocate a reconsideration of the traditional scheduling arrangements and related practices of middle schools. Our thinking is guided by these eight questions:

1. What is an appropriate number of students a middle school teacher should see each day/term/year? Is there a relationship between how a teacher works with students and the number of students assigned to a teacher?

2. What is the appropriate number of teachers for middle school students to see each day/term/year? Is there a relationship between student behavior and "sense of belonging" and the

number of teachers a student is assigned during a day/term/ year?

3. What is the appropriate time balance between core and encore subjects? What factors should be considered in determining this balance?

4. What is the appropriate number of subjects in which a student should be enrolled during any one day/term/year? Is there a relationship between the number of classes for which students are responsible and their success in those classes?

5. How should exploratory classes be scheduled in relation to other subjects?

6. While many middle school schedules *on paper* show the possibility of flexibly combining single periods into longer instructional blocks, *in practice,* we find classes typically are taught in single periods. Does this practice make the middle school experience even more fragmented for both students and teachers? Does such practice create stress and make it difficult for teachers to implement some of the more productive teaching strategies?

7. With the growing diversity of school populations, do we need to plan schedules that permit extended learning time for those students who need additional time to meet course expectations?

8. Should a middle school schedule be compatible with elementary and high school schedules in the same feeder pattern?

As we reflected upon the roots and history of the middle school movement, we kept these key questions at the forefront of our consciousness.

BACKGROUND OF MIDDLE-LEVEL SCHOOLING

When the concept of middle schools was first proposed during the early 1960s, middle schools were seen as a bridge between elementary schools and the traditional high school. It was thought that the existing junior high schools were primarily mini-high schools organized for pre- and young adolescents. Most of the existing junior high schools and their parent high schools had fragmented 50- to 55-minute periods; departmentalized faculties; teacher-directed, lecture-style instruction; and class assignments that left students reshuffled each period, often attending classes with students thought to have similar abilities and academic prowess.

> *In terms of scheduling, what we now find in many middle schools is NOT students being reshuffled for six 50- to 55-minute periods but students being reshuffled 7 to 10 times each day for periods of 38 to 42 minutes. Is such a schedule consistent with what we know about middle school students? Is it consistent with middle school philosophy?*

Middle schools began in different parts of the country for various reasons. In the early days, middle schools were often a local response to a local need or initiative. In some communities, they were organized as a result of student population shifts; in other communities they were organized around space availability. Quite often a new high school was built and the old high school building became the middle school because middle school space, such as gymnasiums, did not require the same standards as high school space. In some sections of the country, middle schools with varying grade levels were offered as a way to deal with integration issues, such as sharing busing equally—for example, one school might be assigned all students in a particular district in grades 7 and 8, while another building site was assigned all students in grades 5 and 6; often both buildings would have the name "middle" somewhere in the title, while some simply were called intermediate schools. This early development of the middle school may have been more a product of the administrative needs of school districts than the instructional needs of students (Smith, 1998).

At about the same time, educational psychologists, sociologists, and educators were documenting the unique developmental characteristics of children approaching and beginning adolescence. For example, it was stated that children in the 10- to 15-year-old group undergo rapid physical, cognitive, emotional and social changes (Lawton, 1993). The rate and extent of growth of this age group is matched during a person's lifetime only between birth and age 3 (Lipsitz, 1984). It also was calculated that children are maturing physically at earlier ages than a few decades ago and that all these changes are factors that should be considered in how children learn (Crockett, 1995, cited in Smith, 1998). Middle schools became the organizational structure designed to teach children in what several writers referred to as the turbulent period of a child's life.

The flexibility of middle school programs, practices and organizational structures was seen to be more responsive to this identified age group than the traditional, somewhat rigid structures of junior high schools. The failure of junior high schools to be "needs responsive to students" again was invoked by Dennis Sabo in his study of middle school climate, as he reported that "middle schools were developed in response to the failure of junior high schools to address the growing knowledge of the needs of early adolescence" (1995, p. 157). It was even stated that middle schools were seen as an opportunity to "re-organize in support of good teaching" (National Education Association, 1966).

> *In view of the above statements, how can we continue to justify short, choppy periods of time as being "needs responsive to middle school students"—and, we might add, "needs responsive to middle school teachers?" How can such a scheduling format support what we know to be good teaching? How do teachers in a daily, single-period schedule engage middle school students in active learning strategies? In short time periods, how do middle school teachers make the best use of technology in today's classrooms?*

The current acceptance of the term and grade grouping known as "middle school" by a majority of school districts across the country is well established. It generally is accepted that middle schools were defined by William Alexander, a recognized leader of the middle school movement, as schools containing grade levels between grades 5 and 8 (Smith, 1998). As recapped in the most recent publication of its basic position paper, *This We Believe: Developmentally Responsive Middle Schools,* the National Middle School Association advocates middle schools that are characterized by:

- Educators committed to young adolescents,
- A shared vision,
- High expectations for all,
- An adult advocate for every student,
- Family and community partnerships, and
- A positive school climate (NMSA,1995).

> *Is a middle school schedule an important factor in providing students with: (1) an adult advocate; (2) a need to belong, which appears to be even more important for today's middle school students than it was 30 years ago; and (3) a positive school climate?*

Such schools would provide:

- Curriculum that is challenging, integrative and exploratory,
- Varied teaching and learning approaches,

♦ Assessment and evaluation that promote learning,

♦ Flexible organizational structures,

♦ Programs that foster health, wellness and safety, and

♦ Comprehensive guidance and support services (NMSA, 1995).

> *If middle schools are to offer curriculum that is challenging, integrative and exploratory, varied in teaching and learning approaches, flexible in structure, and comprehensive in guidance and support services, what would be a defensible scheduling format to facilitate the achievement of such goals? Is the school's schedule an important factor in facilitating the achievement of such goals? Does reshuffling middle school students every day in 7 to 10 single periods of different disciplines facilitate the achievement of these such goals?*

BRIDGING THE GAP BETWEEN BELIEF AND PRACTICE: THE ROLE OF SCHEDULING IN IMPLEMENTING EXEMPLARY MIDDLE SCHOOLS

As we examine the major premises of the middle school movement and match those goals with what we know about teaching and learning, we find little disagreement about what constitutes good education for middle-level students. There are, however, gaps between some of the concepts as described in the literature and what we observe in the daily operations of many middle schools throughout the country. Too often there is a gap between what middle school advocates say they believe regarding "flexible organizational structures" (NMSA, 1995) and the actual middle school schedules utilized throughout the country. We believe that several of the discrepancies between stated middle school beliefs and actual practices have their roots in the school schedule.

It is the schedule that gives teachers sustained instructional periods of time with students; until that time is provided, it is very difficult, if not impossible, for teachers to involve students in the integrated, active, relevant, and application-oriented activities, such as cooperative learning, Socratic seminars, effective use of technology and project-based learning, recommended by middle school advocates (Allen, Splittgerber, & Manning, 1993; Crockett, 1995, cited in Smith, 1998; Doda & George, 1999; George & Alexander, 1993; Lipsitz, 1984; Rafferty, Leinenbach, & Helms, 1999; Scales, 1999; Wiles & Bondi, 1993).

> *If we truly believe middle school instructional practices should include cooperative learning, individual and group projects, and active learning activities, what type of schedule can best facilitate such instructional strategies?*

The organization of teachers into interdisciplinary "teams" is another defining aspect of a middle school (Alexander, 1987; Allen et al., 1993; George & Alexander, 1993; Doda & George, 1999). Grouping teachers into interdisciplinary or modified interdisciplinary teams facilitates the planning and delivery of integrated thematic units. The collaboration on student management and discipline issues is enabled when teacher teams work and plan together on a regular basis.

If implemented correctly, one of the most important benefits of the team concept in the middle school is the relatively small number of teachers and students with whom an individual student must interact. It can be argued that the developmental needs of the young adolescent who is transitioning from a self-contained elementary classroom are better served with a limited number of teacher contacts during any one day/term/year. The schedule design determines the structure and membership of teams; without careful attention to schedule design the benefits of teaming can be lost or diluted.

> *If we believe that middle school students should have a limited number of teacher contacts during any one day/term/year, what does such a belief imply for scheduling? What are we likely to find today in schools operating with a single-period format?*

One of the few absolutely consistent components of a true middle school is the "flexible schedule" (Lipsitz, 1984; Alexander, 1987; George et al., 1992; Allen et al., 1993; George & Alexander, 1993; Wiles & Bondi, 1993). It is through the schedule that administrators begin to meet the important goals of middle school and to respond to the needs of the students (Lipsitz, 1984). It is the schedule that provides a more reasonable workload for teachers and students (Carroll, 1994a, 1994b). It is the schedule that determines the number of students/grades/records for which a teacher must be responsible during any one day/term/year. It is the schedule that can reduce how frequently students and teacher teams change classes (Hackmann, 1995). It is the schedule that determines how many teachers a student must interact with on any given day/term/year.

It is the schedule that can fundamentally affect the relationship among staff and between staff and students (Carter, 1995).

Conversely, however, the school schedule, rather than serving as a positive element in the learning environment, can make teaching and learning more difficult. It is important, therefore, to craft the schedule so that it encourages rather than hinders instructional flexibility. The school schedule can be seen as an infrastructure that either enables or restricts every other aspect of the school's life. When structure and intentions are in conflict, structure rather than intent is likely to dominate (Eisner, 1988). As a classroom teacher was overheard to say: "The schedule is God. You can implement any innovation you want in your classroom as long as you don't mess with the schedule" (Watts & Castle, 1993).

The school schedule is a critical piece of the middle school puzzle, essential to the picture of a student-centered, innovative school that is responsive to the needs of students, teachers, and the community. Programs and practices related to curriculum, instruction, and pupil services are either blunted or thwarted altogether if the *time* for them is not provided efficiently and effectively. This may be why middle school advocates continue to point to the need to improve the school organizational structure. The call to "restructure" middle schools is actually a call to put in practice the concepts and recommendations for instructional practices and scheduling strategies that have been emerging since the 1960s.

This book will help educators responsible for middle-level schooling to answer that call. Flexible block scheduling is a tool for implementing these practices.

REVISITING FLEXIBLE SCHEDULING IN MIDDLE SCHOOL: EXPLORING EIGHT QUESTIONS

From its early days, there has been a lack of detail regarding what specifically is meant by "flexible scheduling" in the middle school. Based on our research and experience in working with hundreds of middle schools throughout the country, we return to the eight defining questions:

1. What is an appropriate number of students a middle school teacher should see each day/term/year? Is there a relationship between how a teacher works with students and the number of students assigned to a teacher?

It is not unusual for middle school teachers to work with 135 to 180 students each day. Most middle schools are organized into interdisciplinary teaching teams, and on a daily basis, each teacher typically instructs 5 or 6 groups of students assigned to the team as the students rotate in groups of 20 to 35 through the schedule. We contend that as long as middle school teachers are assigned to work with such a large number of students daily, they will have difficulty serving students in the personal ways that middle school advocates promote.

In high schools with block schedules where teachers work with only three classes per semester, students often comment: "This year the teacher takes more personal interest in me." "Now the teacher makes me come after school and complete my work." "Yesterday the teacher took me outside the room and talked with me; last year she just lowered my grade."

School policymakers must decide what an appropriate teacher load is, basing the decision on a range of considerations, including the ability of students to deal with a variety of adults at this stage of their development, the need for teacher specialization, the psychological effect on teachers, and the cost. Is it possible to design middle school schedules that also limit the number of students with whom teachers work?

2. What is the appropriate number of teachers for middle school students to see each day/term/year? Is there a relationship between student behavior and "sense of belonging" and the number of teachers a student is assigned during a day/term/year?

In a typical middle school team, usually consisting of English, mathematics, science, and social studies teachers, it is not unusual for students to have a single-period class with each team member, plus exposure during the year to four to six exploratory teachers, one or two elective teachers, such as band and Spanish, and one or two physical education teachers; hence, a typical middle school student, particularly in grades 7 and 8, may have 8 to 12 different teachers during a school year. For example, we once worked with a middle school that operated a six-period schedule. Students had four core classes daily; in the remaining two periods, six-week wheels were scheduled. Consequently, students interacted with a total of 16 different teachers (4 core and 12 encore teachers) over the course of the year. We ask the question: Under such an arrangement, what happens to a student's sense of belonging and security?

We also wonder: If students had fewer teachers each day, would the typical teacher advisor/advisee programs, which are strongly advocated in middle schools, be as necessary? Our question should not imply that we are opposed to *quality* advisor/advisee programs. But based on our observations, and on many teacher comments, some current advisor/advisee programs are artificial and ineffective. We contend that if teachers are inclined to be effective advisors, and if they work with no more than two or three groups of students each day for extended blocks of time, then teachers will provide the needed security and advice to students during their classes and will not need to have a group of students sent to them for 20 to 30 minutes for an advisor/advisee period.

3. What is the appropriate time balance between core and encore subjects? What factors should be considered in determining this balance?

In our work with middle schools across the country, we often ask this question: What percentage of middle school students' time in school should be spent studying these subjects: language arts (including reading), mathematics, social studies, and science? Answer the question yourself. Of course, there is no single "right" answer—and yet the open discussion of our responses is often uncomfortable, for we recognize that the school schedule is the practical expression of the value we place on certain school endeavors. When we allocate two periods daily to language arts, we say that we value skill in this area more than skill in mathematics or science. When we allocate a daily period each to mathematics and physical education, we say, in effect, that they are of relatively equal importance.

Remember, again, that there is no correct allocation; this is a matter for debate, negotiation and decision-making among policymakers. With regard to the schedule, however, school administrators and teachers often wield a great deal of influence as to this division of time.

Back to our question. The most frequent answer given is that 75 percent of a middle school student's time in school should be spent studying language arts, mathematics, social studies, and science. Yet, it is not unusual in many middle schools to find that less than 50 percent of the day is spent in these subjects. We worked in one large school district which operates seven 47-minute periods in nearly all of its middle schools. The school day begins at 7:30 AM and ends at 2:20 PM, a total of 410 minutes. Seventh and eighth grade students are enrolled in these courses: English, mathematics, social studies, science, physical education, and two electives. Consequently, students spend four 47-minute periods, or 188 minutes daily, studying the basic core of schooling—well less than half of the available time.

One could argue that this computation is unfair; we have included the unavoidable lunch period, class change, and home room time in our allocation. Even so, four of seven classes constitutes only 57 percent of the available instructional periods—far less than 75 percent.

Recent criticism of the middle school is focused on the performance of students on standardized tests. In March 1998, the Southern Regional Education Board (SREB) reported: "The middle grades—grades five through eight—are the weak link in American education. Nowhere is the link more fragile than in the states served by the Southern Regional Education Board." The National Assessment of Educational Progress statistics analyzed by the SREB reveal these facts about the middle grades in the states served by SREB:

+ "Almost 50 percent of eighth graders are below the basic level in math;

+ Even in the highest performing SREB states (Maryland, Texas, and Virginia), more than 40 percent of eighth graders are below the basic level; and

+ In the two lowest performing SREB states (Louisiana and Mississippi), nearly two-thirds of eighth graders are below the basic level." (SREB, 1998, p. 1)

We also question whether middle school personnel can continue to ignore what is happening academically to so many students during their first year in high school. Is it possible that middle schools have placed too much emphasis on what some call non-core courses? Based on our work in 40 states, we find that the school grade level having one of the highest failure rates in the country is grade 9. In Virginia, during the 1995–96 school year 13.2 percent of all ninth grade students were retained, nearly double the rate of any other grade level (Virginia Department of Education, 1996). Algebra I seems to lead the list of courses failed, with English 9 a close second.

Some suggest that the poor performance of middle school students on standardized tests and the high failure rate of ninth grade students is proof that the middle school concept is seriously flawed (Bradley, 1998). In response to the SREB report that middle schools are the "weak link" in education, Beane (1999) concludes:

> ...[T]oward the end of the Southern Board's report, the authors describe "high" and "low" performing middle schools in such a way that the former are said to use almost exactly the kind of practices promoted by middle school advocates while the latter are said to use practices middle school advocates typically oppose. (p. 5)

This implies that greater fidelity in the implementation of the middle school concept and practices may result in better performance. In fact, one longitudinal study of middle schools in Illinois suggests that when these concepts are implemented as an integrated set of practices, students' achievement and behavior improve significantly over time (Felner et al., 1997).

We believe in the basic middle school concept and the instructional practices advocated for middle schools. We are concerned, however, with the allocation and organization of time during the school day. Could it be that part of the problem with middle school and ninth grade students' academic performance is the amount of time devoted to these tested subjects? Remember, it is not unusual to find that less than half the school day is spent in English, mathematics, science, and social studies. Does this finding suggest that it would be beneficial to middle school students if, at least for selected students, more time were given to mathematics, reading, and writing? This question becomes even more relevant in states where students are required to pass high-stakes, standards-based tests to be promoted and, ultimately, to graduate (Marsh, 1999, Chap. 6). Could it be that the use of instructional approaches recommended by middle school advocates is nearly impossible in 40-minute periods? Would these practices have a greater level of implementation if schools operated schedules with longer class periods?

4. What is the appropriate number of subjects in which a student should be enrolled during any one day/term/year? Is there a relationship between the number of classes for which students are responsible and their success in those classes?

While the specifics vary from state to state, during the past 15 years numerous courses have been mandated for middle school students. For example, in addition to the traditional four core courses, we often find required courses such as health, technology, foreign language, computer literacy, home economics, and family living. We wonder if middle school students are being expected to deal with too many subjects, often presented in fragmented ways, during a school day or year? In terms of what we know about the characteristics and problems of the middle school student (Lawton, 1993; Carnegie Council on Adolescent Development, 1996, 1989, 1990; George & Alexander, 1993), do we need to revisit what we are asking a 13-year-old student to do, which, in many middle schools, is to be responsible for eight or nine different classes, notebooks, texts, tests, and other class requirements, often every school day? As teachers, would we oppose such expectations for ourselves?

5. How should exploratory classes be taught in relation to other subjects?

It is our understanding that originally exploratory classes were to be what the term implies—an opportunity to explore, to gather information on which to make later decisions—not just another shorter course (Alexander & George, 1981, pp. 61–63; George & Alexander, 1993, pp. 73–76). The initial idea of exploratory classes in the middle school was to offer students a pyramid of experiences (see Figure 6.1, p. 138); for example, maybe in grade 6, six weeks of French, six weeks of Spanish, and six weeks of German. In grade 7, a student who was particularly interested in Spanish might choose nine weeks of Spanish and in grade 8 possibly a semester or a full year of Spanish. Similar pyramids could be built for art, music, and technology opportunities.

We contend that many exploratory courses have become, over time, more like regular classes with homework, tests, notebooks, and grades, except they are scheduled for fewer weeks. Such classes rarely are integrated with or even supportive of the core curriculum. This creates a situation, especially in states with high-stakes testing programs, in which core and encore teachers are placed in opposition to each other, competing for time in the schedule and instructional resources. In their plea to close the gap between exploratory and core classes, Doda and George (1999) state:

> ...[M]ore often than not, teachers in special or exploratory, or unified arts of the curriculum find themselves on the fringes of middle school innovations, especially interdisciplinary teaming. With approximately 55 percent of our nation's middle level schools organized in interdisciplinary teaching teams (McEwin, Dickinson, & Jenkins, 1996) and poised for the promise of cross-disciplinary collaboration, one might expect that in at least a small percentage of these middle schools, collaboration across all subject-area boundaries would be practiced. While some of these schools have teams that engage in varying degrees of interdisciplinary and integrated curriculum planning, the presence of interdisciplinary team organization in middle schools has not guaranteed such collaborative communication between what have come to be called the core and the non-core staff. (Burnaford, 1993)

Before constructing any schedule, the roles of and connections between core and encore teachers must be clarified.

6. While many middle school schedules *on paper* show the possibility of flexibly combining single periods into longer instructional blocks, *in practice*, we find classes typically are taught in single periods. Does this practice make the middle school experience even more fragmented for both students and teachers? Does such practice create stress and make it difficult for teachers to implement some of the more productive teaching strategies?

While many middle schools have been capable of providing blocks of time for instruction, most continue to meet classes for 40 to 50 minutes daily. According to Epstein and MacIver (1990) only 19 percent of middle schools employed flexible scheduling, making this the least implemented of all recommended middle school practices. It is not unusual to find a middle school student in a typical day going to at least seven or eight different classrooms, having seven or eight different teachers with varying expectations, and never having more than 4 minutes to go to his or her locker or to go to the bathroom! How many adults would look forward to such a routine for 180 days of the year? Is such a pace consistent with what we know about this age student?

The following statement, made recently during a conversation with a colleague, expresses the frustrations of at least one middle school teacher: "Everything is so disjointed. The students go from math, then to science, then to....Nothing is connected. And in 45 minutes they shut down science and then go to English. It must be very frustrating to the students. It certainly is to me, and I get two periods off!"

Gallagher (1999) summarized the impetus for block scheduling as follows:

> Although time is always in short supply during the school day, the bigger problem seems to lie in its distribution. When so many subjects are crunched into small time slots, schools tend to operate more like factories on overdrive than as centers of reflective learning. Given the amount of each class period that is devoted to housekeeping—attendance, assignments, and homework collection—teachers have very limited instructional time with students. For example, a 1984 study by researchers at Southwest Texas State University found that on average only 28 minutes of a 50-minute period at the high schools they evaluated were devoted to teaching. (p. 11)

We contend that as long as middle school schedules are built around single periods, much of what we just described will continue. Yes, a few teams in a school may make adjustments and combine two or three periods, but over time the trend is to send students to a different teacher and classroom for each period in the scheduled day. It is simply all too easy a pattern for schools to drift into.

We believe that to be consistent with what we know about middle school students, schedules must be built around blocks of time that limit the number of movements and teacher contacts that can be made in a single day.

7. With the growing diversity of school populations, do we need to plan schedules that permit extended learning time for those students who need additional time to meet course expectations?

With the growing diversity in most school populations today (Marsh, 1999, Chap. 5), we contend that schedules must be created that allow for varying time frames for students to master course content (see Chapter 8 of this book). Also, with the move toward end-of-course tests and other high-stakes examinations in the United States, it is necessary for students to do more than just "cover material" and "get a grade!"[1] We also contend that students should be allotted more time to master material, when necessary, without first having to fail a course. For years we have been willing to give students extended learning time—if they were willing to fail first. We should offer schedules that permit early interventions when students are struggling to master content.

8. Should a middle school schedule be compatible with elementary and high school schedules in the same feeder pattern?

While we understand the particular interest educators have in issues facing their specific level of schooling, we must consider the implications of our decisions within the entire span of K–12 (or perhaps K–16) educational practice. Doesn't a sixth grade student have more in common with a fifth grade student than with an eighth grade student? Perhaps the sixth grade schedule should resemble the elementary schedule more than the schedule designed for eighth grade students. Maybe the eighth grade schedule should more closely mirror the high school plan than the middle school schedule.

Our system of education is particularly inept at managing transitions from level to level of schooling. The result is a well-documented drop in academic performance in the transition years of sixth and ninth grades (Alspaugh, 1998). We believe that considerable thought should be given to planning for these transitions and conceptualizing a more seamless articulation between levels.

To accomplish this formidable challenge we must begin to think within the K–12 context on a variety of issues. For example, earlier we asked: What is the appropriate number of teachers for middle school students to see each day/term/year? This question must be answered within the context of what has happened in elementary school and what will happen in high school. Does it make sense to schedule a sixth grade student with eight different teachers every day, when previously they were exposed to only one or two teachers daily?

Another issue relates attention span to recommended class length. If we adopted class period length simply on the basis of students' relative attention spans, we would provide the shortest classes to kindergarten students and the longest to seniors in high school. Illogically, just the opposite is true; kindergarten students work on a "block" schedule, staying for 6 hours with the same teacher, while high school students are rotated through eight or nine 40-minute periods. Other issues that must be con-

---

1 For additional references on this issue, see Canady and Hotchkiss, 1989; Rettig and Canady, 1998; and Chapters 7 and 8 of this book.

sidered along a developmental continuum include the number of subjects and different expectations students can juggle; the number of students in classes; the length of the school day; the time of the day school is conducted; the need for bathroom breaks; and the need for relevancy and application.

We use these questions to reconceptualize the needs of middle school students and the influence the schedule may have in addressing these needs. With these questions in mind, we describe a variety of schedules in this book.

SCHEDULING DESIGN CONSIDERATIONS

The schedules in this book are designed to address the following issues, which are identified with many middle schools in operation today:

- ◆ In all the proposed schedules, thoughtful consideration was given to the number of students each teacher works with during a school day/term/year and the number of teachers a middle school student reports to during a school day/term/year.

- ◆ In all the proposed schedules, we support some form of teaming for teachers and students. Teaming has been an integral part of the middle school concept from the beginning. In some cases, we propose two-teacher teams, especially for students in the lower grades of a middle-level school. Essentially, we believe that students should be introduced gradually to a larger number of teachers as they move through the grade levels. In some cases, we schedule the traditional four-member interdisciplinary team; in other situations, we schedule modified interdisciplinary teams, such as a two-member teacher team of English/language arts and social studies, paired, for example, on a Day 1/Day 2 basis, with a two-teacher team of mathematics and science.

We also support the idea of Rotating Arts Teams, which, in the early days of middle school programs, often were referred to as RAT teams. The RAT team is a way to reduce the fragmentation in middle school teams and to reduce the number of students special teachers see each week. In a RAT configuration, selected special teachers are assigned to a particular team on a rotating basis for a designated period of time; an example might be assigning an art teacher to a team for 9 weeks and then moving the teacher to another team for 9 weeks. Such assignments usually result in improved integration of core and encore curriculum. To maximize the chances of such integra-

tion occurring, Doda and George (1999) suggest that in advance of teacher assignments the following should occur:

> It is necessary for the entire staff to draft a general curric-
> ulum map which includes all fields. The process of
> school-wide curriculum mapping is an extremely useful
> way to revisit curriculum across the child's day in an ef-
> fort to pull the fragmented puzzle pieces together. Once
> the map is drafted, exploratory staff can anticipate core
> team units of study and align non-core units accordingly.
> This would also be enormously helpful to ESL, special
> education, and media staff in the school who are eager to
> learn of team curriculum plans in advance. Without
> shared planning time, such rotating team alliances bring
> exploratory teachers into the core curriculum conversa-
> tion and away from the periphery. (p. 35)

♦ We support the concept of block scheduling, in various forms,
throughout all the proposed schedules. We believe "blocking"
is the primary way to give middle schools the flexibility recommended in the middle school literature. Blocking also reduces some of the "madness" we see in middle schools with
students being reshuffled every 40 to 50 minutes during the
school day. If middle school students are to experience the
"hands-on," active type of learning described extensively in
the literature, teachers must have time to prepare and to engage students in those types of teaching strategies. Rick
Wormeli (1999), who was named the nation's top English
teacher at the 1996 Disney American Teaching Awards, reported that "…longer class periods gave me the opportunity
to step out of the darkness, as Plato described in his story,
'Cave Allegory,' to the bright illumination of meaning. I now
have the time to teach to the rhythm of my training and experience instead of to the tick of the classroom clock" (p. 17). Also,
as the availability of technology is increased in middle
schools, extended time periods are needed to make best use of
such resources in classrooms.

♦ We believe that the traditional exploratory programs existing
in most middle schools today need to be reexamined. Too often such programs are disjointed, have little relevance to core
content, and are not designed to offer students ways to build
on a special interest area each year they are in middle school.
The original idea of exploratories, as presented by Alexander
and George (1981, pp. 61–63) should be implemented with
greater fidelity. Students should begin in the middle school

with 6 to 9 weeks of study in four to six areas, such as Spanish, family living, art, or technology, for the purpose of *exploring* each topic to see whether further study is wanted. During the following school year, the student might choose two or three of these topics to explore in greater depth. During the third year of middle school a student then might choose a full semester or a full year of one or two subjects, such as Spanish and/or technology. This hierarchical plan of exploratories is different from the series of academic mini-courses that many exploratory programs have become.

♦ Several of the schedules proposed in this book offer a greater allocation of time for some core classes. We realize we are introducing the "ugly head" of a long-time clash between core and encore classes. Our own feelings are that we prefer not to put one set of classes in competition with another set of classes or to imply that a class in math is more important than a music class; however, we also must admit that now, in many states, the "real world" is that the number of classes being required for graduation is increasing. In addition to being required to complete more courses, there is a growing trend to require students to pass barrier examinations in order to receive passing course grades, and ultimately to graduate (Marsh, 1999, Chap. 6). If such are the requirements for students, is it fair to students not to recognize and to address those issues during the middle school years?

This book uses four basic scheduling formats that can be adapted to create a huge variety of middle school schedules. Each chapter introduces the basic scheduling format for a particular design, develops adaptations for a variety of specific situations, and offers advantages and disadvantages of each schedule.

Chapter 2 shows how instructional blocks may be built from 20- to 30-minute modules of time. Chapter 3 illustrates how single periods may be combined to form alternate-day (A/B) block schedules. Chapters 4 and 5 demonstrate the development of four-block and five-block middle school schedules. Chapter 6 describes several different formats for scheduling exploratory and elective classes.

In addition to the basic block schedule designs illustrated, Chapters 7 and 8 show numerous modifications to the schedules that reduce class size and vary the amount of learning time, whether for enrichment or to increase the chances that selected students are able to complete core requirements successfully.

Finally, Chapter 9 addresses the all-important issue of "teaching in the block." We continue to believe that "regardless of a school's time schedule, what happens between individual teachers and students in class-rooms is still most important, and simply altering the manner in which we schedule schools will not ensure better instruction by teachers or in-creased learning by students" (Canady & Rettig, 1995b, p. 240).

2

ADAPTING PRINCIPLES OF MODULAR SCHEDULING FOR THE MIDDLE SCHOOL

A simple way to build a middle school block schedule is to first determine a specific number of time modules possible in a school day; next schedule the activities that must occur outside of team time and then permit teachers on each team to create their own schedule from the remaining time modules. This chapter gives the basic overview of how this type of schedule can be built; we then provide a detailed school schedule utilizing this scheduling format.

To build a block schedule from modules of time, we suggest that one first determine the shortest period of time used throughout the school day. This might be a lunch period of 30 or 40 minutes or an advisor/advisee period of 25 or 30 minutes. The second step is to decide what is the total number of time modules available in the school day. For example, if you determine that you are going to work with 30-minute time modules—possibly because you want lunch periods to be 30 minutes each, and all classes are to be in multiples of 30 (30 minutes, 60, minutes, 90 minutes, etc.). If you have a 390-minute school day, then there are 13 modules of time (13×30) from which to build the schedule. If you have a 400-minute day, you might still work with 13 modules of time, possibly adding 10 minutes to the first block of time to give extra time for homeroom duties. If you have a 400-minute day and desire to have an advisor/advisee period of 25 minutes and also lunch periods of 25 minutes, you could build a schedule using 16 modules of time (16×25).

In Figure 2.1 (p. 20), the basic format for designing a modular block schedule based on 30-minute modules is illustrated for a school that has two teaching teams at each of the three grade levels, a 30-minute homeroom and/or advisory period, and 420 total minutes in the school day.

FIGURE 2.1. MIDDLE SCHOOL MODULAR MASTER SCHEDULE USING 30-MINUTE MODULES—420 TOTAL MINUTES

Team	Team 6-A	Team 6-B	Team 7-A	Team 7-B	Team 8-A	Team 8-B	PE/Expls	EEE
Mod	Homeroom/Advisory (30 minutes)							
1	1	1	1	1	1	1	Plan	1
2	2	2	2	2	2	2	Plan	2
3	3	3	EEE	EEE	PLAN, PE, & EXPLs	PLAN, PE, & EXPLs	Teams 8-A & 8-B	EEE Grade 7
4	4	4	EEE	EEE	PLAN, PE, & EXPLs	PLAN, PE, & EXPLs	Teams 8-A & 8-B	EEE Grade 7
5	Lunch	Lunch	5	5	PLAN, PE, & EXPLs	PLAN, PE, & EXPLs	Teams 8-A & 8-B	5
6	EEE	EEE	6	6	Lunch	Lunch	Lunch	EEE Grade 6
7	EEE	EEE	Lunch	Lunch	7	7	Plan	EEE Grade 6
8	7	7	PLAN, PE, & EXPLs	PLAN, PE, & EXPLs	8	8	Teams 7-A & 7-B	8
9	9	9	PLAN, PE, & EXPLs	PLAN, PE, & EXPLs	9	9	Teams 7-A & 7-B	9
10	10	10	PLAN, PE, & EXPLs	PLAN, PE, & EXPLs	EEE	EEE	Teams 7-A & 7-B	EEE Grade 8
11	PLAN, PE, & EXPLs	PLAN, PE, & EXPLs	11	11	EEE	EEE	Teams 6-A & 6-B	EEE Grade 8
12	PLAN, PE, & EXPLs	PLAN, PE, & EXPLs	12	12	12	12	Teams 6-A & 6-B	12
13	PLAN, PE, & EXPLs	PLAN, PE, & EXPLs	13	13	13	13	Teams 6-A & 6-B	13

Note: Each mod represents 30 minutes. If lunch can be 25 minutes, then this plan could be designed using sixteen 25-minute modules, which adds 30 minutes in the school day for core classes.

PE and exploratory classes meet for 90-minute blocks every other day (EOD). Electives, extended learning time, and enrichment classes (EEE) meet in 60-minute periods.

All numbered modules represent time for which core teachers plan instruction. With this plan, core teachers have control over their time; for example, they may want to schedule more reading and math time for some students than for other students.

The first step in building a schedule from time modules probably should be to mark all the modules needed for lunch periods. In Figure 2.1, Teams 6-A and 6-B go to lunch during Mod 5, Teams 8-A and 8-B during Mod 6, and Teams 7-A and 7-B during Mod 7. If six lunch periods were needed, depending on when the earliest lunch could be scheduled, lunch periods might be scheduled during Mods 4, 5, 6, 7, 8, and 9.

After all lunch periods are appropriately placed in the master schedule, it is best to determine next when team-planning periods can occur. In Figure 2.1, shaded rectangles show that Teams 6-A and 6-B have planning during modules 11, 12, and 13; teams 7-A and 7-B plan during modules 8, 9, and 10; and Teams 8-A and 8-B plan during modules 3, 4, and 5. Here all teams have a planning block consisting of three 30-minute modules, for a total of 90 minutes. When assigning the planning blocks, care must be taken to avoid overlaps; also teams should not be left with one module between a planning block and another scheduled out-of-team activity, such as lunch, because such time is often wasted. The goal is to give all teams at least two or three large blocks (90 minutes or longer) each day, which team members can schedule based on the instructional needs of students and the instructional goals of the particular unit being studied.

In the school shown in Figure 2.1, the "triple E" periods (EEE), consisting of two modules for a total of 60 minutes, are for band and foreign language; these may meet daily or on alternate days. Students not taking band and/or a foreign language during the year could take either another elective or a series of exploratories. We recommend, however, that this be a time to provide students with additional *electives*, *extended* learning time, and *enrichment*; students selected on an individual basis for this period of assistance could be determined by members of each team. For example, 7-A team members may decide that this is a time to regroup selected students for 5 days to rewrite their research papers under the direction of their language arts teacher; the science teacher may want 17 students to return during this period until their science fair projects are completed; and the math teacher may choose to work with 15 students having difficulty with a particular math concept. The social studies teacher might take any remaining students (after band and language students have been assigned to classes) for an enrichment activity lasting 5 days.

CREATING A MODULAR SCHEDULE

Figure 2.2 is a blank worksheet for developing a middle school modular block schedule. Using this tool, we can create a modular schedule based on 16 modules of time consisting of 25 minutes each.

FIGURE 2.2. MIDDLE SCHOOL MODULAR MASTER SCHEDULE WORKSHEET USING 25-MINUTE MODULES—420 TOTAL MINUTES

Mod	Team 6-A	Team 6-B	Team 7-A	Team 7-B	Team 8-A	Team 8-B
Homeroom/Advisory (20 minutes)						
1	1	1	1	1	1	1
2	2	2	2	2	2	2
3	3	3	3	3	3	3
4	4	4	4	4	4	4
5	5	5	5	5	5	5
6	6	6	6	6	6	6
7	7	7	7	7	7	7
8	8	8	8	8	8	8
9	9	9	9	9	9	9
10	10	10	10	10	10	10
11	11	11	11	11	11	11
12	12	12	12	12	12	12
13	13	13	13	13	13	13
14	14	14	14	14	14	14
15	15	15	15	15	15	15
16	16	16	16	16	16	16

STEP 1: PLACE LUNCH PERIODS

In our example, we created six 25-minute lunch periods instead of the three 30-minute periods shown in Figure 2.1 (p. 20). One argument for the shorter lunch period is that it reduces the amount of time students wait in line to be served; however, a major argument against the plan is that teachers have only 25 minutes for lunch. Schools employing this plan tend to give teachers additional planning time to compensate for the shorter lunch break.

We begin by assigning lunch periods by teams (Figure 2.3). Because our sample school begins at 8:30, with homeroom until 8:50, we start lunch with Team 6-A in module 5 (beginning at 10:30) and end with Team 8-B in module 10 (ending at 1:00). If school begins earlier at 8:00, one simple way to avoid beginning lunch at 10:00 is to slide up one module, taking modules 6 to 11 for lunch.

FIGURE 2.3. STEP 1: DETERMINE LUNCH PERIODS

Time	Mod	Team 6-A	Team 6-B	Team 7-A	Team 7-B	Team 8-A	Team 8-B
8:30	Homeroom/Advisory (20 minutes)						
8:50	1	1	1	1	1	1	1
9:15	2	2	2	2	2	2	2
9:40	3	3	3	3	3	3	3
10:05	4	4	4	4	4	4	4
10:30	5	Lunch	5	5	5	5	5
10:55	6	6	Lunch	6	6	6	6
11:20	7	7	7	Lunch	7	7	7
11:45	8	8	8	8	Lunch	8	8
12:10	9	9	9	9	9	Lunch	9
12:35	10	10	10	10	10	10	Lunch
1:00	11	11	11	11	11	11	11
1:25	12	12	12	12	12	12	12
1:50	13	13	13	13	13	13	13
2:15	14	14	14	14	14	14	14
2:40	15	15	15	15	15	15	15
3:05–3:30	16	16	16	16	16	16	16

STEP 2: PLACE TEACHER PLANNING BLOCKS

Second, we add planning periods for each team of teachers with the PE and Exploratory block (Figure 2.4). In this model, planning periods of three modules provide a 75-minute planning block. These are placed carefully in the master schedule to avoid leaving any instructional periods of less than two modules.

FIGURE 2.4. STEP 2: BLOCK PE, EXPLORATORY, AND PLANNING TIME

Time	Mod	Team 6-A	Team 6-B	Team 7-A	Team 7-B	Team 8-A	Team 8-B	PE/ Expls
8:30	Homeroom/Advisory (20 minutes)							
8:50	1	1	1	1	1	PLAN, PE, & EXPLs	1	Team 8-A
9:15	2	2	2	2	2		2	
9:40	3	3	3	3	3		3	
10:05	4	4	4	PLAN, PE, & EXPLs	4	4	4	Team 7-A
10:30	5	Lunch	5		5	5	5	
10:55	6	6	Lunch		6	6	6	
11:20	7	7	7	Lunch	7	7	PLAN, PE, & EXPLs	Team 8-B
11:45	8	8	8	8	Lunch	8		
12:10	9	9	9	9	9	Lunch		
12:35	10	10	10	10	10	10	Lunch	Lunch
1:00	11	11	11	11	PLAN, PE, & EXPLs	11	11	Team 7-B
1:25	12	12	12	12		12	12	
1:50	13	13	13	13		13	13	
2:15	14	PLAN, PE, & EXPLs	PLAN, PE, & EXPLs	14	14	14	14	Teams 6-A & 6-B
2:40	15			15	15	15	15	
3:05–3:30	16			16	16	16	16	

STEP 3: PLACE THE "TRIPLE E" PERIODS

The *elective, extended learning time,* and *enrichment* periods, shown as the EEE period, are added to complete the schedule for the six teams (Figure 2.5). The EEE period consists of two modules of 25 minutes (total

FIGURE 2.5. STEP 3: BLOCK THE EEE TOWER PERIOD; COMPLETED MIDDLE SCHOOL MODULAR MASTER SCHEDULE USING 25-MINUTE MODULES—420 TOTAL MINUTES

Time	Mod	Team 6-A	Team 6-B	Team 7-A	Team 7-B	Team 8-A	Team 8-B	PE /Expls	EEE
8:30		Homeroom/Advisory (20 minutes)							
8:50	1	1	1	1	1	PLAN, PE, & EXPLs	1	Team 8-A	Plan
9:15	2	2	2	2	2		2		
9:40	3	3	3	3	3		3		
10:05	4	4	4	PLAN, PE, & EXPLs	EEE	4	4	Team 7-A	EEE 7-B
10:30	5	Lunch	5			5	5		
10:55	6	6	Lunch		6	6	6		Lunch
11:20	7	7	EEE	Lunch	7	7	PLAN, PE, & EXPLs	Team 8-B	EEE 6-B
11:45	8	8		8	Lunch	8			
12:10	9	EEE	9	9	9	Lunch			EEE 6-A
12:35	10		10	10	10	10	Lunch	Lunch	
1:00	11	11	11	EEE	PLAN, PE, & EXPLs	11	11	Team 7-B	EEE 7-A
1:25	12	12	12			12	12		
1:50	13	13	13	13		EEE	13		EEE 8-A
2:15	14	PLAN, PE, & EXPLs	PLAN, PE, & EXPLs	14	14		14	Teams 6-A & 6-B	
2:40	15			15	15	15	EEE		EEE 8-B
3:05–3:30	16			16	16	16			

time = 50 minutes). To prevent overlaps of these activities, we keep track of the assignment of PE, elective, and exploratory personnel in the right-hand columns of the chart.

Remaining modules for each team are available for the team members to schedule as they see fit. For example team 6-A begins the day with 100 minutes of core time. A second core block of 75 minutes is available after lunch, and a third core block is available after the EEE period. All teams have 250 minutes of core instructional time available daily.

STEP 4: CREATE A TEAM CORE TIME SCHEDULE

While the core time each team is allocated is clearly marked on Figure 2.5 (p. 25), how are the core teachers to divide and schedule this time? There are many possibilities. In Figure 2.6, we suggest one division of time. If students took five subjects (language arts, mathematics, science, social studies, and Spanish), and teachers taught five sections, the available 250 minutes of core time could be divided into three blocks: one 100-minute block and two 75-minute blocks. If we rotate all classes through these blocks, each class would meet three times per week. Following Block I through the week, we see that it meets for 100 minutes (8:50 to 10:30) on Monday, for 75 minutes (1:00 to 2:15) on Wednesday, and for 75 minutes (10:55 to 12:10) on Thursday. Figure 2.7 (p. 28) is a sample student schedule using this division of time. One advantage of this model is that no course must always meet in the early morning or late afternoon block.

Figure 2.8 (p. 29) illustrates a different allocation of the 250 minutes of core time. Classes now meet four times a week in two 50-minute and two 75-minute blocks. Figure 2.9 (p. 30) is a sample schedule for the Team 6-A language arts teacher. Notice again that each of this teacher's five groups meet four times weekly, and that each meeting falls into a different time slot.

Figure 2.10 (p. 31) is an adaptation of the previous schedule. In this plan, one common elective period is scheduled for the entire school at the end of the day (modules 15 and 16), because this is when the band director from the high school is assigned to the middle school. (Of course, the elective period could be placed at any time in the schedule.) All exploratory, PE, core, and elective teachers can be available at this time. The EEE or tower period allows multigrade-level performing arts groups to meet; it also may be used to provide remediation, enrichment, and additional electives for students. Care must be taken to plan student schedules for this time appropriately (see detailed discussion of tower periods in Chapter 4).

(Text continues on page 32, following Figure 2.10)

FIGURE 2.6. 6A TEAM SCHEDULE (OPTION 1):
THREE CORE CLASS MEETINGS PER WEEK
(100 MIN., 75 MIN., AND 75 MIN.)

Time	Mod	Monday	Tuesday	Wednesday	Thursday	Friday
8:30		Homeroom/Advisory (20 minutes)				
8:50	1	Block I	Block IV	Block II	Block V	Block III
9:15	2					
9:40	3					
10:05	4					
10:30	5	Lunch				
10:55	6	Block II	Block V	Block III	Block I	Block IV
11:20	7					
11:45	8					
12:10	9	Electives, Extended Learning Time, and Enrichment				
12:35	10					
1:00	11	Block III	Block I	Block IV	Block II	Block V
1:25	12					
1:50	13					
2:15	14	Teacher Planning, Physical Education, and Exploratories				
2:40	15					
3:05–3:30	16					

FIGURE 2.7. 6A TEAM SCHEDULE (OPTION 1): THREE CORE CLASS MEETINGS PER WEEK (100 MIN., 75 MIN., AND 75 MIN.)— SAMPLE STUDENT SCHEDULE

Time	Mod	Monday	Tuesday	Wednesday	Thursday	Friday
8:30		Homeroom/Advisory (20 minutes)				
8:50	1	Language Arts	Spanish	Math	Social Studies	Science
9:15	2	Language Arts	Spanish	Math	Social Studies	Science
9:40	3	Language Arts	Spanish	Math	Social Studies	Science
10:05	4	Language Arts	Spanish	Math	Social Studies	Science
10:30	5	Lunch				
10:55	6	Math	Social Studies	Science	Language Arts	Spanish
11:20	7	Math	Social Studies	Science	Language Arts	Spanish
11:45	8	Math	Social Studies	Science	Language Arts	Spanish
12:10	9	Electives, Extended Learning Time, and Enrichment				
12:35	10	Electives, Extended Learning Time, and Enrichment				
1:00	11	Science	Language Arts	Spanish	Math	Social Studies
1:25	12	Science	Language Arts	Spanish	Math	Social Studies
1:50	13	Science	Language Arts	Spanish	Math	Social Studies
2:15	14	Teacher Planning, Physical Education, and Exploratories				
2:40	15	Teacher Planning, Physical Education, and Exploratories				
3:05–3:30	16	Teacher Planning, Physical Education, and Exploratories				

FIGURE 2.8. 6A TEAM SCHEDULE (OPTION 2): FOUR CORE CLASS MEETINGS PER WEEK (50 MIN., 50 MIN., 75 MIN., AND 75 MIN.)

Time	Mod	Monday	Tuesday	Wednesday	Thursday	Friday
8:30		Homeroom/Advisory (20 minutes)				
8:50	1	Block I	Block V	Block IV	Block III	Block II
9:15	2					
9:40	3	Block II	Block I	Block V	Block IV	Block III
10:05	4					
10:30	5	Lunch				
10:55	6	Block III	Block II	Block I	Block V	Block IV
11:20	7					
11:45	8					
12:10	9	Electives, Extended Learning Time, and Enrichment				
12:35	10					
1:00	11	Block IV	Block III	Block II	Block I	Block V
1:25	12					
1:50	13					
2:15	14	Teacher Planning, Physical Education, and Exploratories				
2:40	15					
3:05–3:30	16					

FIGURE 2.9. 6A TEAM SCHEDULE (OPTION 2): FOUR CORE CLASS MEETINGS PER WEEK (50 MIN., 50 MIN., 75 MIN., AND 75 MIN.)— SAMPLE TEACHER SCHEDULE

Time	Mod	Monday	Tuesday	Wednesday	Thursday	Friday
8:30		Homeroom/Advisory (20 minutes)				
8:50	1	Language Arts Group I	Language Arts Group V	Language Arts Group IV	Language Arts Group III	Language Arts Group II
9:15	2					
9:40	3	Language Arts Group II	Language Arts Group I	Language Arts Group V	Language Arts Group IV	Language Arts Group III
10:05	4					
10:30	5	Lunch				
10:55	6	Language Arts Group III	Language Arts Group II	Language Arts Group I	Language Arts Group V	Language Arts Group IV
11:20	7					
11:45	8					
12:10	9	Electives, Extended Learning Time, and Enrichment				
12:35	10					
1:00	11	Language Arts Group IV	Language Arts Group III	Language Arts Group II	Language Arts Group I	Language Arts Group V
1:25	12					
1:50	13					
2:15	14	Teacher Planning, Physical Education, and Exploratories				
2:40	15					
3:05–3:30	16					

FIGURE 2.10. COMPLETED MIDDLE SCHOOL MODULAR MASTER SCHEDULE USING 25-MINUTE MODULES—420 TOTAL MINUTES: SCHOOLWIDE TOWER PERIOD DURING MODS 15 AND 16

Time	Mod	Team 6-A	Team 6-B	Team 7-A	Team 7-B	Team 8-A	Team 8-B	PE/Expls/EEE
8:30		Homeroom/Advisory (20 minutes)						
8:50	1	1	1	1	1	PLAN, PE, & EXPLs	PLAN, PE, & EXPLs	Grade 8
9:15	2	2	2	2	2			
9:40	3	3	3	3	3			
10:05	4	4	4	PLAN, PE, & EXPLs	PLAN, PE, & EXPLs	4	4	Grade 7
10:30	5	Lunch	5			5	5	
10:55	6	6	Lunch			6	6	
11:20	7	7	7	Lunch	7	7	7	Lunch
11:45	8	8	8	8	8	Lunch	8	Duty
12:10	9	9	9	9	Lunch	9	9	Plan
12:35	10	PLAN, PE, & EXPLs	PLAN, PE, & EXPLs	10	10	10	Lunch	Grade 6
1:00	11			11	11	11	11	
1:25	12			12	12	12	12	
1:50	13	13	13	13	13	13	13	Plan
2:15	14	14	14	14	14	14	14	
2:40	15	EEE	EEE	EEE	EEE	EEE	EEE	EEE
3:05–3:30	16							

A CASE STUDY

To illustrate how a middle school might develop a master schedule and individual team schedules by using the modular format shown in Figures 2.1 through 2.10, we selected a detailed case study of how one particular school went through the process. Middle schools in this large Virginia school district were confronted with a variety of issues and problems. Modular block scheduling was viewed as one way to address these problems; however, other issues had to be addressed if blocking were to become a reality.

FRAMING THE PROBLEMS[1]

Although many of the middle schools in the district had adopted teaming structures, this school remained entrenched in a traditional junior/senior high school schedule with 47-minute classes. The schedule worked fine for the sixth grade teams, because they were able to combine single periods to create large amounts of time for the core subjects of reading, English, math, science, and social studies. Sixth grade students participated in only two encore periods—daily physical education (PE) and an exploratory wheel—which were scheduled during their core teachers' individual and team-planning times. Thus, when not in PE or exploratory classes, students were "on core" with their sixth grade teachers, who had control of the instructional time and discipline.

Seventh and eighth grade teams did not have this luxury. Students were enrolled in three encore classes—PE and two electives—while the four-teacher teams, with teachers from English, math, science, and social studies, were assigned five classes daily. Although it was possible to allot team teachers a two-period block of time for individual and team planning, during any of the remaining five periods of the day 20 percent of the students were "off core," taking PE or electives. As a result, seventh and eighth grade teams were locked into a period schedule and could never gather all teachers and students together for special activities without disrupting other classes. *While sixth grade teachers had the freedom and flexibility to adapt time to instruction, the seventh and eighth grade teachers had to adapt instruction to 47-minute periods of time.* The fragmented schedule created an environment that was not conducive to good discipline and student learning.

---

1 This section is adapted from Smith, Pitkin, and Rettig, 1998.

CONSENSUS FOR CHANGE

Many teachers and administrators believed that a block schedule would enable teachers to enhance instruction, and that fewer class changes involving masses of students would improve the climate of the school. While some people thought the concepts of block schedules being utilized in high schools across the country (Canady & Rettig, 1995a) might be useful, the situation required a plan unique to middle schools.

In deciding to move to a block schedule, school personnel identified these goals:

- Creating pure teams with a minimum of cross-teaming,
- Maintaining various levels of service for special education and English as a Second Language (ESL) students, provided on-team whenever possible,
- Reducing the number of class changes,
- Maintaining two separate programs for gifted students: a regional program drawing from a wide geographic area and a school-based program,
- Maintaining elective programs, especially in music (which offered three different performing groups—mixed grades, seventh grade, and eighth grade),
- Maintaining a strong foreign language program in the eighth grade, and
- Maintaining heterogeneous teams.

CREATING "PURE" TEAMS

There are at least three ways to create "pure teams"—that is, teams with common students, common teachers, and common time. One way to accomplish this goal in schools with four-person teams is simply to assign the team only four groups of students and a block of time in which to instruct them. This action, however, has a number of possible effects. If students continue to go off-team for three of seven periods, such a move requires either large classes for the core teachers (five groups now divided into four groups) or an increase in core staff to maintain constant class size. In addition, core teachers would teach only four of seven periods, an expensive proposition at best. They could be assigned an additional class—elective or exploratory—outside the team; this fragments the job of the core teacher, although it reduces either class size or the need for staff in exploratory and elective programs. One final possibility is to assign each core teacher an additional core class in a non-teamed situation. For example, if sixth and seventh grades were teamed but the eighth grade was not teamed, sixth and seventh grade teachers could pick up an eighth grade section as their fifth class. This possibility is not recommended because it causes fragmentation both for teachers and for the non-teamed eighth grade students.

Alternatively, if four groups were assigned to each four-person team, they could be given a block of time larger than four of seven periods, perhaps the equivalent of four of six periods. In this scenario, students would travel off-team the equivalent of only two of six periods, which would reduce either class size or staff in elective and exploratory classes. However, this plan would increase the amount of time core teachers work and the amount of time students spend in core. Core time would increase even more if we assign core teachers the equivalent of six of eight periods with their team students.

To maintain a similar ratio of core to encore time, while maintaining class size and creating pure teams, it was decided to add both a subject and a teacher (from current elective and exploratory staff) to each seventh and eighth grade core team to handle the five sections of students. See Figure 2.11 for an analysis of school staffing levels in various scheduling configurations. The decision to add to each team subjects not generally thought of as "core" had implications for staffing and programs. Teachers of elective classes were very anxious. They realized that course enrollments and possibly jobs were at stake.

Criteria for adding subjects and personnel to core teams were considered. What were the possibilities for integrating the new core subjects with existing core subjects? Would current staffing allow the placement of new subjects on core teams? What additions would best fit the needs of the community? What would be the effect of the new additions on the subjects not selected for addition to the core?

The committee debated a variety of possibilities. Because standardized reading test scores for students were low, several staff members felt that a reading course (similar to Grade 6) should be added to the core. However, because the available reading staff would have been insufficient, and a self-contained reading class for all students was contradictory to the reading resource model emphasized in the district, this was not done. Other possibilities included PE/health and the current elective programs such as art, drama, foreign language (eighth grade), music (band, chorus, strings, or general music), reading, technology education, or teen living.

Based on the criteria, the committee decided that a semester of art and a semester of teen living were appropriate additions to the seventh grade core. The combination of a fine arts class and a practical arts class provided balance, and the subject matter of each could be blended easily into the core instructional program. Thus, seventh grade students would be enrolled in language arts, mathematics, science, social studies, and a

FIGURE 2.11. STAFFING REQUIREMENTS FOR VARIOUS SCHEDULING MODELS

Schedule	Core Periods	Ex/El/PE Periods	Teaching Periods	Plan/Duty Periods	Staff Ratio Core: Ex/El/PE	Core Staff	Ex/El/PE Staff	Total Staff
Six-period day	5	1	5	1	5:1	40	8	48
Six-period day*	4	2	5	1	2:1	32	16	48
Six-period day	4	2	4	2	2:1	40	20	60
Seven-period day*	5	2	6	1	5:2	33.3	13.3	46.67
Seven-period day	5	2	5	2	5:2	40	16	56
Seven-period day*	4	3	5	2	4:3	32	24	56
Seven-period day	4	3	4	3	4:3	40	30	70
Eight-period day*	6	2	7	1	3:1	34.3	11.4	45.7
Eight-period day	6	2	6	2	3:1	40	13.3	53.3
Eight-period day*	5	3	6	2	5:3	33.3	20	53.3
Eight-period day	5	3	5	3	5:3	40	24	64
Eight-period day*	4	4	5	3	1:1	32	32	64

This chart assumes: (1) all core teachers and PE, exploratory, and elective teachers instruct equivalent numbers of periods/blocks; (2) section size of 25 and a school of 1000 students; (3) maximum efficiency (never achieved)—meaning that all certifications match, that all class sizes are equivalent, and that all electives are chosen equally. The chart works for equivalent block schedules as well. Core generally means language arts (reading and English), mathematics, social studies, and science. If foreign language is placed on the team, it needs to be classified as core for the relative comparisons made in this chart. Chart data do not include small special education classes.

*Can have pure team, but not pure team time, because one group is in PE, exploratory, or electives during every core period. For pure team time to be achieved, the number of core periods must match the number of teaching periods.

semester each of art and teen living during core time; outside of the core, when the team teachers were planning, they would participate in PE/ health and have one elective choice.

The choice of what to add to the core team in eighth grade was far more problematic. Art and teen living were eliminated because they had been added to core at seventh grade. A second pairing of a fine and a practical art would leave only one elective slot in students' schedules, setting up a forced choice between a select musical performance group and foreign language—an unwise conflict. That left music, PE and health, or foreign language as possibilities for addition to the core.

Although every student took health and physical education, this possibility was rejected for two reasons: the difficulty of integrating physical education with other core subjects, and the logistical problems presented by PE in a flexible core-time schedule. (How would locker room supervision be handled? Would classes starting and stopping at different times in the gymnasium be a problem?) Music was eliminated because only one-third of eighth grade students were involved in band, chorus, or strings, which was not enough to justify placing those courses on core teams.

By contrast, foreign language presented fewer logistical problems and many factors in its favor. Spanish is the second language of the school community, and the local plan for school improvement emphasizes the importance of foreign language instruction. In the fall of 1994, two new programs were introduced: a Spanish immersion program for sixth grade students and the International Baccalaureate program, which emphasizes foreign language, at the high school. Requiring all eighth graders to take a first-year foreign language would support these programs and send a very strong message about academic expectations for students. Although some of the committee feared that many eighth grade students would struggle in what formerly had been a high school course for the academic elite, it was decided to add foreign language to the eighth grade core teams. Thus, all eighth grade students would be enrolled in language arts, mathematics, science, social studies, and either Spanish or French on core team, and students would take PE/health and one elective choice off core.

DESIGNING THE MASTER SCHEDULE

Once the teaming plan was chosen, the master schedule could be designed. As always with scheduling, "the devil is in the details"; and the new teaming plan added several new details. The task was to move from the generalities described above to a practical model. Teams of students had to be created—teams that accommodated core subjects and elective choices. Because not all electives were offered every block of the day, it was necessary to assign students to teams that would be "off core" when their particular electives were available.

The many sort factors included algebra, geometry, Latin, different multigrade levels of music, reading levels, Gifted and Talented Center (GTC) classes, gifted and talented school-based classes (GTSB), LD, ESL, gender and ethnic groups. Creating teams that addressed these factors, yet generally reflected the diversity of the school, was a challenge.

Difficulties arose in scheduling the advanced music programs because of conflicts with the numerous sort factors, specifically GTC, GTSB, and Latin. Creating single sections of advanced performing groups that included both seventh and eighth graders would require the clustering all advanced music students on a few teams, which would unbalance the teams academically. Thus, a decision was made to schedule two separate sections of advanced band, advanced orchestra, and advanced chorus. This allowed the master schedule to run with no schedule conflicts and permitted balanced teams, but dismayed the music instructors.

Figure 2.12 (p. 38) illustrates the master schedule. The day opens with a 20-minute Teacher Advisory (T/A). Four 90-minute blocks form the framework of the schedule for teacher planning time and students' PE and elective classes. These blocks (clearly shaded and labeled PE/Elective in Figure 2.12) meet from 8:05 to 9:35, 9:35 to 11:05, 11:35 to 1:05, and 1:05 to 2:35. Students from several teams travel off core to take PE and electives during each of the four blocks; core teachers utilize this large block of time for team and individual planning. Five 30-minute lunch periods are accommodated easily. Each team of five teachers is allocated 270 minutes for core instruction.

Teachers were challenged to design team schedules from the available 270 minutes to best meet the needs of their students. They were encouraged to have at least one class longer than the others and to "slide" blocks within their core time schedule. In a sliding schedule, classes meet at different times each day throughout a given rotation to share the best and worst instructional times in a school day.

Figure 2.13 (p. 39) shows the team schedule designed by the Champions; classes are of different lengths and meet four times a week on a slide (one 90-minute class, one 70-minute class, and two 55-minute classes weekly). Each teacher has five classes, designated Blocks I–V. Figure 2.14 (p. 39) illustrates the Wave Team schedule, in which teachers meet three classes a day Monday through Thursday; on Friday, they teach a five-period day. (Block V is the same every day because of an unavoidable cross-team connection that was phased out after the first year.)

(Text continues on page 40, following Figure 2.14.)

FIGURE 2.12. SAMPLE MIDDLE SCHOOL MASTER SCHEDULE

Flames, Raptors, Red 'Roos 6	T/A	Core (190 minutes)	Lunch C	Core (80 minutes)	PE/Wheel	[1:05]
Coyotes, Chameleons, Shockwaves 6	T/A	Core (160 minutes)	Lunch B	Core (110 minutes)	PE/Wheel	[1:05]
Dragons 7	T/A	PE/Elective	Core (160 minutes)	Lunch E	Core (110 minutes)	[1:05]
Hotshots 7	T/A	Core (130 minutes)	Lunch A	Core (50 minutes)	PE/Elective	Core (90 minutes) [1:05]
Wave 8	T/A	PE/Elective	Core (130 minutes)	Lunch D	Core (140 minutes)	
Champions 8	T/A	Core (90 minutes)	PE/Elective	Core (70 minutes)	Lunch E	Core (110 minutes)
Phoenix 7	T/A	Core (90 minutes)	PE/Elective	Core (40 minutes)	Lunch D	Core (140 minutes)
PE & Electives	T/A	Dragons, Wave, Superstars (8th)	Champions, Phoenix	Teacher Lunch	Hotshots, Superstars (7th)	All 6th Grade Teams
Superstars (7th) ESL 1	T/A	Core (130 minutes)	Lunch A	Core (50 minutes)	PE/Elective	Core (90 minutes) [1:05]
Superstars (8th) ESL 1	T/A	PE/Elective	Core (40 minutes)	Lunch A	Core (230 minutes)	
TIMES	7:45 8:05 (8:15 on M & F)	9:35	11:05 11:35	1:05		2:35

LUNCH STARTS   A 10:15, B 10:45, C 11:15, D 11:45, E 12:15   *Star Day, periods 2, 4, 6, 8   //Stripe Day, periods 3, 5, 7, 9

PE/Elective classes are 90 minutes on alternate days

FIGURE 2.13. CHAMPIONS' TEAM WEEKLY SCHEDULE

		PE/ ELECTIVES		Lunch		
Monday	Block I		Block II		Block III	Block IV
Tuesday	Block V		Block I		Block II	Block III
Wednesday	Block IV		Block V		Block I	Block II
Thursday	Block III		Block IV		Block V	Block I
Friday	Block II		Block III		Block IV	Block V

8:05   9:35   11:05   12:20   12:57   1:45   2:35

FIGURE 2.14. THE WAVE TEAM WEEKLY SCHEDULE

	8:05	9:35	11:45	12:15	1:45	2:35
Monday	Electives/ PE	Block I	Lunch D	Block II		Block V
Tuesday	Electives/ PE	Block III	Lunch D	Block IV		Block V
Wednesday	Electives/ PE	Block II	Lunch D	Block I		Block V
Thursday	Electives/ PE	Block IV	Lunch D	Block III		Block V
Friday	Electives/ PE	Block I / Block IV	Block II / Block III	Lunch D	Block III / Block II	Block IV / Block I	Block V

NOTE: The Friday schedule alternates weekly.

PE and elective teachers also had choices. They could teach two 43-minute classes or one 90-minute class within each block. They unanimously chose 90-minute classes, meeting every other day; teachers instruct three sections daily. For example, a student might attend band for 90 minutes one day and PE/health for 90 minutes the next. These alternate days are labeled "Star Day" and "Stripe Day." Class changes to elective programs and PE locker room changes were reduced by half. Because students from both seventh and eighth grades were scheduled in electives during the first three elective blocks, it was possible to mix them to create ability-based performing arts groups.

IMPLEMENTATION ISSUES

In addition to the complexity of creating the master schedule, other logistics needed to be worked out.

- ◆ It was necessary to re-register students after receiving central office approval for the plan.

- ◆ Once given the list of students on their team, teachers needed time to form class sections and to create a mini-master schedule for the team. The time needed to accomplish this task was grossly underestimated. Teachers had a week of pre-school workdays; much of the time was spent negotiating sections. It may be wiser, especially when first implementing the block schedule, for the guidance department to create the initial sections within the team to get the school year started. Teams can readjust as they see fit. However, while grouping the students was difficult and time-consuming, it was an excellent team-building experience for the teachers.

- ◆ Funds were needed to provide staff development training in instructional strategies appropriate for teaching in longer blocks of time.

- ◆ Meetings were held with parents to discuss the new schedule. We advise that parents be involved in the process from the start, including as representatives on the scheduling committee. (See Craig, 1995, for an excellent discussion on how to use such a committee.)

- ◆ The needs of special education and ESL students were carefully considered. It was possible to add either special education or ESL students to each team; appropriate support staff then were added to teams as well.

Two major instructional issues arose. The first issue concerned grading in foreign language. The school did not want to penalize students for attempting to complete this high school course. It was decided that students who were earning less than a C during the final grading period could be withdrawn from the class (on paper) so that they did not receive a poor grade as the first entry on their high school transcript; these students would repeat the first year of the language. They also could be given a "Pass" for a language exploratory. In addition, a reading class was created for the few students for whom foreign language participation was deemed inappropriate.

The second concern involved the decision to split advanced-level music classes into two sections, eliminating opportunities within the school day for these groups to practice as a whole. Although there were weekly after-school practice sessions, one of the tradeoffs for implementing this schedule was the reduction of opportunities for whole-group practice. For the 1995–96 school year, the schedule was modified to provide two weekly extended advisory periods during which these groups could meet as a whole.

PROGRESS UPDATE

A dramatic change occurred at this middle school. Certainly, the disciplinary climate improved. During the first year, 1994–95, in-school suspensions were reduced by 20 percent to 465, as compared to 581 during the 1993–94 school year. Similarly, out-of-school suspensions dropped 16.7 percent from 347 to 289. During the second year of the schedule, suspensions during the first semester were down 47 percent. Based on feedback from anonymous surveys administered in both January and June of the second year, faculty were very supportive of the new schedule. Figure 2.15 (p. 41) summarizes the survey results. In addition, the number of student retentions dropped dramatically from 29 to 13 in seventh grade and from 21 to 9 in eighth grade.

This middle school's block schedule combines four unusual elements: nontraditional core subjects added to the interdisciplinary team, an alternate-day block schedule for PE and electives, sliding core-time team schedules, and a partial inclusion model for serving students with special needs. *While the schedule is not an end in itself, it has served as a platform for the improvement of instruction and school climate.*[2] The new block schedule re-energized the staff, gave teams control over core instructional time, and challenged teachers to find innovative instructional approaches.

---

2 See Smith (1998) for further confirmation of this important point.

FIGURE 2.15. SURVEY RESULTS

Staff Perceptions (in %): Block Schedule Format vs. a 7-Period Day

	More/Better		Same		Less/Worse	
	01/95	*06/95*	*01/95*	*06/95*	*01/95*	*06/95*
Students performing better	42	45	50	47	8	8
Teachers covering course content	63	55	27	29	10	16
Students mastering concepts	55	48	36	41	9	11
Students thinking critically/ana-lytically	61	67	35	29	4	4
Control of instructional time	64	64	21	22	15	14
Discussions about curricu-lum/instruction	58	58	33	30	9	12
Experimenting with instructional approaches	76	71	18	24	6	5
Teachers feel successful	49	51	32	30	9	8
Success with learning-disabled students	53	48	38	33	9	19
Classroom behavior	53	53	35	42	12	5
Hallway behavior	80	76	20	17	0	7

	Block Schedule		Undecided		7-Period Day	
	01/95	*06/95*	*01/95*	*06/95*	*01/95*	*06/95*
Prefer block to a 7-period day	74	97	18	0	8	3

3

ALTERNATE-DAY SCHEDULES IN THE MIDDLE SCHOOL

Another popular high school schedule that developed in the United States during the 1990s is referred to as the alternate-day block schedule (Canady & Rettig, 1995b, Chap. 2). In some school districts, this scheduling format may be referred to as a Day 1/Day 2 schedule, an Odd/Even schedule, an A/B schedule, or an eight-block schedule.

In this scheduling plan, students typically meet half of their classes (usually three or four) for 80 to 110 minutes each on one day and the remainder of their classes on the following school day. Core classes alternate daily for the entire school year. Some schools name the alternate school days according to school colors; for example, if a school's colors are purple and gold, they may call one day Purple Day and the other day Gold Day.

This chapter begins by describing the basic format of the alternate-day schedule common in many high schools and some middle schools across the country. This basic model is then adapted for the middle school by adding teams, team planning, and exploratory opportunities to achieve special benefits for both teachers and students.

BASIC FORMS OF THE ALTERNATE-DAY SCHEDULE

Alternate-day schedules typically are derived from the traditional six-, seven-, or eight-period schedule. By doubling each class period and scheduling it every other day, we create the alternate-day schedule. After outlining the basic models, we describe several modifications.

SIX-PERIOD FORMAT

If the school changes to a block schedule from a six-period schedule, students on the six-course alternate-day plan (6 A/B) take three classes each day: for example, classes 1, 3, and 5 meet on Day 1 (the Odd Day) and classes 2, 4, and 6 meet on Day 2 (the Even Day). Figure 3.1 shows the basic structure of an alternate-day block schedule built from six periods.

FIGURE 3.1. BASIC ALTERNATE-DAY BLOCK SCHEDULE BUILT FROM SIX PERIODS

Days	M Day 1 A	T Day 2 B	W Day 1 A	R Day 2 B	F Day 1 A	M Day 2 B
	1	2	1	2	1	2
P	1	2	1	2	1	2
E	3	4	3	4	3	4
R I	3	4	3	4	3	4
O	Lunch					
D S	5	6	5	6	5	6
	5	6	5	6	5	6

In Figure 3.2, a six-period alternate-day schedule is shown as three blocks of time.

FIGURE 3.2. BLOCKED ALTERNATE-DAY SCHEDULE BUILT FOR SIX BLOCKS

Days		M Day 1 A	T Day 2 B	W Day 1 A	R Day 2 B	F Day 1 A	M Day 2 B
P	Block I	1	2	1	2	1	2
E R I	Block II	3	4	3	4	3	4
O	Lunch						
D S	Block III	5	6	5	6	5	6

SEVEN-PERIOD FORMAT

If the school is operating on a seven-period day, in the equivalent block schedule, six classes alternate every other day and one course meets daily in a single period. This short-period class typically is placed in the first, third, fifth, or seventh period slot so that the remaining periods may be doubled and alternated. It is common for lunch periods to be placed before and/or after the single period when it is placed in the third or fifth time slot. Placing the single period in the seventh slot may facilitate sports practices and travel. Placing the single period in the first-period slot often helps a school interface with a regional vocational program or school for the academically gifted. Figure 3.3 shows a seven-course schedule with the everyday class in the fifth period slot.

FIGURE 3.3. BASIC ALTERNATE-DAY BLOCK SCHEDULE BUILT FROM SEVEN PERIODS

Days	M Day 1 A	T Day 2 B	W Day 1 A	R Day 2 B	F Day 1 A	M Day 2 B
P	1	2	1	2	1	2
E	1	2	1	2	1	2
R	3	4	3	4	3	4
I	3	4	3	4	3	4
O	Period 5 and Lunch					
D	7	6	7	6	7	6
S	7	6	7	6	7	6

In Figure 3.4, three major blocks of time are illustrated clearly with Period 5 scheduled as a single period running every day.

FIGURE 3.4. BLOCKED ALTERNATE-DAY SCHEDULE BUILT FOR SEVEN BLOCKS

Days		M Day 1 A	T Day 2 B	W Day 1 A	R Day 2 B	F Day 1 A	M Day 2 B
P E R I O D S	Block I	1	2	1	2	1	2
	Block II	3	4	3	4	3	4
	Period 5	Period 5 and Lunch					
	Block III	7	6	7	6	7	6

EIGHT-PERIOD FORMAT

An eight-period alternate-day schedule, sometimes called an eight-block schedule, is shown in Figure 3.5.

FIGURE 3.5. BASIC ALTERNATE-DAY BLOCK SCHEDULE BUILT FROM EIGHT PERIODS

Days	M Day 1 A	T Day 2 B	W Day 1 A	R Day 2 B	F Day 1 A	M Day 2 B
P E R I O D S	1	2	1	2	1	2
	1	2	1	2	1	2
	3	4	3	4	3	4
	3	4	3	4	3	4
	Lunch					
	5	6	5	6	5	6
	5	6	5	6	5	6
	7	8	7	8	7	8
	7	8	7	8	7	8

If the school is working on an eight-period day, an alternate-day block schedule can be illustrated as four blocks, as shown in Figure 3.6.

FIGURE 3.6. BLOCKED ALTERNATE-DAY SCHEDULE BUILT FOR EIGHT BLOCKS

	Days	M Day 1 A	T Day 2 B	W Day 1 A	R Day 2 B	F Day 1 A	M Day 2 B
P E R I O D S	Block I	1	2	1	2	1	2
	Block II	3	4	3	4	3	4
	Lunch						
	Block III	5	6	5	6	5	6
	Block IV	7	8	7	8	7	8

TYPICAL HIGH SCHOOL MODIFICATIONS OF THE BASIC ALTERNATE-DAY BLOCK SCHEDULE

The basic alternate-day block schedule can be modified in many ways. For example, an activity/seminar period can be created to replace one block, or a school can decide to block some days and operate a single-period schedule other days.

THE ACTIVITY/SEMINAR BLOCK

A modified version of the alternate-day eight-period schedule which offers an activity/seminar period is shown in Figure 3.7 (p. 48). (Of course, the activity period may be assigned a different time block on Day 2.) This period has multiple uses; for example, schoolwide activities such as pep rallies or assembly programs can be scheduled during that block. Although schoolwide activities might have priority in this block of time, it could also be used for providing extended learning time for students needing such assistance. Still other students during this block might be involved in additional exploratories, electives, or scheduled seminars conducted by teachers, guidance counselors, other students, or community members.

FIGURE 3.7. ALTERNATE-DAY BLOCK SCHEDULE BUILT FOR SEVEN COURSES (ONE LUNCH PERIOD; EIGHT BLOCKS; ACTIVITY/SEMINAR PERIOD)

	Blocks and Times	M Day 1 A	T Day 2 B	W Day 1 A	R Day 2 B
P E R I O D S	Block I & HR 8:00–9:36	1	2	1	2
	Block II 9:41–11:11	3	4	3	4
	Lunch 11:16–11:50	LUNCH			
	Block III 11:55–1:25	5	6	5	6
	Block IV 1:30–3:00	7	Activity/ Seminar	7	Activity/ Seminar

THE TWO-DAY BLOCK

A second adaptation of the alternate-day schedule is commonly used to pilot block scheduling. In this model, a regular single-period schedule operates three days a week, and the block schedule operates on two (usually consecutive) days a week. In the example shown in Figure 3.8, block classes are held on Wednesday and Thursday, and single periods occur on Monday, Tuesday, and Friday.

FIGURE 3.8. SIX COURSES; ONE DOUBLE PERIOD WEEKLY

Days	M Day 1	T Day 2	W Day 3	R Day 4	F Day 5
P E R I O D S	1	1	1	2	1
	2	2			2
	3	3	3	4	3
	4	4			4
	Lunch				
	5	5	5	6	5
	6	6			6

THE FOUR-DAY BLOCK

Some schools expand on the model illustrated in Figure 3.8 and block four days per week using Monday or Friday as the single-period day on which all classes meet.

BENEFITS OF THE ALTERNATE-DAY BLOCK SCHEDULE

The alternate-day block schedule offers a variety of benefits for both middle school students and teachers.

♦ The number of class changes is reduced and the time typically used for moving between classes is absorbed into instructional blocks.

Consider what a typical day is like for a student in a traditionally scheduled middle school. The student is likely to go to six, seven, or eight different classes, with that many different teachers. At least half of the classes may have little, if any relationship to the content of other classes. Imagine the stress level for adults if we had to change offices every 45 minutes, with a new supervisor and different expectations at every turn, and never more than 5 minutes to visit the restroom! Limiting the number of class changes reduces discipline problems, and the school environment becomes less stressful for both students and teachers (Angola High School, 1997; Canady & Rettig, 1996; Cawelti, 1997; Conner, 1997; Cunningham, 1997; Eineder, 1996; Fleck, 1996; Freeman, 1996; Guskey & Kifer, 1994; Hundley, 1996; Irvine, 1995; Jones, 1997; King et al., 1975; Kramer, 1997a; Mistretta & Polansky, 1997; North Carolina Department of Public Instruction, 1998; O'Neil, 1995; Phelps, 1996; Pulaski County High School, 1994; Salvaterra & Adams, 1995; Schoenstein, 1995; Sessoms, 1995; Smith, 1998; Snyder, 1997; Staunton, 1997a, 1997b).

♦ Teachers are better able to plan extended lessons that engage students as active learners.

In the initial discussions of middle school philosophy during the 1960s, a major theme was that middle school students needed to be *involved* in their learning; indeed, it has been argued for decades that middle school students need to be active—not passive—learners. Single periods of 40 to 50 minutes certainly limit what teachers can do. In just 45 minutes, how can one seriously engage a group active young students in a science lab? Or immerse them in a Socratic seminar? Involve them in the writing process? Connect them on the Internet with students living in Japan? Take them to a computer lab for problem-based math simulations? (See Canady & Rettig, 1996; Gilkey & Hunt, 1998.)

♦ Teaching with a variety of instructional models is encouraged.

We have learned from our experiences with high schools that block scheduling can be a catalyst for other changes. With adequate and appropriate staff development, many teachers do teach differently in the block. We do see less lecture (Brandenburg, 1995; Bryant, 1995; Canady & Rettig, 1996; Davis et al., 1977; Jones, 1997; King, 1996; King et al., 1975; Kramer, 1996; Mayes, 1997; O'Neil, 1995; Phelps, 1996; Pisapia & Westfall, 1996; Quinn, 1997; Sessoms, 1995; Staunton, 1997b; Vawter, 1998). We do see fewer work sheets; we do see students who are engaged in their learning, not just waiting for 3 o'clock and June; we do see teachers welcoming the time to use various types of technology; we do see more teachers using various instructional models, such as inquiry and concept formation, and cooperative learning strategies (Blaz, 1998; Canady & Rettig, 1996; Conti-D'Antonio, Bertrando, & Eisenberger, 1998; Gilkey & Hunt, 1998, pp. 102–103).

♦ Itinerant teacher schedules can be simplified.

It is quite common for some teachers to teach at more than one middle school or also at a high school in the district. Typically, these are foreign language, music, art, technology, and physical education teachers. Teachers traveling between schools often lose at least one instructional period each day. If all schools sharing teachers choose the same Day 1/Day 2 schedule, then itinerant teachers can be assigned to teach in School "X" on Day 1 and School "Y" on Day 2. This eliminates midday travel time and the school district often gains another instructional period for each itinerant teacher.

♦ Students have fewer classes, quizzes, tests, and homework assignments on any one day.

Because fewer classes meet on any one day, quizzes, tests, and homework assignments can be better balanced than in a single-period schedule. There is evidence, based on high school data, that students who are not highly organized, and sometimes not too excited about school, perform better when they can focus on fewer classes during a quarter, term, or semester.

♦ Work missed because of student absences is easier for students to gather and teachers to monitor.

A student who misses a day misses fewer classes, and the task of seeing teachers for make-up work is reduced. Of course, the student misses more work in each block class; therefore, seeing teachers and making up missed work gains increased importance (Irvine, 1995; Kramer, 1996, 1997b; Jones, 1997; Mistretta & Polansky, 1997). To assist students with make-up work, we recommend that schools with alternate-day block schedules provide some type of "opportunity room" where students can go before and/or after school for assistance. If at all possible, the room should be staffed by a full-time teacher. If budget restrictions do not permit such a position, a full-time paraprofessional can be assigned to assist and monitor students, with teachers added on a rotating basis. Such an "advancement center" or "achievement center" also may be useful in working with transfer students, students needing extended learning time in a particular subject, or students needing help with passing a state exit examination, or for students who have been given a chance to re-take a test (Canady & Rettig, 1995b, Chap. 3).

While some middle and junior high schools are capable of implementing the plans described above successfully, certain aspects of the middle school concept—namely teaming, common planning time, and exploratory rotations—require an alternate-day plan specifically designed for middle schools.

ADAPTING THE ALTERNATE-DAY BLOCK SCHEDULE FOR MIDDLE SCHOOLS: MASTER SCHEDULE I

We begin by describing a master schedule that is similar, in many respects, to the modular plans described in Chapter 2. However, we develop this plan into a full middle school alternate-day schedule. Master Schedule I (Figure 3.9, p. 52) illustrates one example of an alternate-day (A/B), middle school master schedule with a "triple E" or "tower" period.

GRADE SIX TIME SCHEDULE

The school day consists of 420 minutes distributed as follows: All teams in grades 6, 7, and 8 are assigned homeroom time from 8:00 to 8:10.

FIGURE 3.9. MIDDLE SCHOOL MASTER SCHEDULE I:
A/B BLOCK SCHEDULE WITH A TRIPLE E (EEE) OR TOWER PERIOD

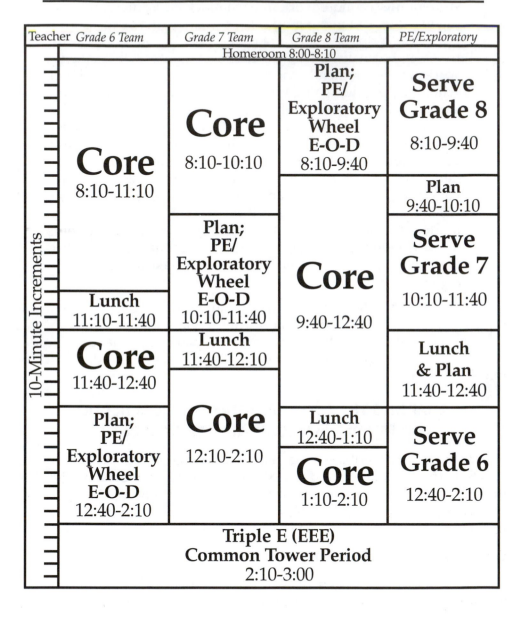

Teacher _Grade 6 Team_	_Grade 7 Team_	_Grade 8 Team_	_PE/Exploratory_
Homeroom 8:00-8:10			
Core 8:10-11:10	**Core** 8:10-10:10	Plan; PE/ Exploratory Wheel E-O-D 8:10-9:40	**Serve Grade 8** 8:10-9:40
			Plan 9:40-10:10
	Plan; PE/ Exploratory Wheel E-O-D 10:10-11:40	**Core** 9:40-12:40	**Serve Grade 7** 10:10-11:40
Lunch 11:10-11:40			
Core 11:40-12:40	Lunch 11:40-12:10		Lunch & Plan 11:40-12:40
Plan; PE/ Exploratory Wheel E-O-D 12:40-2:10	**Core** 12:10-2:10	Lunch 12:40-1:10	**Serve Grade 6** 12:40-2:10
		Core 1:10-2:10	
Triple E (EEE) Common Tower Period 2:10-3:00			

Then the Grade 6 team has a 180-minute block of time for core classes (English, mathematics, science, and social studies); 30 minutes for lunch; another 60 minutes for core classes; and a 90-minute block of time that teachers use for team planning while students attend PE and exploratory classes.

"TRIPLE E" OR "TOWER" PERIOD

Based on the master schedule shown in Figure 3.9, the sixth grade team completes the day with a 50-minute period (EEE) for electives, extended learning, and enrichment. During this EEE period (some middle schools call it a Tower Period), some students may take a foreign language class while other students participate in band, orchestra, or choir. Those students not in an elective may be offered extended learning time in a subject such as mathematics or writing skills, in most cases meeting with selected core teachers. Meanwhile, other core teachers teach an exploratory class and/or an elective. The purpose of scheduling a schoolwide EEE period is to make it possible for students from all grade levels to participate in single-section electives, such as band, choir, and orchestra, without making the schedule too difficult to construct. Although the EEE period in Figure 3.9 is at the end of the day, the period could be placed at any time during the school day. We placed it at the end because in some middle schools itinerant teachers, such as a high school band teacher or Spanish teacher, often come to the middle school either at the beginning or at the end of the school day to teach elective classes.

GRADE SEVEN TIME SCHEDULE

Figure 3.9 shows that Grade 7 teams also have homeroom from 8:00 to 8:10, followed by 120 minutes for core classes, and then 90 minutes for team planning while students are in physical education and exploratory classes. After 30 minutes for lunch, the Grade 7 students have another 120-minute block for core classes, ending the day with the 50-minute EEE period, the same as Grade 6.

GRADE EIGHT TIME SCHEDULE

In Figure 3.9, Grade 8 teachers begin the day with a 90-minute planning block with students in physical education and exploratory, after which Grade 8 teams have 180 minutes for core instruction, which is followed by a 30-minute lunch. After an additional 60 minutes for core instruction, the day ends with the same common EEE period as Grades 6 and 7.

PHYSICAL EDUCATION AND EXPLORATORY SCHEDULE

The physical education and exploratory teachers in Figure 3.9 (p. 52) serve Grade 8 for 90 minutes (8:10 to 9:40). They have a 30-minute preparation time before serving Grade 7 teams for 90 minutes. There is a 60-minute lunch and planning period before serving Grade 6 teams for 90 minutes (12:40 to 2:10). For the PE and exploratory block we recommend that students be divided into two groups. One group should be assigned to physical education (PE) for 90 minutes on an every-other-day (EOD) basis throughout the quarter/semester/year, while the other half of the students can be divided into groups of 20 to 30 for exploratory classes such as art, technology, teen living, foreign languages, and music. These classes also meet every other day, opposite the physical education classes. (See Chapter 6 for a detailed examination of exploratory and elective scheduling options.)

In some schools, physical education and exploratory teachers have another planning period during the common EEE period; in other schools, they serve on a rotating basis to assist with instruction in the electives, enrichment, or extended tutorials for selected students.

ALTERNATE-DAY TEAM SCHEDULES

Having outlined the basic schedule for each grade level, we now illustrate how each team could create an alternate-day schedule for core classes.

GRADE SIX A/B SCHEDULE

The basic school day for teachers and students in sixth grade can be derived from Figure 3.9 (p. 52) as follows:

8:00–8:10	Homeroom
8:10–11:10	Core Instructional Time
11:10–11:40	Lunch
11:40–12:40	Core Instructional Time
12:40–2:10	Planning time for teachers; students alternate between physical education for 90 minutes one day and an exploratory wheel assignment the opposite day.
2:10–3:00	EEE period; core teachers may teach an elective, have additional planning time, or (on a rotating basis) provide extended learning assistance to selected students.

In Figure 3.10 (p. 56), the schedule above is detailed for a Grade 6 four-teacher team working in an alternate-day block schedule. The language arts/reading teacher is paired with the social studies teacher, and the mathematics teacher is paired with the science teacher. We suggest these pairings because we find that teachers of these paired subjects are more likely to integrate their subject content.

DAY 1

Let's take a look at what happens in the schedule illustrated in Figure 3.10. After homeroom on Day 1, the language arts/reading teacher works with student Group A for 120 minutes. At 10:10, the language arts/reading teacher and the social studies teacher exchange groups; the language arts/reading teacher works with student Group B for 60 minutes, goes to lunch at 11:10 for 30 minutes, and then returns to Group B for an additional 60 minutes of core instructional time. Conversely, the social studies teacher works with Group B from 8:10 to 10:10, and then with Group A from 10:10 to 12:40 (with a half-hour break for lunch).

While the language arts/reading and social studies teachers work with student Groups A and B, the mathematics and science teachers follow a similar pattern with student Groups C and D. At 12:40 the four teachers on the Grade 6 team—language arts/reading, social studies, mathematics and science—have 90 minutes for planning while students are in PE and exploratories.

Finally, all Grade 6 teachers and students participate in the various EEE period activities, as explained earlier.

It should be noted that on Day 1, while both Groups A and B have a 120-minute core instructional block for language arts/reading and another for social studies, Group B's language arts/reading time and Group A's social studies time is divided by lunch into two 60-minute periods. To equalize the perceived advantages and/or disadvantages of this schedule, we suggest that these two teachers simply flip early and late blocks as they think best. For example, they could decide to switch the core blocks every other week, or they could follow a quarter-on/quarter-off pattern. (See Canady & Rettig, 1995b, Chapter 4 for additional information on quarter-on/quarter-off schedules.)

DAY 2

On Day 2, the language arts/reading and social studies teachers work with student Groups C and D, while the mathematics and science teachers work with student Groups A and B. This means that groups C and D will only mix with Groups A and B during the PE/exploratory/elective block.

**FIGURE 3.10. GRADE SIX FOUR-TEACHER TEAM
A/B BLOCK SCHEDULE WITH A TRIPLE E (EEE) TOWER PERIOD**

Teachers	LA/Read	SS	Math	Science
Homeroom 8:00–8:10				
Day 1	LA/Read Group A 8:10–10:00	SS Group B 8:10–10:10	Math Group C 8:10–10:10	Science Group D 8:10–10:10
Day 2	LA/Read Group C 8:10–10:10	SS Group D 8:10–10:10	Math Group A 8:10–10:10	Science Group B 8:10–10:10
Day 1	LA/Read Group B 10:10–11:10	SS Group A 10:10–11:10	Math Group D 10:10–11:10	Science Group C 10:10–11:10
Day 2	LA/Read Group D 10:10–11:10	SS Group C 10:10–11:10	Math Group B 10:10–11:10	Science Group A 10:10–11:10

Time scale: 8:00, 8:10, 8:20, 8:30, 8:40, 8:50, 9:00, 9:10, 9:20, 9:30, 9:40, 9:50, 10:00, 10:10, 10:20, 10:30, 10:40, 10:50, 11:00

Time		
11:10		
11:20	Lunch 11:10–11:30	
11:30		
11:40		
11:50	Day 1 LA/Read Group B 11:40–12:40	Day 2 LA/Read Group D 11:40–12:40	Day 1 SS Group A 11:40–12:40	Day 2 SS Group C 11:40–12:40	Day 1 Math Group D 11:40–12:40	Day 2 Math Group B 11:40–12:40	Day 1 Science Group C 11:40–12:40	Day 2 Science Group A 11:40–12:40
12:00		
12:10		
12:20		
12:30		
12:40		
12:50		
1:00	Planning time for teachers on this sixth grade team; physical education and related arts classes (exploratories) meet every other day (EOD) for 90 minutes 12:40–2:10	
1:10		
1:20		
1:30	Note: This block of time could be divided into two 43-minute periods with 4 minutes for transitions; however, for instructional reasons we tend not to recommend the two shorter periods.	
1:40		
1:50		
2:00		
2:10	Triple E (EEE) Period 2:10–3:00	
2:20		
2:30	This 50-minute Triple E (EEE) period is common to all three grade levels in this middle school. We recommend this time for classes and activities that pull students on a schoolwide basis, such as band, choir, foreign language, orchestra, and club activities. For students not in such classes, it can be a time for extended instructional assistance. Core teachers may assist during this block.	
2:40		
2:50		

GRADE SEVEN A/B SCHEDULE

Figure 3.11 (p. 60) shows the schedule for a Grade 7 four-teacher team working in an alternate-day block schedule.

DAY 1

Following homeroom time on Day 1, the language arts/reading teacher has a 120-minute instructional block with Group A, the social studies teacher with Group B, the mathematics teacher with Group C, and the science teacher with Group D.

At 11:10, all four teachers on this team have a 90-minute planning block while their assigned students attend physical education and exploratories on an EOD basis. Teachers and students have lunch from 12:40 until 1:10. In the afternoon, the language arts/reading and social studies teachers exchange groups, as do the mathematics and science teachers, for a 120-minute instructional block with their second group of students for the day. Beginning at 2:10, teachers and students in this team participate in a 50-minute EEE period with Grades 6 and 8.

DAY 2

On Day 2, the same schedule is followed except teachers work with the other two student groups assigned to this team; that is, the language arts/reading and social studies teachers work with Groups C and D, while the mathematics and science teachers work with Groups A and B.

GRADE EIGHT A/B SCHEDULE

Figure 3.12 (p. 62) shows the schedule for Grade 8 for a four-teacher team working in this sample alternate-day middle school schedule. Following homeroom, the four teachers have a 90-minute planning period while students are in physical education and exploratories on an EOD basis.

DAY 1

Beginning at 9:40, the language arts/reading teacher works with student Group A for a 120-minute instructional block, the social studies teacher instructs Group B, the mathematics teacher works with Group C, and the science teacher has Group D. At 11:40, the language arts/reading and social studies teachers exchange instructional groups A and B while the mathematics and science teachers exchange instructional groups C and D. The new groups receive 60 minutes of instruction, go to lunch from 12:40 until 1:10, and then return for another 60-minute period of instruction to complete their 120 minutes of core time in that subject for the day. At 2:10, all Grade 8 students and teachers on this sample team have a 50-minute EEE period with Grades 6 and 7.

DAY 2

On Day 2, the same schedule operates with each teacher instructing different groups. The language arts/reading social studies teachers work with Groups C and D, while the mathematics and science teachers work with Groups A and B.

ALTERNATE-DAY MASTER SCHEDULE II

In Master Schedule II (Figure 3.13, p. 64), we modify the plan shown in Figure 3.9 so that all three teams have at least 60 minutes of core time early in the day and the PE and exploratory teachers have an unbroken planning time of 60 minutes. The planning block and lunch period for Grade 7 also are changed.

GRADE-LEVEL TIME SCHEDULES

The time schedule remains the same for the Grade 6 team. Following homeroom, Grade 7 has core instruction for 150 minutes. This could be divided into various configurations: two 75-minute classes, one 100-minute class and one 50-minute class, or three 50-minute classes. This instructional block is followed by lunch for 30 minutes, then planning for 90 minutes, then 90 minutes of additional core time, and finally the 50-minute common EEE period.

The Grade 8 team has a 60-minute period for core instructional time, followed by a 90-minute planning time for teachers while students are in physical education and exploratories on an EOD basis. At 10:40 the Grade 8 team has another 60-minute period for core, followed by lunch from 11:40 until 12:10. After lunch the Grade 8 team has a 120-minute block for core classes. The day ends with a 50-minute common tower period.

PE AND EXPLORATORY SCHEDULES

In this same schedule, physical education and exploratory teachers (assuming they have no homeroom assignments) begin the day with a 60-minute planning block; they then serve Grade 8 teams and have lunch from 10:40 until 11:10. After lunch they serve Grade 7 teams for a 90-minute block, followed by Grade 6 students for 90 minutes. They end the day with the common EEE period, where they may be assigned teaching duties on a rotating basis and/or have another planning period.

(Text continues on page 64, following Figure 3.13.)

FIGURE 3.11. GRADE SEVEN FOUR-TEACHER TEAM
A/B BLOCK SCHEDULE WITH A TRIPLE E (EEE) TOWER PERIOD

Teachers	LA/Read	SS	Math	Science
8:00		Homeroom 8:00–8:10		
8:10				
8:20				
8:30				
8:40				
8:50	Day 1 LA/Read Group A 8:10–10:10	Day 1 SS Group B 8:10–10:10	Day 1 Math Group C 8:10–10:10	Day 1 Science Group D 8:10–10:10
9:00	Day 2 LA/Read Group C 8:10–10:10	Day 2 SS Group D 8:10–10:10	Day 2 Math Group A 8:10–10:10	Day 2 Science Group B 8:10–10:10
9:10				
9:20				
9:30				
9:40				
9:50				
10:00				
10:10				
10:20				
10:30				
10:40				
10:50				
11:00				

Planning time for teachers on this seventh grade team; physical education and related arts classes (exploratories) meet every other day (EOD) for 90 minutes 10:10–11:40

Note: This block of time could be divided into two 43-minute periods with 4 minutes for transitions; however, for instructional reasons we tend not to recommend the two shorter periods.

Lunch 11:40–12:00

Time	Day 1 LA/Read Group B	Day 2 LA/Read Group D	Day 1 SS Group A	Day 2 SS Group C	Day 1 Math Group D	Day 2 Math Group B	Day 1 Science Group C	Day 2 Science Group A
11:10								
11:20								
11:30								
11:40								
11:50								
12:00								
12:10	12:10–2:10	12:10–2:10	12:10–2:10	12:10–2:10	12:10–2:10	12:10–2:10	12:10–2:10	12:10–2:10
12:20								
12:30								
12:40								
12:50								
1:00								
1:10								
1:20								
1:30								
1:40								
1:50								
2:00								
2:10								
2:20								
2:30								
2:40								
2:50								

Triple E (EEE) Period 2:10–3:00

This 50-minute Triple E (EEE) period is common to all three grade levels in this middle school. We recommend this time for classes and activities that pull students on a school-wide basis, such as band, choir, foreign language, orchestra, and club activities. For students not in such classes, it can be a time for extended instructional assistance. Core teachers may assist during this block.

FIGURE 3.12. GRADE EIGHT FOUR-TEACHER TEAM
A/B BLOCK SCHEDULE WITH A TRIPLE E (EEE) TOWER PERIOD

Teachers	LA/Read	SS	Math	Science
8:00	Homeroom 8:00–8:10			
8:10				
8:20				
8:30	Planning time for teachers on this eighth grade team; physical education and related arts classes (exploratories) meet every other day (EOD) for 90 minutes 8:10–9:40			
8:40				
8:50				
9:00	Note: This block of time could be divided into two 43-minute periods with 4 minutes for transitions; however, for instructional reasons we tend not to recommend the two shorter periods.			
9:10				
9:20				
9:30				
9:40	**Day 1** **LA/Read Group A** **9:40–11:40** / Day 2 LA/Read Group C 9:40–11:40	**Day 1** **SS Group B** **9:40–11:40** / Day 2 SS Group D 9:40–11:40	**Day 1** **Math Group C** **9:40–11:40** / Day 2 Math Group A 9:40–11:40	**Day 1** **Science Group D** **9:40–11:40** / Day 2 Science Group B 9:40–11:40
9:50				
10:00				
10:10				
10:20				
10:30				
10:40				
10:50				
11:00				

Time	LA/Read Group B	LA/Read Group D	SS Group A	SS Group C	Math Group D	Math Group B	Science Group C	Science Group A
11:10								
11:20								
11:30								
11:40–12:40	**Day 1** **LA/Read** **Group B**	Day 2 LA/Read Group D	**Day 1** **SS** **Group A**	Day 2 SS Group C	**Day 1** **Math** **Group D**	Day 2 Math Group B	**Day 1** **Science** **Group C**	Day 2 Science Group A
12:40–1:10	Lunch							
1:10–2:10	**Day 1** **LA/Read** **Group B**	Day 2 LA/Read Group D	**Day 1** **SS** **Group A**	Day 2 SS Group C	**Day 1** **Math** **Group D**	Day 2 Math Group B	**Day 1** **Science** **Group C**	Day 2 Science Group A
2:10–3:00	Triple E (EEE) Period							

Triple E (EEE) Period 2:10–3:00

This 50-minute Triple E (EEE) period is common to all three grade levels in this middle school. We recommend this time for classes and activities that pull students on a school-wide basis, such as band, choir, foreign language, orchestra, and club activities. For students not in such classes, it can be a time for extended instructional assistance. Core teachers may assist during this block.

FIGURE 3.13. MIDDLE SCHOOL MASTER SCHEDULE II:
A/B BLOCK SCHEDULE WITH A TRIPLE E (EEE) OR TOWER PERIOD

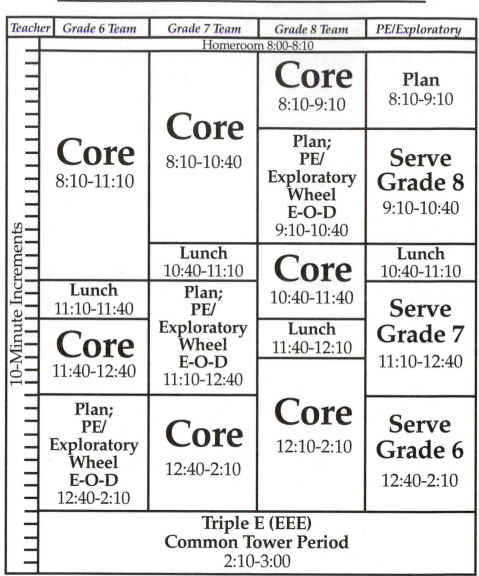

Teacher	Grade 6 Team	Grade 7 Team	Grade 8 Team	PE/Exploratory
	Homeroom 8:00-8:10			
10-Minute Increments	**Core** 8:10-11:10	**Core** 8:10-10:40	**Core** 8:10-9:10	Plan 8:10-9:10
			Plan; PE/ Exploratory Wheel E-O-D 9:10-10:40	**Serve Grade 8** 9:10-10:40
		Lunch 10:40-11:10	**Core** 10:40-11:40	Lunch 10:40-11:10
	Lunch 11:10-11:40	Plan; PE/ Exploratory Wheel E-O-D 11:10-12:40	Lunch 11:40-12:10	**Serve Grade 7** 11:10-12:40
	Core 11:40-12:40			
	Plan; PE/ Exploratory Wheel E-O-D 12:40-2:10	**Core** 12:40-2:10	**Core** 12:10-2:10	**Serve Grade 6** 12:40-2:10
	Triple E (EEE) Common Tower Period 2:10-3:00			

FOUR LUNCH PERIODS

Each of the previous master schedules shows only three lunch periods. What if a school needs four? Figure 3.14 shows how a middle school in an alternate-day block schedule can have up to four lunch periods. In this example, a 25-minute time period for teacher advisory groups was added to the schedule and all instructional blocks were shortened accordingly to 85 minutes.

Figure 3.14 shows that we have chosen to build lunch periods before and after Block III. To have four lunch periods, we schedule one-quarter of the students for lunch from 11:10 to 11:35 and one-quarter of the students into an activity class or advisory during the same time period; after 25 minutes, the two groups switch. In Figure 3.14, these lunches are shown as Lunches A and B. Lunches C and D are scheduled for the remaining one-half of the students, and those schedules are achieved in the same way as Lunches A and B except they occur after students have completed Block III.

FIGURE 3.14. BLOCK III AND FOUR LUNCH PERIODS

	11:10–11:35	*11:35–12:00*	*12:05–1:30*	
¼ of School	Lunch A	Activity or Advisory	Day 1	Course 5
			Day 2	Course 6
¼ of School	Activity or Advisory	Lunch B	Day 1	Course 5
			Day 2	Course 6
	11:10–12:35		*12:40–1:05*	*1:05–1:30*
¼ of School	Day 1	Course 5	Lunch C	Activity or Advisory
	Day 2	Course 6		
¼ of School	Day 1	Course 5	Activity or Advisory	Lunch D
	Day 2	Course 6		

VARIATIONS ON THE ALTERNATE-DAY THEME: TWO INTERESTING EXAMPLES

Some schools find it difficult to provide students with many choices and still devote significant time to core instruction. Many parents want students to take a foreign language, be in the band, and still participate in exploratory offerings. Sometimes these requests are difficult to schedule without diluting the time available for core instruction to an unacceptable level. Two schools in Maryland designed block schedules that attempt to provide it all. Figure 3.15 (p. 66) illustrates the first of these schedules.

Each grade level has six core classes: reading, English, mathematics, science, social studies, and either a foreign language or another block of additional mathematics and/or language arts. Each of these six classes

FIGURE 3.15. A/B BLOCK SCHEDULE WITH ROTATING CORE, A/B EXPLORATORY, AND DAILY BAND: MASTER SCHEDULE

	8:00–9:25 (85 minutes)		9:30–10:50 (80 minutes)		10:55–1:35 (160 minutes)				1:40–3:00 (80 minutes)	
Periods	1	2	3	4	5	6	7	8	9	10
Grade 6	Day 1 Class 1		Class 3		10:55–11:30	11:35–12:10	12:15–1:35 Class 7		Day 1, 3, 5 Related Arts	
	Day 2 Class 2		**Class 4**		Band, Advisory, Skills/Enrichment	LUNCH	**Class 8**			
	Day 3 Class 3		Class 7				Class 1			
	Day 4 Class 4		**Class 8**				**Class 2**			
	Day 5 Class 7		Class 1				Class 3			
	Day 6 Class 8		**Class 2**				**Class 4**		Health/ PE Day 2, 4, 6	
Grade 7	Day 1, 3, 5 Related Arts		Day 1 Class 3		10:55–11:30	11:35–12:55 Class 6		1:00–1:35	Class 9	
			Day 2 Class 4			**Class 7**		Band, HR, Advisory, Skills/Enrichment	**Class 10**	
			Day 3 Class 6		LUNCH	Class 9			Class 3	
			Day 4 Class 7			**Class 10**			**Class 4**	
			Day 5 Class 9			Class 3			Class 6	
	Health/ PE Day 2, 4, 6		**Day 6 Class 10**			**Class 4**			**Class 7**	
Grade 8	Day 1 Class 1		Day 1, 3, 5 Related Arts		10:55–12:15 Class 5		12:20–12:55	1:00–1:35	Class 9	
	Day 2 Class 2				**Class 6**			Band, HR, Advisory, Skills/Enrichment	**Class 10**	
	Day 3 Class 5				Class 9		LUNCH		Class 1	
	Day 4 Class 6				**Class 10**				**Class 2**	
	Day 5 Class 9				Class 1				Class 5	
	Day 6 Class 10		Health/ PE Day 2, 4, 6		**Class 2**				**Class 6**	

Note: This is a master schedule for both teachers and students. For a teacher, "Class 3" means the group of students the teacher would have in Period 3 if this were a single-period schedule. For students, "Class 3" means the class they would have during Period 3 if this were a single-period schedule. Core periods rotate and alternate; PE/health and exploratory periods alternate only; lunch and band/extension are in fixed periods. Shading is added to show how teachers could be shared across grade levels. A teacher could instruct Classes 1, 3, and 7 in Grade Six (unshaded) and Classes 10, 2, and 6 in Grade Eight (shaded). See text for a detailed explanation of this schedule.

---

meets every other day (EOD) for 80 minutes. In addition to the core classes, students have 5 minutes added onto the first block for homeroom, an 80-minute block that alternates EOD between PE/health and exploratory offerings, 35 minutes for either band, advisory, or a skills class, 35 minutes for lunch, and 25 minutes for class changes. The master schedule is built on ten periods, of which eight are blocked and two (lunch and band) are not.

Let's examine the sixth grade schedule. The core blocks for sixth grade fall into periods 1–2, 3–4, and 7–8; thus, we call the six core classes sixth grade students take Class 1, Class 2, Class 3, Class 4, Class 7, and Class 8. These classes rotate and alternate on an EOD basis. Each core teacher works with six classes. For example, after homeroom on Day 1, all core teachers in Grade 6 instruct Class 1 (their first period group in a single-period schedule) from 8:00 to 9:25 and Class 3 from 9:30 to 10:50. Band, advisory and skills/enrichment meet during Period 5 (10:55–11:30). Lunch follows in Period 6 (11:35–12:10). Students and teachers return to core for Class 7, from 12:15 to 1:35. Finally, the PE/health and related arts block meets in Periods 9 and 10. PE/health alternates EOD with a related arts class. Core teachers plan during this time. On Day 2, teachers instruct and students attend core Classes 2, 4, and 8. Classes 1, 3, and 7 always meet on "odd" days, which are unshaded on Figure 3.15. Core Classes 2, 4, and 8 always meet on "even" days, which are shaded on Figure 3.15. On Day 3, sixth grade Classes 1, 3, and 7 meet, but in different time slots. Class 3 meets first thing after homeroom, from 8:00 to 9:25. Class 7 follows, from 9:30 to 10:50. After periods 5 and 6, Class 1 meets from 12:15 to 1:35. The day concludes for teachers with planning time and for students with the PE/health and related arts block.

Figure 3.16 (p. 68) shows three teacher schedules—one sixth, one seventh, and one eighth. As this example illustrates, each of the teachers' six groups meets every other day for 80 minutes, and each meeting falls during a different block. Each teacher also is scheduled for 80 minutes of team and individual planning time, 35 minutes of lunch and 35 minutes of skills/enrichment time.

FIGURE 3.16. A/B BLOCK SCHEDULE WITH ROTATING CORE, A/B EXPLORATORY, AND DAILY BAND: THREE TEACHERS' SCHEDULES

	8:00–9:25 (85 minutes)		9:30–10:50 (80 minutes)		10:55–1:35 (160 minutes)			1:40–3:00 (80 minutes)		
Periods	1	2	3	4	5	6	7	8	9	10
Teacher 6A	Day 1 Group 6-1		Group 6-3		10:55–11:30 Band, HR, Advisory, Skills/Enrichment	11:35–12:10 LUNCH	12:15–1:35 Group 6-5	Team and Individual Planning Time		
	Day 2 Group 6-2		Group 6-4				Group 6-6			
	Day 3 Group 6-3		Group 6-5				Group 6-1			
	Day 4 Group 6-4		Group 6-6				Group 6-2			
	Day 5 Group 6-5		Group 6-1				Group 6-3			
	Day 6 Group 6-6		Group 6-2				Group 6-4			
Teacher 7A	Team and Individual Planning Time		Day 1 Group 7-1		10:55–11:30 LUNCH	11:35–12:55 Group 7-3		1:00–1:35 Band, HR, Advisory, Skills/Enrichment	Group 7-5	
			Day 2 Group 7-2			Group 7-4			Group 7-6	
			Day 3 Group 7-3			Group 7-5			Group 7-1	
			Day 4 Group 7-4			Group 7-6			Group 7-2	
			Day 5 Group 7-5			Group 7-1			Group 7-3	
			Day 6 Group 7-6			Group 7-2			Group 7-4	
Teacher 8A	Day 1 Group 8-1		Team and Individual Planning Time		10:55–12:15 Group 8-3		12:20–12:55 LUNCH	1:00–1:35 Band, HR, Advisory, Skills/Enrichment	Group 8-5	
	Day 2 Group 8-2				Group 8-4				Group 8-6	
	Day 3 Group 8-3				Group 8-5				Group 8-1	
	Day 4 Group 8-4				Group 8-6				Group 8-2	
	Day 5 Group 8-5				Group 8-1				Group 8-3	
	Day 6 Group 8-6				Group 8-2				Group 8-4	

Figure 3.17 (p. 70) illustrates three sample student schedules. Each of these students attends six core classes which meet every other day in different blocks, 80 minutes of either PE or a related arts (exploratory) class, 35 minutes of lunch and 35 minutes for either band or skills/enrichment.

For example, our eighth grade student attends English from 8:00 to 9:25 on Day 1 followed by his related arts class from 9:30 to 10:50. Algebra class meets on Day 1 from 10:55 to 12:15. After lunch and band or skills/enrichment our student has social studies. On Day 2, the student's reading class meets first, followed by PE/health. His French class meets from 10:55 to 12:15. After lunch and band or skills/enrichment, earth science meets from 1:40 to 3:00. On Day 3 his algebra class meets again, but this time from 8:00 until 9:25. Our student then returns to his related arts class from 9:30 to 10:50 followed by social studies from 10:55 to 12:15. After lunch and band or skills/enrichment, his English class meets again. The schedule progresses in this manner with classes meeting every other day on a rotational basis.

In the school for which this schedule was designed, staffing was tight; unfortunately, it was necessary to share teachers across grade levels. The shading shown in Figure 3.15 (p. 66) simplifies possible sharing arrangements. Teachers can easily work in two grade levels; just make sure they work on "odd" or unshaded days in one grade and "even" or shaded days for a different grade. For example, a foreign language teacher might instruct three classes of French for Grade 7 (Classes 3, 6, and 9), as well as three classes of French for Grade 8 (Classes 2, 6, and 10). These six classes never conflict.

Sharing a core teacher across three grade levels is more problematic. It is not possible to teach two core classes at each grade level. It is possible to instruct three at one grade level and one or two at each of the other two grades. For example, a teacher could instruct three sections of seventh grade (Classes 3, 6, and 9), as well as two sections of Grade 8 (Classes 2 and 6), and one section of Grade 6 (Class 8). All three sections of seventh grade are on "odd" days; the two sections of eighth grade and one section of sixth grade are on "even" days and do not conflict with each other.

This schedule allows a mixed-grade-level band, something many band directors prefer. From 1:00 to 1:35, the seventh and eighth grade band meets. Seventh grade students not skillful enough to play in this group can join the sixth grade band by switching lunch periods.

FIGURE 3.17. A/B BLOCK SCHEDULE WITH ROTATING CORE, A/B EXPLORATORY, AND DAILY BAND: THREE STUDENTS' SCHEDULES

	8:00–9:25 (85 minutes)		9:30–10:50 (80 minutes)		10:55–1:35 (160 minutes)				1:40–3:00 (80 minutes)	
Periods	1	2	3	4	5	6	7	8	9	10
Grade 6 Student	Day 1 English		Math		10:55–11:30 Band, HR, Advisory, Skills/Enrichment	11:35–12:10 LUNCH	12:15–1:35 Social Studies		Day 1, 3, 5 Related Arts	
	Day 2 Reading		Science				Spanish			
	Day 3 Math		Social Studies				English			
	Day 4 Science		Spanish				Reading			
	Day 5 Social Studies		English				Math		Health/ PE Day 2, 4, 6	
	Day 6 Spanish		Reading				Science			
Grade 7 Student	Day 1, 3, 5 Related Arts		Day 1 Science		10:55–11:30 LUNCH	11:35–12:55 English		1:00–1:35 Band, HR, Advisory, Skills/Enrichment	Social Studies	
			Day 2 Math			Reading			Remedial	
			Day 3 English			Social Studies			Science	
			Day 4 Reading			Remedial			Math	
	Health/ PE Day 2, 4, 6		Day 5 Social Studies			Science			English	
			Day 6 Remedial			Math			Reading	
Grade 8 Student	Day 1 English		Day 1, 3, 5 Related Arts		10:55–12:15 Algebra		12:20–12:55 LUNCH	1:00–1:35 Band, HR, Advisory, Skills/Enrichment	Social Studies	
	Day 2 Reading				French				Earth Science	
	Day 3 Algebra				Social Studies				English	
	Day 4 French				Earth Science				Reading	
	Day 5 Social Studies		Health/ PE Day 2, 4, 6		English				Algebra	
	Day 6 Earth Science				Reading				French	

A second interesting schedule, which is similar to the plan shown in Figure 3.15 (p. 66) but is designed for five core-class scheduling slots, is shown in Figure 3.18 (p. 72).

In this schedule, students take five core classes and teachers teach five sections of core. The classes are English, mathematics, social studies, science, and either reading or foreign language. In addition, students participate in either band or a core extension class, the PE/health and related arts block, and lunch. Core classes meet three times a week on a rotational schedule. Twice a week each class meets for an 85-minute block. Once a week, each class meets for 40 minutes, after which all band students leave. Students who are not in band remain for an additional 40 minutes of core extension: practice, reinforcement, and enrichment.

Let's examine the Grade 7 schedule. Because seventh grade core blocks fall in periods 1–2, 5, and 8–9, we denote their classes as Classes 1, 2, 5, 8, and 9. On Day 1, after homeroom, from 8:00 to 9:25 teachers instruct and students attend Class 1, the class that would meet in period 1 if this were a single-period schedule. From 9:30 to 10:55, students attend the PE/health and related arts block while their core teachers plan; on one day students attend a PE/health class for 85 minutes and the next day they attend a related arts class for 85 minutes. Class 9 meets from 11:00 to 11:40. Following lunch, music students leave for band and all non-band students return to Class 9 from 12:30 to 1:10. To complete the day, students attend Class 2 from 1:15 to 2:45. On Day 2, students attend Class 5, a split Class 2 and Class 8. The pattern continues so that by the end of the week each class has met for two 85-minute blocks and a 40-minute period plus a 40-minute extension, which band students do not attend. Similar rotations occur for both sixth and eighth grade students.

Figure 3.19 (p. 74) illustrates three sample teacher schedules. An eighth grade math teacher has her team and individual planning time after homeroom. On Day 1, she meets section 8.1 for Algebra I from 9:30 to 10:55. After lunch, she meets with her Math 8 class (section 8.5), for 40 minutes from 11:45 to 12:25, after which any band students leave. She continues with the remaining students providing practice, reinforcement, and enrichment until 1:10. She instructs section 8.2 in Pre-algebra (PA) from 1:15 until 2:45. On Day 2, after planning time, she instructs section 8.3 in Algebra I. After lunch she then meets with section 8.2 for Pre-algebra; after 40 minutes all band students depart and the remaining students receive practice, reinforcement, and enrichment until 1:10. She completes the day with section 8.4 in Pre-algebra. The schedule continues in this manner with each class meeting for 85 minutes twice a week in addition to a 40-minute period with a 40-minute extension for practice, reinforcement, and enrichment (or band).

FIGURE 3.18. FIVE-DAY ROTATIONAL BLOCK WITH ROTATING CORE, A/B PE/EXPLORATORY, AND DAILY BAND: MASTER SCHEDULE

			7:45–7:55	8:00–9:25	9:30–10:55	11:00–1:10			1:15–2:45	
		Periods	*1*	*2*	*3*	*4*	*5*	*6*	*7*	*8*	*9*
		Day 1		Class 1		Class 2	11:00–11:40 Class 6 ➡	11:45–12:25 Band/Extension ➡ Class 6	12:30–1:10	"A" Day Related Arts	
Grade 6	Homeroom	Day 2		Class 3		Class 4	Class 2 ➡	➡ Class 2	L U N C H		
		Day 3		Class 6		Class 1	Class 4 ➡	➡ Class 4			
		Day 4		Class 2		Class 3	Class 1 ➡	➡ Class 1			
		Day 5		Class 4		Class 6	Class 3 ➡	➡ Class 3		Health/ PE "B" Day	
		Day 1		Class 1	"A" Day Related Arts		11:00–11:40 Class 9 ➡	11:45–12:25	12:30–1:10 Band/Extension ➡ Class 9	Class 2	
Grade 7	Homeroom	Day 2		Class 5			Class 2 ➡	L U N C H	➡ Class 2	Class 8	
		Day 3		Class 9			Class 8 ➡		➡ Class 8	Class 1	
		Day 4		Class 2			Class 1 ➡		➡ Class 1	Class 5	
		Day 5		Class 8	Health/ PE "B" Day		Class 5 ➡		➡ Class 5	Class 9	

7:45–7:55			8:00–9:25		9:30–10:55		11:00–1:10			1:15–2:45	
Periods			1	2	3	4	5	6	7	8	9
Grade 8	Homeroom	Day 1	"A" Day Related Arts		Class 3		11:00–11:40	11:45–12:25 Class 9 ➡	12:30–1:10 Band/Extension ➡ Class 9	Class 4	
		Day 2			Class 5		L U N C H	Class 4 ➡	➡ Class 4	Class 8	
		Day 3			Class 9			Class 8 ➡	➡ Class 8	Class 3	
		Day 4			Class 4			Class 3 ➡	➡ Class 3	Class 5	
		Day 5	Health/PE "B" Day		Class 8			Class 5 ➡	➡ Class 5	Class 9	

Note: Where the ➡ is shown, this class is extended into the next instructional period for all students who are not in band. Each of the five core classes is extended for 40 minutes once a week. Band students miss this extended class. Core classes rotate. PE/health and exploratories alternate on an EOD basis. Band meets in the same two periods daily (Periods 6 and 7). Grade 7 students who qualify can be in the Grade 8 band. Sixth grade students who qualify for either the Grade 7 or Grade 8 band switch lunch to Period 6 and join the appropriate band in Period 7. If the high school band director is unavailable for Grade 8 band, the schedule is altered to allow for three separate band classes to avoid a conflict (see Figure 3.21, p. 78, for this option).

FIGURE 3.19. FIVE-DAY ROTATIONAL BLOCK WITH ROTATING CORE, A/B PE/EXPLORATORY, AND DAILY BAND: THREE SAMPLE TEACHER SCHEDULES

7:45–7:55			8:00–9:25		9:30–10:55		11:00–1:10			1:15–2:45	
Periods			1	2	3	4	5	6	7	8	9
Grade 6	*Homeroom*	Day 1	Language Arts 6.1		Language Arts 6.2		11:00–11:40 LA 6.5 ➡	11:45–12:25 Band/ Extension ➡ LA 6.5	12:30–1:10 L U N C H	Team and Individual Planning Time	
		Day 2	Language Arts 6.3		Language Arts 6.4		LA 6.2 ➡	➡ LA 6.2			
		Day 3	Language Arts 6.5		Language Arts 6.1		LA 6.4 ➡	➡ LA 6.4			
		Day 4	Language Arts 6.2		Language Arts 6.3		LA 6.1 ➡	➡ LA 6.1			
		Day 5	Language Arts 6.4		Language Arts 6.5		LA 6.3 ➡	➡ LA 6.3			
Grade 7	*Homeroom*	Day 1	Social Studies 7.1		Team and Individual Planning Time		11:00–11:40 SS 7.5 ➡	11:45–12:25 L U N C H	12:30–1:10 Band/ Extension ➡ SS 7.5	Social Studies 7.2	
		Day 2	Social Studies 7.3				SS 7.2 ➡		➡ SS 7.2	Social Studies 7.4	
		Day 3	Social Studies 7.5				SS 7.4 ➡		➡ SS 7.4	Social Studies 7.1	
		Day 4	Social Studies 7.2				SS 7.1 ➡		➡ SS 7.1	Social Studies 7.3	
		Day 5	Social Studies 7.4				SS 7.3 ➡		➡ SS 7.3	Social Studies 7.5	

7:45–7:55		8:00–9:25		9:30–10:55		11:00–1:10			1:15–2:45	
Periods		1	2	3	4	5	6	7	8	9
G r a d e 8	**H o m e r o o m**			Algebra I 8.1 (Day 1)		11:00–11:40	11:45–12:25 M8 8.5 ➡	12:30–1:10 Band/Extension ➡ M8 8.5	Pre-algebra 8.2	
		Team and Individual Planning Time (Day 2)		Algebra I 8.3		L U N C H	PA 8.2 ➡	➡ PA 8.2	Pre-algebra 8.4	
		(Day 3)		Math 8 8.5			PA 8.4 ➡	➡ PA 8.4	Algebra I 8.1	
		(Day 4)		Pre-algebra 8.2			AI 8.1 ➡	➡ AI 8.1	Algebra I 8.3	
		(Day 5)		Pre-algebra 8.4			AI 8.3 ➡	➡ AI 8.3	Math 8 8.5	

Note: Numbers denote sections; for example, "8.1" means "section 8.1." Groups need not be platooned. Where the ➡ is shown, this class is extended into the next instructional period for all students who are not in band. Each of a teacher's five sections is extended for 40 minutes once a week. Band students miss this extended class. Core classes rotate. (M8 = Math 8; PA = Pre-algebra; AI = Algebra I.)

Three student schedules are shown in Figure 3.20 (p. 76). On Day 1, the seventh grade student follows homeroom with his Pre-algebra class from 8:00 to 9:25. Next comes his related arts class (9:30–10:55). Social studies meets for 40 minutes, followed by lunch. Then our student attends band, while non-band students return to social studies. Science 7 ends Day 1. After homeroom on Day 2 he attends Language Arts 7 followed by PE/health. Science 7 meets for 40 minutes. After lunch, our student attends band, while non-band students return to science. Day 2 ends with Spanish Ia. As the week continues each core class meets three times: two 85-minute blocks and one 40-minute period (extended for an additional 40 minutes for non-band students).

In the examples illustrated by Figures 3.18 to 3.20, seventh and eighth grade bands meet during the same period (7), although any sixth grade students who qualify may attend the seventh or eighth grade band by switching lunch times. The high school band director instructs the eighth grade band. If the high school band director is unavailable for this assignment, we would alter the schedule to avoid the conflict. The master schedule shown in Figure 3.18 could be changed by rescheduling periods 5 to 7.

FIGURE 3.20. FIVE-DAY ROTATIONAL BLOCK WITH ROTATING CORE, A/B PE/EXPLORATORY, AND DAILY BAND: THREE SAMPLE STUDENT SCHEDULES

			7:45–7:55	8:00–9:25		9:30–10:55		11:00–1:10			1:15–2:45	
		Periods		*1*	*2*	*3*	*4*	*5*	*6*	*7*	*8*	*9*
Grade 6	*Homeroom*	Day 1		Math 6		Reading 6		11:00–11:40 SS 6 ➡	11:45–12:25 Band/ Extension ➡ SS 6	12:30–1:10 L U N C H	"A" Day Related Arts	
		Day 2		Science 6		Language Arts 6		Read 6 ➡	➡ Read 6			
		Day 3		Social Studies 6		Math 6		LA 6 ➡	➡ LA 6			
		Day 4		Reading 6		Science 6		Math 6 ➡	➡ Math 6			
		Day 5		Language Arts 6		Social Studies 6		Sci 6 ➡	➡ Sci 6		Health/ PE "B" Day	
Grade 7	*Homeroom*	Day 1		Pre-algebra		"A" Day Related Arts		11:00–11:40 SS 7 ➡	11:45–12:25 L U N C H	12:30–1:10 Band/ Extension ➡ SS 7	Science 7	
		Day 2		Language Arts 7				Sci 7 ➡		➡ Sci 7	Spanish Ia	
		Day 3		Social Studies 7				SP Ia ➡		➡ SP Ia	Pre-algebra	
		Day 4		Science 7				Pre A ➡		➡ Pre A	Language Arts 7	
		Day 5		Spanish Ia		Health/ PE "B" Day		LA 7 ➡		➡ LA 7	Social Studies 7	

7:45–7:55	8:00–9:25		9:30–10:55		11:00–1:10			1:15–2:45	
Periods	1	2	3	4	5	6	7	8	9
G r a d e 8 — H o m e r o o m	Day 1 — "A" Day Related Arts		Algebra I		11:00–11:40	11:45–12:25 — Eng 8 ➡	12:30–1:10 Band/ Extension ➡ Eng 8	Spanish Ib	
	Day 2		Earth Science		L U N C H	SP Ib ➡	➡ SP Ib	World Studies I	
	Day 3		English 8			WS I ➡	➡ WS I	Algebra I	
	Day 4		Spanish Ib			Alg I ➡	➡ Alg I	Earth Science	
	Day 5	Health/ PE "B" Day	World Studies I			E Sci ➡	➡ E Sci	English 8	

Note: Where the ➡ is shown, this class is extended into the next instructional period for all students who are not in band. Each of the five core classes is extended for 40 minutes once a week. Band students miss this extended class. Core classes rotate. PE/health and exploratories alternate on an EOD basis. (SPIa = Spanish I, Part A; SPIb = Spanish I, Part B; WSI = World Studies I.)

Figure 3.21 (p. 78) illustrates one possibility. Sixth grade students follow lunch with the first 40 minutes of class from 11:45 to 12:25. Band students leave and any remaining students receive practice, reinforcement or enrichment activities from 12:30 to 1:10. Seventh grade students attend band from 11:00 to 11:40. In this case the practice, reinforcement, and enrichment session precedes the regular class, which is held after lunch from 12:30 to 1:10. Eighth grade students have class from 11:00 to 11:40, band or extension from 11:45 to 12:25, and lunch from 12:30 to 1:10. A sixth grade student, who qualifies for the seventh grade band would switch lunch and band periods (band in period 5; lunch in period 7). A seventh grade student, who qualifies for the eighth grade band would do the same, eating lunch during period 5 and attending band with eighth grade students during period 6.

We believe the alternate-day block schedule detailed in this chapter has several advantages for middle school students and teachers over the traditional single-period daily schedule.

Some of those advantages are:

◆ Students have no more than five classes and no more than three core classes on any one day.

FIGURE 3.21. FIVE-DAY ROTATIONAL BLOCK WITH ROTATING CORE, A/B PE/EXPLORATORY, AND DAILY BAND: MASTER SCHEDULE (3 BAND PERIODS)

			8:00–9:25	9:30–10:55	11:00–1:10			1:15–2:45
7:45–7:55		*Periods*	*1* / *2*	*3* / *4*	*5*	*6*	*7*	*8* / *9*
Grade 6	*Homeroom*	Day 1	Class 1	Class 2	11:00–11:40 L U N C H	11:45–12:25 Class 6 ➡	12:30–1:10 Band/ Extension ➡ Class 6	"A" Day Related Arts Health/PE "B" Day
		Day 2	Class 3	Class 4		Class 2 ➡	➡ Class 2	
		Day 3	Class 6	Class 1		Class 4 ➡	➡ Class 4	
		Day 4	Class 2	Class 3		Class 1 ➡	➡ Class 1	
		Day 5	Class 4	Class 6		Class 3 ➡	➡ Class 3	
Grade 7	*Homeroom*	Day 1	Class 1	"A" Day Related Arts Health/PE "B" Day	11:00–11:40 Band/ Extension Class 9 ➡	11:45–12:25 L U N C H	12:30–1:10 ➡ Class 9	Class 2
		Day 2	Class 5		Class 2 ➡		➡ Class 2	Class 8
		Day 3	Class 9		Class 8 ➡		➡ Class 8	Class 3
		Day 4	Class 2		Class 1 ➡		➡ Class 1	Class 5
		Day 5	Class 8		Class 5 ➡		➡ Class 5	Class 9

7:45–7:55		8:00–9:25		9:30–10:55		11:00–1:10			1:15–2:45	
Periods		*1*	*2*	*3*	*4*	*5*	*6*	*7*	*8*	*9*
G r a d e *8*	*H o m e r o o m*	Day 1	"A" Day Related Arts	Class 3		11:00–11:40 ⟍ Class 9 ➡	11:45–12:25 Band/ Extension ➡ Class 9	12:30–1:10	Class 4	
		Day 2		Class 5		Class 4 ➡	➡ Class 4	L U N C H	Class 8	
		Day 3		Class 9		Class 8 ➡	➡ Class 8		Class 3	
		Day 4		Class 4		Class 3 ➡	➡ Class 3		Class 5	
		Day 5	Health/ PE "B" Day	Class 8		Class 5 ➡	➡ Class 5		Class 9	

Note: Where the ➡ is shown, this class is extended into the next instructional period for all students who are not in band. Each of the five core classes is extended for 40 minutes once a week. Band students miss this extended class. Core classes rotate. PE/health and exploratories alternate on an EOD basis. Band meets in Period 5 for Grade 7, Period 6 for Grade 8, and Period 7 for Grade 6. Grade 6 students who qualify for the Grade 7 band eat lunch during Period 7 and join the Grade 7 band during Period 5. Grade 7 students who qualify can be in the Grade 8 band; they eat lunch during Period 5 and join the Grade 8 band during Period 6.

- ♦ Core teachers never have more than three classes on any one day.
- ♦ Physical education/exploratory teachers typically never work with more than three groups of students on any one day.
- ♦ Both teachers and students benefit from having the possibility of scheduling all instructional groups at various times during the week/quarter/term/semester/year for extended blocks of time for core classes.

Physical education and exploratory teachers, by working on an alternating-day format, have 80 to 90 minutes of time for their active instructional needs. The main issue to arise from implementation of the alternate-day schedule is instruction. Can teachers effectively adapt instruction to the longer time frame and the every-other-day class meeting schedule? We address this question in detail in Chapter 9.

4

THE FOUR-BLOCK SCHEDULE: ADAPTING THE 4/4 HIGH SCHOOL BLOCK SCHEDULE FOR MIDDLE SCHOOLS

During the 1990s, the 4/4 semester block schedule became one of the most widely implemented high school block schedules in the United States. In some states, this popular scheduling model is referred to as the "accelerated" schedule, primarily because it permits students to acquire 24 credits in 3 years and to graduate early. In other states, the model is called the "four-period day" or the "Block 4" schedule, while in some school districts it is referred to as semestering (see Canady & Rettig, 1995b, Chapter 3 for a detailed discussion of this high school model).

Regardless of the name given, the common description of what we refer to as the high school 4/4 schedule is that students meet daily in a time range of 80 to 100 minutes for one semester, completing four courses, and then repeat the same schedule format during the second semester, usually by completing four additional courses. In most school districts, teachers in the 4/4 schedule teach three classes each semester. This chapter describes how the 4/4 high school block schedule can be adapted to the middle school concept to achieve some unique benefits for both teachers and students.

THE BASIC FOUR-BLOCK SCHEDULE

Figure 4.1 is a simple model of the four-block schedule for a middle school student. In this schedule, students receive a block of language arts and reading daily, a block of mathematics daily, a block of social studies for one semester and science the next, and one block devoted to physical education, exploratories, and electives.

FIGURE 4.1. FOUR-BLOCK MIDDLE SCHOOL STUDENT SCHEDULE

	Semester 1	Semester 2
Block I	Reading/Language Arts	
Block II	Mathematics	
LUNCH		
Block III	Science	Social Studies
Block IV	Day 1 PE	Day 2 Elective/Expl.

In Figure 4.1, the student is scheduled for a daily reading and language arts block during Block I for both the fall and spring semesters, mathematics daily during Block II for both semesters (180 days), science during Block III in the fall (90 days), social studies in Block III for the spring (90 days), and physical education every other day (EOD) opposite an elective or an exploratory rotation in Block IV.

This student schedule can be created from a variety of teaming arrangements. In the following sections, we describe the possibilities for teams of two, three, four, and six teachers.

TWO-TEACHER TEAM

Two-teacher teams often work well for sixth grade teachers with 60 or fewer students. In this teaming situation, typically one of the teachers becomes the language arts/social studies teacher for all students; the other teacher becomes the math/science (and perhaps health) teacher for all students. It is possible for these two teachers simply to divide the available time into two equal parts and switch groups midway through this time. A disadvantage of this plan is that students from one half of the team are never mixed with students from the other half.

Figure 4.2. illustrates an alternative time division for teachers in the four-block, two-teacher team. This plan allows more mixing of the students and ensures that students receive 90 minutes of language arts, 90

FIGURE 4.2. FOUR-BLOCK SCHEDULE, TWO-TEACHER TEAM

Times	8:00–8:10	Block I 8:10–9:40	Block II 9:45–11:15	11:20–11:50	Block III 11:55–1:25	Block IV 1:30–3:00
Teacher A **Language Arts & Social Studies**	HR	Group 1 Language Arts	Group 2 Language Arts	Lunch	Social Studies Group 2 (Sem. 1) Group 1 (Sem. 2)	Teachers: Individual and Team Planning Time
Teacher B **Math & Science**	HR	Group 2 Math	Group 1 Math	Lunch	Science Group 1 (Sem. 1) Group 2 (Sem. 2)	Students: PE & Exploratory Block

minutes of math, and 90 minutes of science and/or social studies daily. From 8:10 until 9:40, Teacher A works with Group 1 in language arts and reading, while Teacher B works with Group 2 for 90 minutes of mathematics. At 9:40 the teachers exchange groups, teaching their subject to the new group for the next 90 minutes. At 11:55, after lunch, Teacher A puts on the social studies hat and works with Group 2 again for 90 minutes. Teacher B instructs Group 1 in science. While it is suggested in Figure 4.2 that Groups 1 and 2 remain separate all day, this is not necessary. After mathematics and language arts instruction is completed, Groups 1 and 2 can be remixed for social studies and science; they also can be remixed during Block IV when PE, electives, or exploratory classes meet.

This model also shows students participating in one semester of social studies and one semester of science. Some have argued that this might not be wise if life science is being taught and the seasons come into play. Also, during election years it might be advantageous for the social studies teacher to have access to both groups of students in the fall. The schedule permits other alternations besides the semester exchange. The two teachers could decide to exchange students every 9 weeks or perhaps every 4½ weeks so that a grade is received in both subjects each marking period. If desired, social studies and science classes could meet EOD. It also is possible, although we would argue not advisable, to divide the block into two 45-minute "skinnies" and meet both classes daily. Regardless, a great deal of flexibility is available. While it seems more logical to have one teacher instruct language arts and social studies and the second instruct math and science, the pairings could be changed—the language arts teacher could teach science and the math teacher could teach social studies.

Another scheduling strategy for the two-person team is for each teacher to work with one group for 180 minutes. For example, Teacher A might work with Group 2 during Blocks I and II for math and science, while Teacher B instructs Group 1 in language arts and social studies. During Block III, Teacher A would work with Group 2 in language arts, and Teacher B would instruct Group 1 in mathematics. When the groups are alternated for science and social studies, for example every 3 weeks, the double block would be changed.

THREE-TEACHER TEAM

A three-teacher team, serving 90 or fewer students, also is possible in the four-block schedule (Figure 4.3). One teacher instructs three classes of language arts/reading; the second team member instructs three classes of mathematics; and the final team member teaches three groups of students science *and* social studies on some alternating basis—daily, by unit, by 9 weeks, or by semester.

FIGURE 4.3. FOUR-BLOCK SCHEDULE, THREE-TEACHER TEAM

Times	8:00–8:10	Block I 8:10–9:40	Block II 9:45–11:15	11:20–11:50	Block III 11:55–1:25	Block IV 1:30–3:00
Teacher A Language Arts	HR	Group 1 Language Arts	Group 2 Language Arts	Lunch	Group 3 Language Arts	Teachers: Individual and Team Planning Time
Teacher B Math	HR	Group 3 Math	Group 1 Math	Lunch	Group 2 Math	
Teacher C Social Studies & Science	HR	Group 2 Science (Sem. 1) Social Studies (Sem. 2)	Group 3 Science (Sem. 1) Social Studies (Sem. 2)	Lunch	Group 1 Science (Sem. 1) Social Studies (Sem. 2)	Students: PE & Exploratory Block

As shown in Figure 4.3, Teacher A instructs language arts with three different groups, 90 minutes a day each, for the complete school year. Teacher B works with three different math groups, each for 90 minutes a day for the year. Teacher C works with only three groups but must teach both science and social studies on some alternating basis. Again, although Figure 4.3 implies that students in Group A must travel together throughout the day, it is possible to reconfigure classes after each block. For example, after language arts, Group A could be split, with some students going to Teacher B for mathematics and others traveling to Teacher C for science and social studies.

FOUR-TEACHER TEAM

Because of the prominence of preexisting four-person teams (English, mathematics, science, and social studies), we now discuss how to adapt that teaming structure to the time divisions of the four-block schedule for groups of fewer than 120 students. This adaptation requires one "pure" language arts teacher, one "pure" mathematics teacher, a science teacher who teaches one block of mathematics, and a social studies teacher who instructs one block of language arts (Figure 4.4).

FIGURE 4.4. FOUR-BLOCK SCHEDULE, FOUR-TEACHER TEAM

Times	*8:00– 8:10*	*Block I 8:10–9:40*	*Block II 9:45–11:15*	*11:20–11:50*	*Block III 11:55–1:25*	*Block IV 1:30–3:00*
Teacher A *Language Arts*	HR	Group 1 Language Arts	Group 2 Language Arts	Lunch	Group 4 Language Arts	Teachers: Individual and Team Planning Time
Teacher B *Math*	HR	Group 2 Math	Group 1 Math	Lunch	Group 3 Math	
Teacher C *Language Arts & Social Studies*	HR	Social Studies Group 3 (Sem. 1) Group 4 (Sem. 2)	Group 3 Language Arts	Lunch	Social Studies Group 1 (Sem. 1) Group 2 (Sem. 2)	Students: PE & Exploratory Block
Teacher D *Math & Science*	HR	Science Group 4 (Sem. 1) Group 3 (Sem. 2)	Group 4 Math	Lunch	Science Group 2 (Sem. 1) Group 1 (Sem. 2)	

Teachers A and B, the two "pure" teachers, work with three groups of either language arts or mathematics each day. Teacher C instructs all of the social studies in Blocks I and III; these groups are alternated with Teacher D, who teaches science. Teacher C also must work with Group 3 in language arts; Teacher D instructs Group 4 in mathematics—both during Block II. Obviously, in some states, certification limitations may make this adaptation untenable; however, in other states, it is an ideal way to deal with teachers in grades 7 and 8 who have secondary subject certification but are able and permitted to teach one class out of area. In addition to this potential problem, a second issue arises with the four-person adaptation of this schedule. One precept of middle school teaming is the notion that all teachers on a team should become familiar with all students on the team. While this adaptation offers many advantages, language arts Teacher A never instructs Group 3, and mathematics Teacher B never works with Group 4. This same issue arises in the more departmentalized six-teacher version of this schedule.

SIX-TEACHER TEAM

A six-teacher team does allow, however, for each team member to work in a single discipline and provide instruction for up to 180 students. As shown in Figure 4.5, the basic plan requires two language arts teachers, two math teachers, one science teacher, and one social studies teacher. Each language arts and mathematics teacher instructs only three groups each day for the entire school year. Social studies and science instructors work with six groups over the course of the year, but with only three groups during any one time period. Again, one disadvantage of this plan is that language arts and mathematics teachers do not see all students on the team.

THE BASIC MASTER FOUR-BLOCK SCHEDULE

The simplest format for master scheduling in the four-block middle school schedule allocates three blocks to core instruction for each grade level, one block for physical education, electives and/or exploratories, and a 30-minute period for lunch[1] (see Figure 4.6, p. 88). After a 10-minute homeroom period, sixth grade students and teachers work during Blocks I and II. After lunch, core time is completed with Block III. In Block IV sixth grade students attend their PE/elective/exploratory classes and the sixth grade teachers have individual and team planning time.

Seventh grade students and teachers work in core during Blocks I and II. Following lunch, Block III is spent by teachers in planning and by students in PE/elective/exploratory classes. Block IV is the third core block for seventh grade.

---

1 We realize that one 30-minute lunch period will not work for most schools; later in the chapter, we suggest several scheduling adaptations for multiple lunch periods.

FIGURE 4.5. FOUR-BLOCK SCHEDULE, SIX-TEACHER TEAM

Times	8:00–8:10	Block I 8:10–9:40	Block II 9:45–11:15	11:20–11:50	Block II 11:55–1:25	Block IV 1:30–3:00
Teacher A Language Arts	HR	Group 1 Language Arts	Group 2 Language Arts	Lunch	Group 3 Language Arts	
Teacher B Math	HR	Group 3 Math	Group 1 Math	Lunch	Group 2 Math	
Teacher C Social Studies	HR	Social Studies Group 2 (Sem. 1) Group 4 (Sem. 2)	Social Studies Group 3 (Sem. 1) Group 5 (Sem. 2)	Lunch	Social Studies Group 1 (Sem. 1) Group 6 (Sem. 2)	Teachers: Individual and Team Planning Time
Teacher D Science	HR	Science Group 4 (Sem. 1) Group 2 (Sem. 2)	Science Group 5 (Sem. 1) Group 3 (Sem. 2)	Lunch	Science Group 6 (Sem. 1) Group 1 (Sem. 2)	Students: PE & Exploratory Block
Teacher E Language Arts	HR	Group 5 Language Arts	Group 6 Language Arts	Lunch	Group 4 Language Arts	
Teacher F Math	HR	Group 6 Math	Group 4 Math	Lunch	Group 5 Math	

Teachers A and B see the same students; teachers E and F see the same students. Teachers C and D see all students. It is also possible to re-mix groups after each block.

FIGURE 4.6. FOUR-BLOCK MASTER SCHEDULE—ONE LUNCH PERIOD; GRADE-LEVEL EXPLORATORY, ELECTIVE, AND PLANNING BLOCK

Teams	8:00–8:10	Block I 8:10–9:40	Block II 9:45–11:15	11:20–11:50	Block III 11:55–1:25	Block IV 1:30–3:00
Grade 6	HR	Block I	Block II	Lunch	Block III	Block IV Team and Individual Planning
Grade 7	HR	Block I	Block II	Lunch	Block III Team and Individual Planning	Block IV
Grade 8	HR	Block I	Block II Team and Individual Planning	Lunch	Block III	Block IV
PE/H		Team and Individual Planning	Day 1: 8-A	Lunch	Day 1: 7-A	Day 1: 6-A
			Day 2: 8-B		Day 2: 7-B	Day 2: 6-B
Exploratory and/or Elective		Team and Individual Planning	Day 1: 8-B	Lunch	Day 1: 7-B*	Day 1: 6-B
			Day 2: 8-A*		Day 2: 7-A	Day 2: 6-A

* 8-A means half of the eighth grade; 7-B means half of the seventh grade. If a school shares staff, for example, a band director who only comes in the afternoon, the exploratory blocks can be flipped from morning to afternoon every other day. If all seventh grade band students were in the grouping shown as 7-B (half the 7th grade, not a single section), the band director could work with the seventh grade from 11:35 to 1:00 on Day 1 and the eighth grade during the same time period on Day 2. All other elective/exploratory classes would follow suit. This plan works especially well if there are two sections of sixth grade band and one section each of seventh and eighth grade band.

Seventh grade students and teachers work in core during Blocks I and II. Following lunch, Block III is spent by teachers in planning and by students in PE/elective/exploratory classes. Block IV is the third core block for seventh grade.

In eighth grade, core Block I follows homeroom. Block II is spent in planning for teachers, and PE and electives or exploratories for students. After lunch the eighth grade team completes core instruction in Blocks III and IV.

The master schedule shown in Figure 4.6 depicts one means of providing PE, health, exploratories, and electives. All physical education, health, and elective/exploratory teachers plan during Block I. During Block II, half of the eighth grade students (8-A) attend PE/health for 90 minutes on Day 1, while the other half of the eighth grade students (8-B) participate in either electives or exploratory. On Day 2, the 8-B half of the eighth grade goes to PE/health, and the 8-A half participates in electives or exploratory. We strongly suggest that these classes meet in this fashion, every other day for 90 minutes, rather than every day for 43 minutes (43 + 4 + 43 = 90). Obviously, though, a variety of rotations is possible for PE, elective, and exploratory classes. Classes also could meet every day in blocks on a quarter-on, quarter-off basis, or every day in blocks for a semester (see Canady & Rettig, 1995b, Chap. 4).

During Block III, grade 7 students participate in the same alternation described for grade 8 students, with half of the students (7-A) attending PE/health and half (7-B) participating in electives or exploratory classes on Day 1; the 7-A and 7-B groups switch on Day 2. The same pattern holds for grade 6 during Block IV.

BENEFITS TO STUDENTS

The benefits of the four-block schedule for middle school students are:

♦ Students focus on fewer classes each day and each term.

In view of how middle-school-aged students are described in the literature, we feel it is imperative that we look seriously at the typical "class load" middle school students are assigned in the traditionally-scheduled middle school. Again, it is not unusual for a middle school student to have 7 to 8 different classes (and teachers) during a school day and as many as 12 to 15 core, exploratory, or elective classes with different teachers each school year. A student must be extremely well organized and disciplined to contend with such a class load successfully. In the four-block schedule, typically a student never needs to meet requirements for more than five classes; two of those classes can be noncore classes, which usually have fewer notebooks to keep, fewer tests to take, and less homework to complete.

♦ Students experience reduced stress in the four-block schedule because they are not trying to get to lockers and bathrooms and to "see their friends" seven or eight times per day.

If some socialization time (S-time) is desired, a specific period of time can be built into the schedule between blocks. This S-time is possible in most schools because less time in the schedule is being used for class changes. For example, a school might complete Block I in the morning and then declare a 15-minute break for students and teachers to socialize. During this time, milk, juices, fruit, and yogurt might be available in the food service areas. If it were not desirable to have the entire school "out of class" during the same 15-minute block, one grade level could move homeroom time to another block during the day, then the 15-minute break could be staggered over a period of 15 to 30 minutes. Another way to stagger the break is to vary the advisor-advisee time by grade levels, or if the school shows a daily news broadcast, that time could vary by grade levels, which would create varying times for the morning blocks. Of course, such changes would mean that the bell schedule must be altered, possibly by having no bells from the morning tardy bell to the first lunch bell.

♦ Students in the four-block schedule may be assigned varying amounts of time to master course material.

For example, if some students need extended time to complete a math curriculum successfully, math could be scheduled for four, five, six, seven, or even eight quarters of 4½ to 5 weeks each; a term of 4½ weeks in the four-block schedule is equivalent to 9 weeks in a traditional single-period schedule. In the four-block schedule, it is possible to provide the equivalent of 2 years of instruction within the time period of one school year by allocating double time (90 minutes per day vs. 45 minutes per day) for 180 days in a school year. For example, during eighth grade it may be possible for a student to take Algebra I spread over two semesters, or take Algebra I first semester and geometry second semester, or take Pre-algebra first semester and Algebra I during the second semester (see Figure 4.7). (For a detailed description of this possibility see Chapter 8 of this book, or Rettig & Canady, 1998.)

FIGURE 4.7. POSSIBLE MATHEMATICS SEQUENCES FOR EIGHTH GRADE STUDENTS IN THE FOUR-BLOCK SCHEDULE

	Semester 1	Semester 2
Sequence 1	Algebra I	Algebra I continued
Sequence 2	Algebra I	Geometry
Sequence 3	Pre-algebra	Algebra I Part 1
Sequence 4	Algebra I	Elective (e.g., foreign language)

Sequence 4 assumes that the Algebra I teacher could teach a second semester course or supervise a math lab. The foreign language teacher might work an exploratory rotation for seventh grade during first semester.

♦ With longer blocks of time for classes, it should be easier for teachers to engage students in more active learning activities, which is consistent with the literature on how middle school students learn best. From the origination of the middle school concept, it has been argued that students of this age need to be involved in active learning, with ample opportunity for socialization. The block schedule should facilitate such instruction (Smith, 1998).

♦ Because middle school students become accustomed to the time schedule of the high school, the four-block schedule provides a logical transition to the high school 4/4 plan.

♦ Seventy-five percent of students' time is spent in the basic core instructional areas of language arts, mathematics, science and social studies. This allocation is a requirement in Virginia, for example, and it may become critical as states move to end-of-course testing.

BENEFITS TO TEACHERS

Benefits of the four-block schedule for middle school teachers include:

♦ Teachers prepare for fewer courses each day.

We contend that if teachers are going to lecture less and move toward providing more active learning for students, major ways to help teachers (in addition to staff development) are (a) to provide them with fewer students to teach during any one day and during any one time period; (b) to give them longer instructional periods that can best accommodate active learning strategies; (c) to reduce the number of preparations they must make each day; and (d) to increase the number of uninterrupted minutes given teachers for planning. This planning time needs to be an uninterrupted block; it is very difficult to accomplish long-term, serious instructional planning in a single short period. After even the briefest personal errands, there is not much time left in a 40- to 45-minute period.

♦ Teachers see fewer students each day/term/year.

In high schools having block schedules, students often report that many teachers express greater interest in them. For example, students have reported that "teachers talk with me more" (Sessoms, 1995); that "teachers keep me after class for a few minutes to help me," and that "teachers are more likely to conference with me." If teachers are dealing with fewer students, classes, and preparations, teachers who are inclined to be more student-centered exhibit the types of behaviors that students have reported.

♦ Teachers have fewer records and grades to keep track of during any one term.

Teachers throughout the country report that they are overburdened with paperwork; some contend that computers have not reduced the paper load because more reports and records are now expected. We see merit in a schedule that permits teachers to spend more of their time preparing for classes and working with students and less time with record keeping.

♦ Schedules for itinerant teachers can be simplified.

Often middle schools share some teachers with another school. For example, it is not unusual for foreign language, art, music, and physical education teachers to be shared with a high school. When teachers are shared with more than one building, it is not unusual for a teacher to lose one teaching period each day. With shared teaching assignments, itinerant teachers also must deal with a large number of students from two different buildings. If a middle school operates on the four-block schedule and the high school uses the 4/4 schedule, it may be possible to share some exploratory or elective teachers by semester. Such an arrangement permits itinerant teachers to remain in one building for an entire semester, and often to work with fewer students and multiple-level classes during any one semester; it also may provide each teacher another teaching block, because time is not lost in traveling.

♦ Teachers are able to extend lessons; variety in the use of instructional strategies is encouraged.

Daily single class periods make it very difficult to use technology and active teaching strategies effectively. We contend that the single-period class format almost forces teachers into a particular instructional mode, which often is 20 to 30 minutes of lecture—possibly with some chalkboard or overhead-projector work—maybe a few questions to selected members of the class, a brief discussion, and then an assignment to be completed that evening. For students who will not work just for a grade, whose learning style demands "hands-on" work, and who have limited, if any, support at home, this familiar mode of instruction needs attention. We have found, at least at the high school level, that many teachers make instructional changes once they are teaching in an extended block of time (Brandenburg, 1995; Bryant, 1995; Canady & Rettig, 1996; Davis et al., 1977; Jones, 1997; King, 1996; King et al., 1975; Kramer, 1996; Mayes, 1997; O'Neil, 1995; Phelps, 1996; Pisapia & Westfall, 1996; Quinn, 1997; Sessoms, 1995; Staunton, 1997b; Vawter, 1998).

ADAPTING THE FOUR-BLOCK SCHEDULE

The model presented above has been described in the simplest of forms to begin the discussion of its possibilities; however, the basic four-block schedule can be modified in a variety of ways to suit specific purposes.

ADAPTING FOR MULTIPLE LUNCH PERIODS

SLIDING LUNCH SCHEDULE

Obviously, most schools require more than one lunch period. One way to accomplish multiple lunch periods is to add 30 minutes to a block, such as Block III in Figure 4.6 (p. 88), and then devise a schedule whereby classes are scheduled into the lunchroom every 5 minutes for 30 minutes of lunch. Figure 4.8 illustrates this idea. Notice that a 10-minute interval is left between the arrival of the last class in one grade level and the first class in the next grade level; this gives the cafeteria staff an opportunity to restock. Also, tables in the cafeteria vacated by one group can be used soon thereafter by another group. For example, tables used by group 6-1 could be used by group 7-1; 5 minutes is left between group 6-1's departure and group 7-1's arrival for cleaning tables. No more than six homerooms occupy the cafeteria at any one time. Obviously, in schools with more than 18 homerooms, or in schools who need to complete lunch in less than 2

FIGURE 4.8. SLIDING LUNCH SCHEDULE
LUNCH AND BLOCK III 11:20 TO 1:25

Teacher	11:20	11:25	11:30	11:35	11:40	11:45	11:50	11:55	12:00	12:05	12:10	12:15	12:20	12:25	12:30	12:35	12:40	12:45	12:50	12:55	1:00	1:05	1:10	1:15	1:20
6-1	Lunch																								
6-2		Lunch																							
6-3			Lunch																						
6-4				Lunch																					
6-5					Lunch																				
6-6						Lunch																			
7-1								Lunch																	
7-2									Lunch																
7-3										Lunch															
7-4											Lunch														
7-5												Lunch													
7-6													Lunch												
8-1																Lunch									
8-2																	Lunch								
8-3																		Lunch							
8-4																			Lunch						
8-5																				Lunch					
8-6																					Lunch				

hours, more than one class would need to be scheduled during each 5-minute arrival slot.

While the lunch plan in Figure 4.8 has several advantages, it also has a major disadvantage: Block III instruction is interrupted by lunch for most teachers and students. For example, group 6-3 has 10 minutes of Block III followed by 30 minutes of lunch, and then the remaining 80 minutes of Block III. The short 10-minute segment is essentially lost for instructional use. Many groups face the same loss of instructional time. One means of ameliorating this problem is to make Block III 5 to 10 minutes longer than other blocks, thus actually making it equivalent in usable instructional time. Another way to equalize the disruption caused is to rotate classes weekly or monthly through different lunch periods over the course of the year. Laboratory or hands-on classes, such as science, art, or PE, should not have broken-block classes because of the problems this would cause with material set-up and clean-up. The lunch plan shown in Figure 4.8 works very well in a middle school schedule built from modules of time as discussed in Chapter 2.

TWO LUNCH PERIODS

It may be possible to serve all students in two lunch periods, thereby keeping Block III instructional time intact. Figure 4.9 (p. 96) illustrates this adaptation. Grade 6, joined by half of the eighth grade, eats first lunch period from 11:20 to 11:50. Block III for these groups meets from 11:55 to 1:25. For grade 7 and the other half of grade 8, Block III occurs from 11:20 to 12:50, after which they eat during the second lunch period from 12:55 to 1:25. While this schedule keeps Block III instructional time from being fragmented, it does separate grade 8 into two different lunch and academic schedules during third block. A second problem with this plan is that the two lunch periods are more than an hour apart. What do cafeteria staff do between lunch periods? While it is possible that they could prepare food for the next day, this down time may cause a problem in many schools; however, if fifth grade is part of the middle school or if the cafeteria is shared with an adjoining elementary or high school, the down time shown here could be useful.

FIGURE 4.9. FOUR-BLOCK MASTER SCHEDULE: TWO 30-MINUTE LUNCH PERIODS; GRADE-LEVEL EXPLORATORY, ELECTIVE, AND PLANNING

	8:00–8:10	Block I 8:10–9:40	Block II 9:45–11:15	Lunch & Block III 11:20–1:25		Block IV 1:30–3:00
Grade 6	HR	Block I	Block II	Lunch A 11:20–11:50	Block III 11:55–1:25	Block IV Team and Individual Planning
Grade 7	HR	Block I	Block II	Block III Team and Individual Planning	Lunch B 12:55–1:25	Block IV
Grade 8	HR	Block I	Block II Team and Individual Planning	Half 8th Grade Block III 11:20–12:50 / Lunch A 11:20–11:50	Lunch B 12:55–1:25 / Half 8th Grade Block III 11:55–1:25	Block IV
PE/Health Teachers		Team and Individual Planning	Day 1: 8-A / Day 2: 8-B	Day 1: 7-A / Day 2: 7-B	Lunch	Day 1: 6-A / Day 2: 6-B
Exploratory and/or Elective Teachers		Team and Individual Planning	Day 1: 8-B / Day 2: 8-A	Day 1: 7-B / Day 2: 7-A	Lunch	Day 1: 6-B / Day 2: 6-A

THREE LUNCH PERIODS

If the cafeteria can serve multiple classes at a time in several serving lines, it is possible to keep Block III intact for two-thirds of the school's population by offering three lunch periods. Figure 4.10 illustrates this possibility. Students in grade 7 are scheduled first for lunch from 11:20 to 11:50; their Block III class meets from 11:55 to 1:25. Grade 6 eats next from 12:05 to 12:35 after the first half of their Block III class, which meets from 11:20 to 12:05. Grade 6 completes Block III from 12:40 to 1:25. Grade 8 students have lunch from 12:55 to 1:25, after completing Block III. In this adaptation, the seventh and eighth grades both have an unbroken third block; the sixth-grade block is broken into two very usable 45-minute periods. The grade level assigned the broken block could rotate its three core classes so that all sections are affected equally. Alternately, teachers could be allowed to elect which lunch period they prefer. Some subject teachers—for example, foreign language, mathematics, or keyboarding—may prefer the break the broken block provides. We do believe it is unwise, however, to break the PE and exploratory block for lunch.

FIGURE 4.10. FOUR-BLOCK MASTER SCHEDULE: THREE 30-MINUTE LUNCH PERIODS; GRADE-LEVEL EXPLORATORY, ELECTIVE, AND PLANNING

	8:00–8:10	*Block I* *8:10–9:40*	*Block II* *9:45–11:15*	*Lunch & Block III* *11:20–1:25*			*Block IV* *1:30–3:00*
Grade 6	HR	Block I	Block II	Block IIIa	Lunch 12:05–12:35	Block IIIb	Block IV Team and Individual Planning
Grade 7	HR	Block I	Block II	Lunch 11:20–11:50	Block III Team and Individual Planning		Block IV
Grade 8	HR	Block I	Block II Team and Individual Planning	Block III		Lunch 12:55–1:25	Block IV
PE/Health Teachers		Team and Individual Planning	Day 1: 8-A	Lunch	Day 1: 7-A		Day 1: 6-A
			Day 2: 8-B		Day 2: 7-B		Day 2: 6-B
Exploratory and/or Elective Teachers		Team and Individual Planning	Day 1: 8-B	Lunch	Day 1: 7-B		Day 1: 6-B
			Day 2: 8-A		Day 2: 7-A		Day 2: 6-A

Many middle schools operate a "tower" period, or what we call a "Triple E" period, to provide a convenient scheduling space for multigrade-level singletons. This strategy is used most often for band, orchestra, and choir. In general, these performing arts groups meet during a 40 to 50 minute period, while students and teachers not involved in these groups engage in other activities. Other common uses for this time include providing tutorial help, study hall, or D.E.A.R. ("Drop Everything and Read") time. In general, we do not recommend the use of this scheduling technique; schools considering the tower period must be prepared for significant detail work and planning. Care also must be taken to provide substantive activity for the nonmusic students, or this period can become an unfortunate waste of valuable instructional time and a source of student behavior problems.

Careful placement of the tower period, however, can facilitate the development of a lunch schedule. For example, Figure 4.11 illustrates a master schedule format that allots 75 minutes for both lunch and the tower period for all three grade levels. In the schedule shown in Figure 4.12, three lunch periods are created from this block of time. Students in the band eat lunch first, and then move to band at 11:25. Students in choir and orchestra attend these groups from 10:55 to 11:40 and then move to lunch.

FIGURE 4.11 FOUR-BLOCK MASTER SCHEDULE: THREE 25-MINUTE LUNCH PERIODS; GRADE-LEVEL EXPLORATORY, MIXED-GRADE-LEVEL PERFORMING GROUPS

	8:00–8:05	Block I 8:05–9:25	Block II 9:30–10:50	Lunch and Tower Period 10:55–12:10	Block III 12:15–1:35	Block IV 1:40–3:00
Grade 6	HR	Block I	Block II	Three lunch periods, band, choir, orchestra, extended learning time, enrichment, clubs, etc., are possible during this time. (See Figure 4.12 for more details regarding lunch and tower periods.)	Block III	Block IV Team and Individual Planning
Grade 7	HR	Block I	Block II		Block III Team and Individual Planning	Block IV
Grade 8	HR	Block I	Block II Team and Individual Planning		Block III	Block IV
PE/Health Teachers		Team and Individual Planning	Day 1: 8-A		Day 1: 7-A	Day 1: 6-A
			Day 2: 8-B		Day 2: 7-B	Day 2: 6-B
Exploratory and/or Elective Teachers		Team and Individual Planning	Day 1: 8-B		Day 1: 7-B	Day 1: 6-B
			Day 2: 8-A		Day 2: 7-A	Day 2: 6-A

FIGURE 4.12. FOUR-BLOCK MIDDLE SCHOOL SCHEDULE: TOWER PERIOD AND THREE 25-MINUTE LUNCH PERIODS

	10:55 . . . . 12:10		
Band Students	Lunch A 10:55–11:20	Band 11:25–12:10	
Students not in band, choir, and orchestra are assigned to various classes and lunch periods based on need and/or choice.	Lunch A 10:55–11:20	Extended learning time, enrichment, clubs, etc. are possible during this time. 11:25–12:10	
	Extended learning time, enrichment, clubs, etc. are possible during this time. 10:55–11:17	Lunch B 11:20–11:45	Activities continued… 11:48–12:10
	Extended learning time, enrichment, clubs, etc. are possible during this time. 10:55–11:40		Lunch C 11:45–12:10
Choir and Orchestra Students	Choir and Orchestra 10:55–11:40		Lunch C 11:45–12:10

A Triple E or tower period, also discussed in Chapter 3, allows for mixed-grade-level participation in schoolwide activities, such as band, chorus, and clubs. Overlapping the schedules for all three performing arts groups also allows for an occasional combined choir and band rehearsal. Of course, this plan assumes several critical factors: separate practice rooms for each band, orchestra, and choir group, and the existence of only one band, one orchestra, and one choir.

Any scheduling plan requires adaptation for the specific circumstances existing in any particular school. For example, what if your school had only one practice room available for performing arts groups? First, we might consider not placing these activities in a tower period, so that each group could meet at different times throughout the day. Second, we might extend the lunch and tower block to 90 minutes and shorten the tower periods to 30 minutes each. A 30-minute period then would be available for each group to meet daily. Third, a decision could be made not to meet each performing group on a daily basis. For example, on a 6-day cycle, band could meet on Day 1 and Day 4; orchestra could meet on Day 2 and Day 5; and choir could meet on Day 3 and Day 6 (see Figure 4.13, p. 100). Students then would be able to participate in all three groups if desired. A variety of other solutions, each with pro and cons, is also possible.

Figure 4.13. Four-Block Middle School Schedule: Tower Period and Three 25-Minute Lunch Periods— Rotating Performing Arts Schedule

	10:55 . . . . 12:10		
		Tower Period 11:25–12:10	
		Day 1	Band
		Day 2	Orchestra
Band, Orchestra, and Choir Students	Lunch A 10:55–11:20	Day 3	Choir
		Day 4	Band
		Day 5	Orchestra
		Day 6	Choir
Students not in band, choir, and orchestra are assigned to various classes and lunch periods based on need and/or choice.	Lunch A 10:55–11:20	Extended learning time, enrichment, clubs, etc. are possible during this time. 11:25–12:10	
	Extended learning time, enrichment, clubs, etc. are possible during this time. 10:55–11:17	Lunch B 11:20–11:45	Activities continued… 11:48–12:10
	Extended learning time, enrichment, clubs, etc. are possible during this time. 10:55–11:40		Lunch C 11:45–12:10

What if your school has sufficient space for each performing group to meet separately, but there are several groups at different levels for each band, orchestra, and choir? Again, in this case, it may be wise to abandon the tower period as the scheduling structure. As discussed in the previous example, however, it is possible to extend the combined tower and lunch period to 90 minutes and create three 30-minute periods. Beginning band could meet for the first 30 minutes, followed by concert band during the next 30 minutes, followed by the wind ensemble in the final 30 minutes. It also would be possible to meet each level during the same period but on a 6-day rotational schedule, similar to the plan illustrated in Figure 4.13.

Each of these options has advantages and disadvantages. For example, most leaders of performing arts groups want daily contact; in several of the adaptations described, groups meet only two of six days. While this may be acceptable in some schools (most notably in the Northeast, where this kind of rotational schedule for band, orchestra, and choir is most common), others would find the plans unacceptable. In several of the plans described above, performing arts groups meet daily, but for only 30 minutes. Given the difficulties of getting any rehearsal started—putting instruments together, warming up, tuning up, getting up on the risers—it is obvious that a 30-minute class will result in far less usable practice time. The critical issue for a tower period, however, is not what provisions are made for the performing arts groups that meet during this time; rather, the critical issue is how the needs of nonmusic students are addressed. If the activities provided for these students are perceived as being "made up" simply to make scheduling the music programs work, teachers and students alike will be dissatisfied; the music programs may be blamed for the waste of students' time. If it is possible, as we suggested with the Triple E period, to provide additional elective and/or exploratory opportunities for all students during this time, the plan has a better chance for success.

FOUR LUNCH PERIODS

Figures 4.14 to 4.17 show schedules for four lunch periods. The block of time shown in each of these figures corresponds to the combination of lunch and Block III shown in Figure 4.10 (p. 97). Two hours and five minutes is sufficient to schedule four lunch periods with 5-minute transitions.

If the fourth lunch period is necessary because one grade level is too large to be accommodated together in the cafeteria, the schedule in Figure 4.14 (p. 102) could be utilized. Both seventh and eighth grades are shown eating separately, while the sixth grade (often the largest group) is split in half. Grade 8 eats lunch from 11:20 to 11:50 and then participates in Block III classes from 11:55 until 1:25. Grade 7 has the first 30 minutes of Block III, followed by Lunch B from 11:50 to 12:20. Seventh grade then reconvenes for the final 60 minutes of Block III from 12:25 to 1:25. Please note that groups with a split block are allocated an additional 5 minutes of lunch time to facilitate class changes. One-half of grade 6 participates in Block III from 11:20 until 12:50 and then eats Lunch D from 12:55 to 1:25. The second half of sixth grade has an hour of Block III, followed by Lunch C, followed by the remaining 30 minutes of Block III.

Figure 4.15 (p. 102) illustrates one possibility for four lunch periods if one grade cannot be divided in half. Three-quarters of the sixth grade students eat Lunch A from 11:20 to 11:50. Their third block follows immediately, from 11:55 to 1:25. After 30 minutes of Block III, one-fourth of the sixth grade, one-fourth of the seventh grade, and one-fourth of the eighth grade join for Lunch B from 11:50 to 12:20. The remaining hour of Block III meets from 12:25 to 1:25. Three-quarters of the seventh grade has an hour of Block III from 11:20 to 12:20, followed by Lunch C from 12:25 to 12:55.

FIGURE 4.14. FOUR-BLOCK MIDDLE SCHOOL SCHEDULE:
BLOCK III AND FOUR 30-MINUTE LUNCH PERIODS
(ALTERNATIVE 1)

Grade 8	Lunch A 11:20–11:50	Block III 11:55–1:25		
Grade 7	Block IIIa 11:20–11:50	Lunch B 11:50–12:20	Block IIIb 12:25–1:25	
½ of Grade 6	Block IIIa 11:20–12:20		Lunch C 12:25–12:55	Block IIIb 12:55–1:25
½ of Grade 6	Block III 11:20–12:50			Lunch D 12:55–1:25

FIGURE 4.15. FOUR-BLOCK MIDDLE SCHOOL SCHEDULE:
BLOCK III AND FOUR 30-MINUTE LUNCH PERIODS
(ALTERNATIVE 2)

	11:20–11:50	*11:50–12:20*	*12:25–12:55*	*12:55–1:25*
¼ of Grade 6	Lunch A	Block III		
¼ of Grade 6	Lunch A	Block III		
¼ of Grade 6	Lunch A	Block III		
¼ of Grade 6	Block IIIa	Lunch B	Block IIIb	
¼ of Grade 7	Block IIIa		Lunch C	Block IIIb
¼ of Grade 7	Block IIIa		Lunch C	Block IIIb
¼ of Grade 7	Block IIIa		Lunch C	Block IIIb
¼ of Grade 7	Block IIIa	Lunch B	Block IIIb	
¼ of Grade 8	Block IIIa	Lunch B	Block IIIb	
¼ of Grade 8	Block III			Lunch D
¼ of Grade 8	Block III			Lunch D
¼ of Grade 8	Block III			Lunch D

Block III is completed from 12:55 to 1:25. Three-quarters of the eighth grade has Block III from 11:20 to 12:50 and eat Lunch D from 12:55 to 1:25. Again, teachers could choose the split-block lunch period if it met their instructional needs.

Figure 4.16 shows an alternative grouping of homerooms for lunch: Lunch A—three-quarters of grade 6; Lunch B—one-fourth of grade 6 and two-fourths of grade 7; Lunch C—two-fourths of grade 7 and one-fourth of grade 8; and Lunch D—three-fourths of grade 8.

FIGURE 4.16. FOUR-BLOCK MIDDLE SCHOOL SCHEDULE: BLOCK III AND FOUR 30-MINUTE LUNCH PERIODS (ALTERNATIVE 3)

	11:20–11:50	11:50–12:20	12:25–12:55	12:55–1:25
¼ of Grade 6	Lunch A	Block III		
¼ of Grade 6				
¼ of Grade 6				
¼ of Grade 6	Block IIIa	Lunch B	Block IIIb	
¼ of Grade 7				
¼ of Grade 7				
¼ of Grade 7	Block IIIa		Lunch C	Block IIIb
¼ of Grade 7				
¼ of Grade 8				
¼ of Grade 8	Block III			Lunch D
¼ of Grade 8				
¼ of Grade 8				

By adding a 25-minute time period for teacher advisory groups, it also is possible to create four lunch periods. All instructional blocks must be shortened to 85 minutes. Figure 4.17 shows this possibility. One-fourth of the school eats during Lunch A while another fourth of the school participates in teacher advisory; after 25 minutes they switch activities. Both groups then have their third-block classes from 12:05 to 1:30. The other half of the students and teachers has Block III from 11:10 to 12:35. After Block III the lunch/advisory switch is repeated between 12:40 and 1:30.

FIGURE 4.17. FOUR-BLOCK MIDDLE SCHOOL SCHEDULE: BLOCK III AND FOUR 25-MINUTE LUNCH PERIODS AND TEACHER ADVISORY (ALTERNATIVE 4)

	11:10–11:35	*11:35–12:00*	*12:05–1:30*	
¼ *of School*	Lunch A	Activity or Advisory	Block III	
¼ *of School*	Activity or Advisory	Lunch B	Block III	
	11:10–12:35		*12:40–1:05*	*1:05–1:30*
¼ *of School*	Block III		Lunch C	Activity or Advisory
¼ *of School*	Block III		Activity or Advisory	Lunch D

Building time for lunch into the middle school block schedule involves attending to a variety of factors, some seemingly unrelated to lunch. To accomplish this task appropriately, these questions must be answered:

♦ What is the seating capacity of the cafeteria?

♦ What are the working hours of the cafeteria staff?

♦ Must cafeteria facilities be shared with other programs or schools?

♦ Is a teacher advisory period desired?

♦ How are performing groups scheduled?

♦ What is the availability of lunchroom supervision?

♦ Is recess valued for middle school students?

The more each of these issues affects the lunch schedule, the more the available choices are restricted.

ADAPTING FOR SOCIAL STUDIES AND SCIENCE INSTRUCTION

The four-block middle school schedule obviously values basic instruction in language arts and mathematics. Some observers contend that the schedule devalues social studies and science, because only half as much time is spent in these disciplines as in language arts and mathematics. In that sense, this observation is true. If, however, we view the time allocated to social studies and science in comparison to current schedules, such devaluing is less clear. In most middle school schedules, social studies and science each are allocated approximately 45 minutes of daily instruction. In the four-block schedule, they are given approximately 90 minutes together, usually on some alternating basis. Math instruction, however, increases to 90 minutes. Where does that time come from? Usually the additional time for mathematics comes from several sources: unneeded transitions that can be folded into instructional time, a slight reduction in the time allocated to encore subjects, a slight reduction in the time allocated to language arts (if two periods were allocated previously), and possibly the elimination of the traditional advisory period.

For example, in a 420-minute day with seven periods, time might be divided as follows: 20 minutes for advisory, 30 minutes for lunch, eight 4-minute transitions, six 48-minute periods, and one 52-minute period (extended seventh period for announcements). Many middle schools allocate two of these periods to language arts (reading and English), one to math, one to social studies, one to science, and two to the encore subjects. Figures 4.2 to 4.5 illustrate the new division of time in the four-block middle school schedule: 10 minutes for homeroom, 30 minutes for lunch, four 5-minute transitions, and four 90-minute blocks. One block is devoted to language arts, one to mathematics, one to both science and social studies, and one block to the encore subjects.

In comparing the actual amounts of time allocated to each subject in the schedule, we see little difference except for mathematics (Figure 4.18, p. 106). Language arts receives 90 minutes in the four-block schedule, versus 96 minutes in the seven-period day; math is allocated 90 minutes versus 48 minutes; social studies and science each receive the equivalent of 45 minutes daily, versus 48 minutes; and the encore subjects are each allocated the equivalent of 45 minutes daily, versus 48 minutes a day. It can be argued however, that classes offered in 90-minute blocks are at least equivalent to two 48-minute classes, once start-up and class-closing routines are considered.

How to offer the social studies and science instruction is another issue that must be addressed in the four-block schedule. There are a variety of methods for scheduling these subjects throughout the year. It is possible simply to divide the block in half and meet each class for 43 minutes, allowing 4 minutes for travel time between science and social studies (see Figure 4.19, p. 106). This, however, leaves at least three major concerns: science laboratories are nearly impossible to complete because of the short class length, students still are responsible for both of these subjects the entire year, and instructional possibilities are limited by the short period. We can solve the lab problem and allow for more instructional flexibility by meeting these classes every other day in blocks (see Figure 4.20). Still, however, students are responsible for the homework, tests, and projects of both classes for the entire year.

FIGURE 4.18. TIME ALLOCATION COMPARISON:
FOUR-BLOCK MIDDLE SCHOOL SCHEDULE VS. SEVEN-PERIOD DAY

Activity/Subject	Seven-Period Day	Four-Block Schedule
Homeroom/ Advisory	20 minutes for Advisory 4 minutes of Period 7 for announcements	10 minutes for homeroom
Lunch	30 minutes	30 minutes
Transitions	8×4 minutes = 32 minutes	4×5 minutes = 20 minutes
Language Arts	2×48 minutes = 96 minutes	90 minutes
Mathematics	48 minutes	90 minutes
Social Studies	48 minutes	45 minutes (90 minutes EOD)
Science	48 minutes	45 minutes (90 minutes EOD)
Encore	2×48 minutes = 96 minutes	90 minutes (90 minutes EOD)
Total	420 minutes	420 minutes

FIGURE 4.19. FOUR-BLOCK MIDDLE SCHOOL SCHEDULE:
SOCIAL STUDIES AND SCIENCE SCHEDULING
OPTION 1: SKINNIES

	Semester 1	Semester 2
Block I 90 minutes	Reading/ Language Arts	
Block II 90 minutes	Mathematics	
	LUNCH	
Block III 90 minutes	Science (43 minutes)	
	Social Studies (43 minutes)	
Block IV 90 inutes	Day 1 PE	Day 2 Elect./Expl.

FIGURE 4.20. FOUR-BLOCK MIDDLE SCHOOL SCHEDULE:
SOCIAL STUDIES AND SCIENCE SCHEDULING
OPTION 2: EVERY OTHER DAY BLOCK

	Semester 1	Semester 2
Block I 90 minutes	Reading/Language Arts	
Block II 90 minutes	Mathematics	
	LUNCH	
Block III 90 minutes	D1 / D2 / D1 / D2 / D1 / D2 SS / SC / SS / SC / SS / SC	
Block IV 90 minutes	Day 1 PE	Day 2 Elect./Expl.

This stress can be alleviated by scheduling classes either by semester (Figure 4.21, p. 108) or on a quarter-on, quarter-off basis (Figure 4.22, p. 108); students then are responsible for only one of the classes during any one term. It may be inadvisable to schedule some classes by semester: a life science class may be dependent on seasonal changes; the social studies course may include a major unit related to a November election; and state examinations may be administered at the end of the school year, creating an inadvisable gap between the end of the course and the state assessment. Another alternative is to schedule social studies and science by units. For example one class might participate in social studies for a 3-week unit, while the second group has science for that time; teachers and students switch after 3 weeks. For this plan, the social studies and science teachers need to prepare units of equal length. If state examinations were administered in the spring, both teachers undoubtedly would want access to students prior to the testing date for review. Two weeks before the exam teachers could switch to an every-other-day block schedule, thus providing more recent exposure to the content that is to be tested.

ADAPTING FOR FOREIGN LANGUAGE INSTRUCTION

There are at least five basic ways to add foreign language instruction to the four-block schedule:

FIGURE 4.21. FOUR-BLOCK MIDDLE SCHOOL SCHEDULE: SOCIAL STUDIES AND SCIENCE SCHEDULING OPTION 3: SEMESTERIZING

	Semester 1	Semester 2
Block I 90 minutes	Reading/Language Arts	
Block II 90 minutes	Mathematics	
LUNCH		
	Semester 1	Semester 2
Block III 90 minutes	Science	Social Studies
Block IV 90 minutes	Day 1 PE	Day 2 Elect./Expl.

FIGURE 4.22. FOUR-BLOCK MIDDLE SCHOOL SCHEDULE: SOCIAL STUDIES AND SCIENCE SCHEDULING OPTION 4: QUARTER-ON, QUARTER-OFF

	Semester 1		Semester 2	
Block I 90 minutes	Reading/Language Arts			
Block II 90 minutes	Mathematics			
LUNCH				
Block III 90 minutes	9W	9W	9W	9W
	SS	SC	SS	SC
Block IV 90 minutes	Day 1 PE			Day 2 Elect./Expl.

- Require that foreign language be one of the choices made in the encore block;
- Replace half of the language arts block with foreign language;
- Replace half of the math block with foreign language;
- Replace the equivalent of one-fourth of the language arts block and one-fourth of the mathematics block with foreign language; or
- Add a "ninth" or "tower" period to the day.

OPTION 1: FOREIGN LANGUAGE AS A CHOICE IN THE ENCORE BLOCK

If a school has a small foreign language program, it may be possible to allow students to enroll in this subject as their elective during the two-period encore block. This option preserves the greatest amount of time for the core areas of language arts, mathematics, social studies, and science, but creates a number of potential problems, as well. Foreign language participation would be put in direct conflict with enrollment in performing arts groups and other exploratory or elective classes. This option will be poorly received by teachers of these classes, especially if the school community values foreign language as a priority. If the two-period encore block is the only time available for students to take PE, fine arts, foreign language, and practical arts classes, the number of possible activities is limited.

OPTION 2: FOREIGN LANGUAGE IN PLACE OF HALF OF THE ENGLISH LANGUAGE BLOCK

Another option is to substitute foreign language for half of the language arts block (Figure 4.23, p. 110). This alternative has been implemented in single-period schedules for years. Many schools with separate English and reading courses allow qualifying students to replace reading with foreign language study. Students and teachers meet English language arts every other day, opposite foreign language class. This choice is logical because students still are engaging in language arts study, albeit foreign "language arts."

OPTION 3: FOREIGN LANGUAGE IN PLACE OF HALF OF THE MATHEMATICS BLOCK

It also is possible to replace half of the allotted time for mathematics with foreign language study and maintain a full daily block for language arts (Figure 4.24, p. 110). Again, the mathematics class would meet in a block every other day opposite foreign language study.

FIGURE 4.23. FOUR-BLOCK MIDDLE SCHOOL SCHEDULE: FOREIGN LANGUAGE SCHEDULING OPTION 2

	Day 1	Day 2
Block I 90 minutes	Reading/ Lang. Arts	Foreign Language
Block II 90 minutes	Mathematics	
LUNCH		
	Semester 1	Semester 2
Block III 90 minutes	Science	Social Studies
Block IV 90 minutes	Day 1 PE	Day 2 Elect./Expl.

FIGURE 4.24. FOUR-BLOCK MIDDLE SCHOOL SCHEDULE: FOREIGN LANGUAGE SCHEDULING OPTION 3

Block I	Reading/Language Arts	
	Day 1	Day 2
Block II	Mathematics	Foreign Language
LUNCH		
	Semester 1	Semester 2
Block III	Science	Social Studies
Block IV	Day 1 PE	Day 2 Elect./Expl.

Implementing either of these two options within the constraints of teaming can be difficult. In a six-person team, as shown in Figure 4.5 (p. 87), a foreign language teacher could replace either a language arts or mathematics teacher, depending on which option were employed. If this one teacher were to serve all students on the team, this would mean that all students would be involved in foreign language, whatever foreign language this teacher could instruct. If the school were fortunate to have a multicertified teacher, more than one foreign language would be available; if not, students would have access to only one foreign language.

OPTION 3A: FOREIGN LANGUAGE OFF TEAM IN PLACE OF HALF OF THE MATHEMATICS BLOCK

Better, perhaps, would be to alter the team to create a five-person team with six groups, where one group of students leaves the team for foreign language instruction, other electives, or exploratories each block. For example, in Figure 4.25 (p. 112) we can follow the schedule of Group 1, which has a language arts class every day during Block I. During Block II this group has mathematics one day and participates in either a foreign language, another elective, or an exploratory class on the opposite day. Group 1 has social studies during Block III first semester and science second semester (remember that these classes can alternate in different patterns as well). Group 1 students then attend PE and a second exploratory, foreign language, or elective during Block IV. The two classes in which students are engaged during the PE/Exploratory/Elective block alternate every other day in blocks. (See Chapter 6 for an in-depth discussion of elective and exploratory classes.)

OPTION 4: FOREIGN LANGUAGE IN PLACE OF ONE-FOURTH OF THE LANGUAGE ARTS BLOCK AND ONE-FOURTH OF THE MATHEMATICS BLOCK

One might question the advisability of either of these previous options. Why should more time be devoted to language arts than to mathematics? Why should more time be devoted to mathematics than to language arts? Figure 4.26 (p. 113) illustrates a student schedule for a plan that provides an additional half-block of time for both mathematics and language arts every other day. On Day 1, the student attends language arts in Block I and then a block of mathematics. After lunch, the student participates in either social studies or science during Block III; the encore courses meet during Block IV. On Day 2, the student attends foreign language class during Block I; during Block II, the student attends 43 minutes of language arts and then 43 minutes of math. After lunch, the student has social studies in Block III, followed by an elective or exploratory class in Block IV.

FIGURE 4.25. FOUR-BLOCK SCHEDULE FIVE-TEACHER TEAM, DROP-ONE SCHEDULE: FOREIGN LANGUAGE OPTION 3A

Times	8:00–8:10	Block I 8:10–9:40	Block II 9:45–11:15	11:20–11:50	Block III 11:55–1:25	Block IV 1:30–3:00
Teacher A Language Arts	HR	Group 1 Language Arts	Group 2 Language Arts	Lunch	Group 3 Language Arts	
Teacher B Math	HR	Day 1 Group 3 ········· Day 2 Group 6	Day 1 Group 1 ········· Day 2 Group 4	Lunch	Day 1 Group 2 ········· Day 2 Group 5	
Teacher C Social Studies	HR	Social Studies Group 2 (Sem. 1) Group 4 (Sem. 2)	Social Studies Group 3 (Sem. 1) Group 5 (Sem. 2)	Lunch	Social Studies Group 1 (Sem. 1) Group 6 (Sem. 2)	Teachers: Individual and Team Planning Time Students: PE & Exploratory Block
Teacher D Science	HR	Science Group 4 (Sem. 1) Group 2 (Sem. 2)	Science Group 5 (Sem. 1) Group 3 (Sem. 2)	Lunch	Science Group 6 (Sem. 1) Group 1 (Sem. 2)	
Teacher E Language Arts	HR	Group 5 Language Arts	Group 6 Language Arts	Lunch	Group 4 Language Arts	
Foreign Language, Additional Elective, or Exploratory		Day 1 Group 6 ········· Day 2 Group 3	Day 1 Group 4 ········· Day 2 Group 1	Lunch	Day 1 Group 5 ········· Day 2 Group 2	

FIGURE 4.26. FOUR-BLOCK MIDDLE SCHOOL SCHEDULE: FOREIGN LANGUAGE SCHEDULING OPTION 4

	Day 1	Day 2
Block 1	Reading/ Lang. Arts	Foreign Language
Block 2	Mathematics	Read/LA
		Math
LUNCH		
Block 3	Science	Social Studies
Block 4	PE	Elective or Exploratory

Although this schedule seems relatively straightforward when viewing the student's schedule, difficulties arise when implementing this plan in a team format. To provide students with the necessary language arts and mathematics, each teacher can instruct only four groups—one-and-a-half blocks every other day for four different groups equals six of eight blocks over 2 days—a full load. Thus to serve a four-group team, full-time language arts and mathematics teachers are needed, but only four blocks every 2 days of each teacher is needed to serve students in social studies, science, and foreign language, as Figure 4.27 (p. 114) shows. Teacher A's schedule would be as written in Figure 4.28 (p. 115).

This schedule is accomplished most easily by "platooning," which means having a group of students travel to all of their core classes together. It is possible to mix students somewhat, as illustrated with the sample student schedule shown in Figure 4.29 (p. 115).

This adaptation of the four-block schedule actually converts it to an alternate-day schedule. After homeroom on Day 1, the student has 90 minutes of language arts with Group 1, followed by 90 minutes of science with Group 2. After lunch, the student attends 90 minutes of mathematics and then 90 minutes of PE/health. On Day 2, 90 minutes of foreign language with Group 2 follows homeroom. The student then attends 43 minutes of math followed by 43 minutes of language arts. Ninety minutes of social studies with Group 2 after lunch precedes a 90-minute elective.

(Text continues on page 116, following Figure 4.29)

FIGURE 4.27. FOUR-BLOCK SCHEDULE: OPTION 4—TEAM SCHEDULE

Times	8:00–8:10	Block I 8:10–9:40	Block II 9:45–11:15 (Per. 3-4)		11:20–11:50	Block II 11:55–1:25	Block IV 1:30–3:00
Teacher A Language Arts	HR	Day 1 Group 1 · · · Day 2 Group 4	D1 G3 · · · D2 G2	D1 G4 · · · D2 G1	Lunch	Day 1 Group 2 · · · Day 2 Group 3	Teachers: Individual and Team Planning Time
Teacher B Math	HR	Day 1 Group 2 · · · Day 2 Group 3	D1 G4 · · · D2 G1	D1 G3 · · · D2 G2	Lunch	Day 1 Group 1 · · · Day 2 Group 4	
Teacher C Social Studies	HR	Assigned to Other Team or to Explore.	Day 1 Group 1 Day 2 Group 3		Lunch	Day 1 Group 4 Day 2 Group 2	Students: PE & Exploratory Block
Teacher D Science	HR	Day 1 Group 3 Day 2 Group 1	Day 1 Group 2 Day 2 Group 4		Lunch	Assigned to Other Team or to Explore.	
Foreign Language	HR	Day 1 Group 4 · · · Day 2 Group 2	Assigned to Other Team or to Explore.		Lunch	Day 1 Group 3 · · · Day 2 Group 1	

FIGURE 4.28. TEACHER A'S SCHEDULE

	Day 1	*Day 2*
8:00–8:10	Homeroom	Homeroom
8:10–9:40	Language Arts Group 1 (90 minutes)	Language Arts Group 4 (90 minutes)
9:45–10:28	Language Arts Group 3 (43 minutes)	Language Arts Group 2 (43 minutes)
10:32–11:15	Language Arts Group 4 (43 minutes)	Language Arts Group 1 (43 minutes)
11:20–11:50	Lunch	Lunch
11:55–1:25	Language Arts Group 2 (90 minutes)	Language Arts Group 3 (90 minutes)
1:30–3:00	Team and Individual Planning	Team and Individual Planning

FIGURE 4.29. A SAMPLE STUDENT'S SCHEDULE

	Day 1	*Day 2*
8:00–8:10	Homeroom	Homeroom
8:10–9:40	Language Arts Group 1 (90 minutes)	Foreign Language Group 2 (90 minutes)
9:45–11:15	Science Group 2 (90 minutes)	Math Group 1 (43 minutes)
		Language Arts Group 1 (43 minutes)
11:20–11:50	Lunch	Lunch
11:55–1:25	Math Group 1 (90 minutes)	Social Studies Group 2 (90 minutes)
1:30–3:00	PE/Health	Elective

OPTION 5: FOREIGN LANGUAGE BY ADDING THE TOWER OR EEE PERIOD

Finally, it also is possible to adapt the four-block schedule and allow participation in PE/health, music, and foreign language by adding a ninth period—a tower or Triple E period—as shown in Figure 4.30. The sixth grade tower period begins at 10:52, lasts for 38 minutes, and is followed by lunch. The eighth grade tower period and the seventh grade lunch periods are held from 12:16 to 12:54. The seventh grade tower period and eighth grade lunch follow, from 12:58 to 1:36. During the tower periods band, orchestra, and chorus can be held. Other exploratory or elective classes can be provided for students who are not involved in performing arts groups. Mixed-grade-level performing arts groups are possible in seventh and eighth grade. If the symphonic band practiced during the eighth grade tower period, a seventh grade student could participate; the student would eat lunch during eighth grade lunch. Similarly, it would be possible for an eighth grade student to be assigned to the concert band during the seventh grade tower period and eat during the seventh grade lunch period. Both foreign language and PE/health or other electives could be taken during the PE/exploratory/foreign language/ elective block, thereby removing the conflict between foreign language and music.

ADAPTING THE FOUR-BLOCK SCHEDULE TO ACCOMMODATE A SEPARATE READING CLASS

Although many educators argue against dividing language arts into separate reading and English classes, many middle schools do believe in, and operate schedules that reflect, this practice. The four-block schedule can be modified in several ways to provide this option. Options are different if all team members teach reading, rather than one teacher specializing in reading. Separate reading classes in middle school are most common in sixth grade and least common in eighth grade. In addition, if reading is taught in sixth grade it is more typical that all team members teach reading; if reading is taught in eighth grade, it is more typical that one teacher instructs all the reading groups. We look first at options where all team members teach reading.

ALL CORE TEACHERS INSTRUCT READING

When all team members instruct a reading class it is common for the team to regroup students into reading skill groups and to carve 40 to 50 minutes from the core time for reading instruction. For example, in the four-block schedule it is typical to have three 90-minute blocks of core and one 90-minute block for PE, exploratories, and electives. It would be possible to take 15 minutes from each of the three core blocks, shortening them to 75 minutes, to create a 45-minute reading class.

FIGURE 4.30. FOUR-BLOCK SCHEDULE PLUS TOWER: FOREIGN LANGUAGE OPTION 5

Teams	8:00–9:24	9:28–10:48	10:52–11:30	11:34–12:12	12:16–12:54	12:58–1:36	1:40–3:00
Grade 6	HR and Block I	Block II	Tower	Lunch	Block III		PE/Elective/Exploratory/FL
Grade 7	HR and Block I	PE/Elective/Exploratory/FL	Block II		Lunch	Tower	Block III
Grade 8	HR and PE/Elective/Exploratory/FL	Block I	Block II		Tower	Lunch	Block III
PE/H Explore/Elective/FL	Grade 8	Grade 7	Tower Exploratories, Planning, and Lunch		Tower Exploratories, Planning, and Lunch		Grade 6
Band, Orchestra and Chorus	General Music, Lessons, and Plan	General Music, Lessons, and Plan	Grade 6	Lunch	Grade 7/8	Grade 7/8	General Music, Lessons, and Plan

Figure 4.31 (p. 118) offers a schedule with separate 45-minute reading periods taught by all team members. The sixth grade begins school with a short homeroom class, followed by 45 minutes of reading. The teachers on the team regroup students into skill groups as needed during this class. The reading class is followed by three 75-minute core blocks and then lunch, from 12:55 to 1:25. The day ends with teachers planning and students attending an exploratory class, an elective, or PE. The late lunch may be avoided by splitting the third core block. The first half of sixth grade core Block III would meet from 11:35 to 12:15. Lunch would follow at 12:20 and end at 12:50. Block II would be completed between 12:55 and 1:25. Seventh and eighth grade schedules are similar.

Another option for a separate reading class is for the entire school to be scheduled for reading at the same time. Cross-grade-level groupings would be possible. Figure 4.32 (p. 120) illustrates this possibility. The entire school holds reading classes between 8:00 and 8:50. Each grade level then has three 75-minute core blocks and one 90-minute PE, exploratory, or elective block. Notice that it was necessary to split the last grade 6 core block to provide three separate lunch periods.

FIGURE 4.31. FOUR-BLOCK MIDDLE SCHOOL SCHEDULE WITH GRADE-LEVEL READING PERIODS

Grade-Level Schedules

	8:00	8:10	8:20	8:30	8:40	8:50	9:00	9:10	9:20	9:30	9:40	9:50	10:00	10:10	10:20	10:30	10:40	10:50	11:00	11:10	11:20	11:30	11:40	11:50	12:00	12:10	12:20	12:30	12:40	12:50	1:00	1:10	1:20	1:30	1:40	1:50	2:00	2:10	2:20	2:30	2:40	2:50

- **Grade 6**: Homeroom & Reading 8:00–8:50 · Core Block I 8:55–10:10 · Core Block II 10:15–11:30 · Core Block III 11:35–12:50 · Lunch 12:55–1:25 · PE/Exploratory/Elective 1:30–3:00
- **Grade 7**: Homeroom & Core Block I 8:00–9:20 · Core Block II 9:25–10:40 · Lunch 10:45–11:15 · PE/Exploratory/Elective 11:20–12:50 · Reading 12:55–1:40 · Core Block III 1:45–3:00
- **Grade 8**: Homeroom & Reading 8:00–8:50 · PE/Exploratory/Elective 8:55–10:25 · Core Block I 10:30–11:45 · Lunch 11:50–12:20 · Core Block II 12:25–1:40 · Core Block III 1:45–3:00

PE, Exploratory, and Elective Schedules

Planning Time	Grade 8
Planning Time	Grade 7
Lunch	
	Grade 6

If the schedule shown in Figure 4.32 were adapted to the model shown in Figure 4.33 (p. 121), noncore teachers (properly trained) could be involved in providing this reading instruction. This would reduce class size during reading time. To involve both core and noncore teachers in reading instruction requires shortening the PE, exploratory, and elective block to 80 minutes, lengthening the core blocks to 80 minutes, and shortening the reading class to 40 minutes. All teachers in the building then could teach three 80-minute blocks plus the 40-minute reading class. Teachers would have 80 minutes of planning daily. With each of these adaptations, three core instructional blocks remain: one for language arts, one for mathematics, and one to be shared by science and social studies. Although the times would change, any of the team schedules shown in Figures 4.2 (p. 83), 4.3 (p. 84), 4.4 (p. 85), and 4.5 (p. 87) could be utilized.

SPECIALIST TEACHES READING

In many schools, when reading continues to be a separate class, one teacher per team is assigned to provide this instruction and must be added to the rotation of groups. The four-block schedule can be adapted easily to support this alternative. One means of accomplishing this schedule change with the purely departmentalized six-teacher team is to replace one of the language arts teachers with a reading teacher. The English teacher then alternates groups every other day with the reading instructor, just as social studies and science might be alternated. Figure 4.34 (p. 122) is a transformation of the six-teacher schedule into this format.

CONCLUSION

The four-block middle school schedule offers a practical means for providing an appropriate transition from elementary school to high school, especially if the high school operates a 4/4 semester schedule. A logical progression might include two-teacher teams in sixth grade, three-teacher teams in seventh grade, and the six-teacher team in eighth grade. The schedule can be modified to accomplish a variety of refinements, limited only by the skill and creativity of the scheduler.

FIGURE 4.32. FOUR-BLOCK MIDDLE SCHOOL SCHEDULE WITH SCHOOLWIDE READING PERIOD

Grade-Level Schedules

Time	Grade 6	Grade 7	Grade 8
8:00–8:50	Grade 6 Homeroom & Reading 8:00–8:50	Grade 7 Homeroom & Reading 8:00–8:50	Grade 8 Homeroom & Reading 8:00–8:50
8:55–10:10	Grade 6 Core Block I 8:55–10:10	Grade 7 Core Block I 8:55–10:10	Grade 8 PE/Exploratory/ Elective 8:55–10:25
10:15–11:30	Grade 6 Core Block II 10:15–11:30	Grade 7 Core Block II 10:15–11:30	Grade 8 Core Block I 10:30–11:45
11:35–12:20	Grade 6 Core Block IIIa 11:35–12:20	Grade 7 PE/Exploratory/ Elective 11:35–1:05	Grade 8 Lunch 11:50–12:20
12:25–12:50	Grade 6 Lunch 12:25–12:50		Grade 8 Core Block II 12:25–1:40
12:55–1:25	Grade 6 Core Block IIIb 12:55–1:25		
1:10–1:40		Grade 7 Lunch 1:10–1:40	
1:30–3:00	Grade 6 PE/Exploratory/ Elective 1:30–3:00		
1:45–3:00		Grade 7 Core Block III 1:45–3:00	Grade 8 Core Block III 1:45–3:00

PE, Exploratory, and Elective Schedules

Planning Time	Plan & Lunch		Break
Grade 8		Grade 7	Grade 6

FIGURE 4.33. FOUR-BLOCK MIDDLE SCHOOL SCHEDULE WITH SCHOOLWIDE READING PERIOD WITH ALL STAFF

Grade-Level Schedules

	Grade 6	Grade 7	Grade 8
Homeroom & Reading	8:00–8:45	8:00–8:45	8:00–8:45
Core Block I	8:50–10:10	8:50–10:10	8:50–10:10
10:15–11:35	Core Block II	Core Block II	PE/Exploratory/Elective
	Lunch 11:40–12:10	PE/Exploratory/Elective 11:40–1:00	Core Block IIa 11:40–12:20
	Core Block III 12:15–1:35		Lunch 12:25–12:55
		Lunch 1:05–1:35	Core Block IIb 1:00–1:35
1:40–3:00	PE/Exploratory/Elective	Core Block III	Core Block III

PE, Exploratory, and Elective Schedules

Reading		Grade 8	Grade 7	Lunch	Grade 6
Plan					

FIGURE 4.34. FOUR-BLOCK SCHEDULE:
SIX-TEACHER TEAM SEPARATE READING CLASS

Times	8:00–8:10	Block I 8:10–9:40	Block II 9:45–11:15	11:20–11:50	Block II 11:55–1:25	Block IV 1:30–3:00
Teacher A English	HR	English Day 1 Group 1 Day 2 Group 5	English Day 1 Group 2 Day 2 Group 6	Lunch	English Day 1 Group 3 Day 2 Group 4	Teachers: Individual and Team Planning Time Students: PE and Exploratory Block
Teacher B Math	HR	Math Group 3	Group 1 Math	Lunch	Math Group 2	
Teacher C Social Studies	HR	Social Studies Group 2 (Sem. 1) Group 4 (Sem. 2)	Social Studies Group 3 (Sem. 1) Group 5 (Sem. 2)	Lunch	Social Studies Group 1 (Sem. 1) Group 6 (Sem. 2)	
Teacher D Science	HR	Science Group 4 (Sem. 1) Group 2 (Sem. 2)	Science Group 5 (Sem. 1) Group 3 (Sem. 2)	Lunch	Science Group 6 (Sem. 1) Group 1 (Sem. 2)	
Teacher E Reading	HR	Reading Day 1 Group 5 Day 2 Group 1	Reading Day 1 Group 6 Day 2 Group 2	Lunch	Reading Day 1 Group 4 Day 2 Group 3	
Teacher F Math	HR	Math Group 6	Math Group 4	Lunch	Math Group 5	

5

THE FIVE-BLOCK MIDDLE SCHOOL SCHEDULE

A five-block middle school schedule is a very flexible plan that can be utilized either to focus predominantly on core instruction or to offer students many opportunities for exploratories and electives. If the school has a 420-minute school day, the schedule could contain five 70-minute blocks with 10 minutes added to Block I to accommodate homeroom duties, 30 minutes for lunch, and 30 minutes for transitions between blocks. Figure 5.1 is a sample bell schedule.

FIGURE 5.1. FIVE-BLOCK BELL SCHEDULE: VARIATION A (70-MINUTE BLOCKS; THREE LUNCH PERIODS; NO BROKEN BLOCKS)

HR 8:00–8:10			
Block I 8:15–9:25			
Block II 9:30–10:40			
Lunch and Blocks III and IV	Lunch A 10:45–11:15	Block III 10:45–11:55	Block III 10:45–11:55
	Block III 11:20–12:30	Lunch B 12:00–12:30	Block IV 12:00–1:10
	Block IV 12:35–1:45	Block IV 12:35–1:45	Lunch C 1:15–1:45
Block V 1:50–3:00			

In Figure 5.1, homeroom could be combined with Block I to provide 85 minutes for homeroom, advising, and the Block I class. Block II, containing 70 minutes, runs from 9:30 until 10:40. Blocks III and IV are both 70 minutes, but the times vary depending on which lunch is utilized. (See Chapter 4 for additional ideas for scheduling lunch periods in various block schedules.) This bell schedule is problematic because there are 45 minutes between lunch periods. It could work, however, if the middle school shared the cafeteria with an elementary or high school that could attend lunch during these open times, or if a large middle school required five lunch periods.

Figure 5.2 is another variation of a 70-minute five-block schedule with three lunch periods. Here lunch times are scheduled closer together, but one-third of the classes have Block III broken, which we consider a major disadvantage. If a school adopts this schedule, some teachers, such as keyboarding, mathematics, or foreign language teachers, might choose the broken block and not see it as a disadvantage. We hope that teachers in areas such as art, physical education, and science would not choose (or be forced into) the split lunch block. If enough teachers do choose the broken block, then all other classes can be assigned to the two unbroken midday periods. If not, we suggest that Lunch B be rotated in such a way that no one set of classes has that lunch for the entire year.

FIGURE 5.2. FIVE-BLOCK BELL SCHEDULE: VARIATION B (70-MINUTE BLOCKS; THREE LUNCH PERIODS; ONE BROKEN BLOCK)

HR 8:00–8:10			
Block I 8:15–9:25			
Block II 9:30–10:40			
Lunch and Block III 10:45–12:30	Lunch A 10:45–11:15	Block IIIA	Block III 10:45–11:55
	Block III 11:20–12:30	Lunch B 11:25–11:55	
		Block IIIB	Lunch C 12:00–12:30
Block IV 12:35–1:45			
Block V 1:50–3:00			

In Figure 5.3, lunch periods are paired with a 30-minute advisory period. In this variation, Blocks I, II, IV, and V are 65 minutes long and occur at the same time for all teachers and students; Block III, although unbroken, varies in its placement depending upon which lunch and advisory periods are selected for a particular middle school grade level.

FIGURE 5.3. FIVE-BLOCK BELL SCHEDULE: VARIATION C (FOUR LUNCH PERIODS; NO BROKEN BLOCKS; ADVISORY)

Block I 8:00–9:15			
Block II 9:20–10:25			
Lunch A 10:30–11:00	Advisory 10:30–11:00	Block III 10:30–11:35	Block IV 10:30–11:35
Advisory 11:00–11:30	Lunch B 11:00–11:30		
Block III 11:35–12:40	Block III 11:35–12:40	Lunch C 11:40–12:10	Advisory 11:40–12:10
		Advisory 12:10–12:40	Lunch D 12:10–12:40
Block IV 12:45–1:50			
Block V 1:55–3:00			

Figure 5.4 is another configuration with two lunch periods. Five 74-minute blocks were created with 30 minutes for lunch and 5 minutes for transitions between blocks. Half of the school eats before Block III and half of the school eats after Block III.

FIGURE 5.4. FIVE-BLOCK BELL SCHEDULE: VARIATION D (74-MINUTE BLOCKS; TWO LUNCH PERIODS)

Block I & Homeroom 8:00–9:19	
Block II 9:24–10:38	
Lunch A 10:38–11:03	Block III 10:43–11:57
Block III 11:08–12:22	Lunch B 11:57–12:22
Block IV 12:27–1:41	
Block V 1:46–3:00	

The five-block middle school schedule often is seen in schools with four grade levels because the schedule allows the specialists' team to work with each grade level for one block and have one block for planning time. Figure 5.5 is a simple master block schedule for the five-block plan designed for four grade levels. After homeroom, each grade level is allocated four 70-minute blocks for core instruction. In addition, one block is provided for students to attend PE, electives, and exploratory classes. Five minutes are allowed for class changes. In the example shown, fifth grade plans during Block V; sixth grade plans during Block IV; seventh grade plans in Block III; and eighth grade plans during Block II. The specialists plan during the first block. The schedule illustrated in Figure 5.5 also could be used by a school with four teams. For example, if there were two teams at Grade 6, one team at Grade 7, and one team at Grade 8, each team could be assigned one block for planning, with the fifth block assigned to the specialists for planning. A school with only seventh and eighth grades and two teams at each grade level also might be well-served by this model.

FIGURE 5.5. FIVE-BLOCK MASTER SCHEDULE: GRADES 5, 6, 7, AND 8

Times	8:00–8:10	Block I 8:15–9:25	Block II 9:30–10:40	Block III 10:45–11:55	12:00–12:30	Block IV 12:35–1:45	Block V 1:50–3:00
Grade 5	HR	Core Block I	Core Block II	Core Block III	Lunch	Core Block IV	PE/Explor.
Grade 6	HR	Core Block I	Core Block II	Core Block III	Lunch	PE/Explor.	Core Block IV
Grade 7	HR	Core Block I	Core Block II	PE/Explor.	Lunch	Core Block III	Core Block IV
Grade 8	HR	Core Block I	PE/Explor.	Core Block II	Lunch	Core Block III	Core Block IV
PE Electives Exploratory	HR	Plan	Grade 8	Grade 7	Lunch	Grade 6	Grade 5

The major issue that must be addressed in the five-block schedule is how to allocate the blocks. Many possibilities exist; for example, one block each could be given to language arts, science, mathematics, and social studies. The final block could be allocated to physical education and exploratories. Figures 5.6 and 5.7 are examples of how the five-block middle school schedule might be staffed in this manner. Figure 5.6 illustrates a typical middle school interdisciplinary team of reading/language arts, mathematics, science, and social studies teachers. Between 80 and 120 students would be assigned to this team. During four blocks teachers instruct their core classes; one block is used for planning while students have physical education and an elective or exploratory class. PE and the exploratory or elective classes meet every other day for a full block.

FIGURE 5.6. FIVE-BLOCK SCHEDULE: FOUR-TEACHER TEAM

Times	8:00-8:10	Block I 8:15-9:25	Block II 9:30-10:40	10:45-11:55	Block III 12:00-12:30	Block IV 12:35-1:45	Block V 1:50-3:00
Teacher A Language Arts	HR	Group 1 Language Arts	Group 2 Language Arts	Lunch	Group 3 Language Arts	Group 4 Language Arts	Teachers Individual and Team Planning Time

Students PE and Exploratory Block on an every-other-day basis |
Teacher B Math	HR	Group 2 Math	Group 1 Math	Lunch	Group 4 Math	Group 3 Math	
Teacher C Social Studies	HR	Group 3 Social Studies	Group 4 Social Studies	Lunch	Group 1 Social Studies	Group 2 Social Studies	
Teacher D Science	HR	Group 4 Science	Group 3 Science	Lunch	Group 2 Science	Group 1 Science	

Allocating 80 percent of the available instructional time (four of five blocks) to the basic core forces all other activities into the PE/exploratory/elective block. If students desire to take band and a foreign language, but still want to be involved in PE and exploratories, one of five blocks is insufficient time to allow this flexibility. The schedule shown in Figure 5.7 (p.) reduces the amount of time allocated to science and social studies, and provides another block for exploratory or elective classes.

Here four groups are assigned to a three-teacher team, which in this case includes a reading/language arts teacher, a mathematics teacher, and an instructor who teaches both social studies and science. During each block one of the four groups is off-team taking an additional exploratory or elective class. During Block I, Group 1 is in a language arts class; Group 2 is in a mathematics class; Group 3 is in a science/social studies class,

FIGURE 5.7. FIVE-BLOCK SCHEDULE:
THREE-TEACHER TEAM

Times	8:00–8:10	Block I 8:15–9:25	Block II 9:30–10:40	Block III 10:45–11:55	12:00–12:30	Block IV 12:35–1:45	Block V 1:50–3:00
Teacher A Language Arts	HR	Group 1 Language Arts	Group 2 Language Arts	Group 3 Language Arts	Lunch	Group 4 Language Arts	Teachers: Individual and Team Planning Time

Students: PE and Exploratory Block on an every-other-day basis |
Teacher B Math	HR	Group 2 Math	Group 1 Math	Group 4 Math	Lunch	Group 3 Math	
Teacher C Social Studies and Science	HR	Group 3 Social Studies and Science	Group 4 Social Studies and Science	Group 1 Social Studies and Science	Lunch	Group 2 Social Studies and Science	
Additional Elective and/or Exploratory Off-Team	HR	Group 4 Additional Elective and/or Exploratory	Group 3 Additional Elective and/or Exploratory	Group 2 Additional Elective and/or Exploratory	Lunch	Group 1 Additional Elective and/or Exploratory	

which is taught on some kind of alternating basis; and Group 4 travels off-team to participate in additional elective or exploratory classes. In this variation, students spend 60 percent of their class time in basic core subjects and 40 percent in other course work.

It is possible for a student to participate in a foreign language class every other day opposite an exploratory rotation scheduled during one of the 65-minute blocks, in addition to taking physical education and band every other day. It also is possible to have a science teacher on one team and a social studies teacher on a second team; these two teachers could switch teams on a regular basis (by quarter, by semester, by unit). Figure 5.8 illustrates these possibilities.

An alternative use of Block IV is suggested in Figure 5.9. In this example, four exploratory courses meet daily for 9 weeks. Physical education again meets every other day opposite band.

FIGURE 5.8. FIVE-BLOCK SAMPLE STUDENT SCHEDULE A
(FOUR LUNCH PERIODS; NO BROKEN BLOCKS; ADVISORY)

Block I *8:00–9:15*	Language Arts				
Block II *9:20–10:25*	Science 9 Weeks	Social Studies 9 Weeks	Sci 4.5 Weeks	SS 4.5 Weeks	Day 1 Science / Day 2 SS
Block III *10:30–11:35*	Mathematics				
11:40–12:10	Lunch A; Advisory A				
12:10–12:40	Advisory B; Lunch B				
Block IV *12:45–1:50*	Day 1 Foreign Language / Day 2 Four 9–Week Exploratories				
Block V *1:55–3:00*	Day 1 Physical Education / Day 2 Band				

FIGURE 5.9. FIVE-BLOCK SAMPLE STUDENT SCHEDULE B
(FOUR LUNCH PERIODS; NO BROKEN BLOCKS; ADVISORY)

Block I *8:00–9:15*	Language Arts				
Block II *9:20–10:25*	Science 9 Weeks	Social Studies 9 Weeks	Sci. 4.5 Weeks	SS 4.5 Weeks	Day 1 Science / Day 2 SS
Lunch A *10:30–11:00*	Lunch				
Advisory *11:00–11:30*	Advisory				
Block III *11:35–12:40*	Mathematics				
Block IV *12:45–1:50*	Geography 9 Weeks	Technology 9 Weeks	Health 9 Weeks		Exploratory Foreign Language 9 Weeks
Block V *1:55–3:00*	Day 1 Physical Education / Day 2 Band				

With the schedule shown in Figure 5.10, we create a totally departmentalized six-member team consisting of two language arts teachers, two mathematics teachers, one social studies teacher, and one science teacher. Eight groups of students are assigned to this team; during each block two of these groups are off-team attending physical education, foreign language, exploratory classes, or other electives.

Perhaps a happy medium is achievable with regard to the apportionment of basic core versus PE/elective/exploratory time if we create a schedule that allot 70 percent of class time for core. If we think of the five-block schedule as a 10-block schedule over 2 days, this becomes possible. Figure 5.11 (p. 132) illustrates just such a time allotment: 7 of 10 blocks are assigned to core for the team shown; for 3 blocks, students attend PE/elective/exploratory classes. Team teachers can be assigned planning for all three blocks, or more likely, planning for two blocks and a duty for one block.

How would a team use the available core time? Consider the traditional four-teacher team with approximately 80 to 120 students divided into four sections. We could rotate classes among the four teachers. Because seven instructional blocks are available over 2 days, the shortest rotation that would come out evenly would be an 8-day cycle. (Figure 5.12, p. 132, is a sample 8-day cycle student schedule and Figure 5.13, page , is a sample 8-day cycle teacher schedule.) Each of the four core sections would meet seven times over the 8-day rotation, resulting in 490 minutes of instruction or an average of more than 60 minutes daily in each class.

Let's examine a sample student's schedule (Figure 5.12, p. 132). After homeroom on Day 1, the student attends language arts class for 70 minutes in Block I, followed by 70 minutes of mathematics in Block II, and 70 minutes of science in Block III. After lunch our student attends a PE and health class in Block IV. This class meets every other day for 70 minutes. Social studies follows in Block V. On Day 2 the student again begins with language arts in Block I followed by mathematics in Block II. During Block III the student leaves the team to attend a Spanish class for the first time. This class meets every other day for 70 minutes. After lunch the student attends band in Block IV; the day ends with a science class during Block V. This rotation continues for 8 days until each core class has met seven times; then the rotation begins anew.

Let's examine the sample teacher schedule (Figure 5.13, p. 133). On Day 1 of the cycle, each of the four core teachers meets with Section 1 during Block I, followed by Section 2 in Block II and Section 3 in Block III. After lunch, planning time occurs during Block IV; students attend a PE/exploratory/elective class. The day concludes with Section 4 in Block V. On Day 2, the teachers again meet with Section 1 in Block I and Section 2 in

(Text continues on page 133, following Figure 5.13.)

FIGURE 5.10. FIVE-BLOCK SCHEDULE SIX-TEACHER TEAM; EIGHT GROUPS OF STUDENTS

Times	8:00–8:10	Block I 8:15–9:25	Block II 9:30–10:40	Block III 10:45–11:55	12:00–12:30	Block IV 12:35–1:45	Block V 1:50–3:00
Teacher A Language Arts	HR	Group 1 Language Arts	Group 2 Language Arts	Group 3 Language Arts	Lunch	Group 4 Language Arts	Teachers: Individual and Team Planning Time Students: PE and Exploratory Block on an every-other-day basis
Teacher B Language Arts	HR	Group 5 Language Arts	Group 6 Language Arts	Group 7 Language Arts	Lunch	Group 8 Language Arts	
Teacher C Math	HR	Group 2 Math	Group 1 Math	Group 4 Math	Lunch	Group 3 Math	
Teacher D Math	HR	Group 6 Math	Group 5 Math	Group 8 Math	Lunch	Group 7 Math	
Teacher E* Social Studies	HR	Group 3 Social Studies	Group 4 Social Studies	Group 1 Social Studies	Lunch	Group 2 Social Studies	
Teacher F* Science	HR	Group 7 Science	Group 8 Science	Group 5 Science	Lunch	Group 6 Science	
Additional Elective and/or Exploratory	HR	Additional Elective and/or Exploratory Groups 4, 8	Additional Elective and/or Exploratory Groups 3, 7	Additional Elective and/or Exploratory Groups 2, 6	Lunch	Additional Elective and/or Exploratory Groups 1, 5	

* Science and social studies teachers alternate groups on some basis, either by day, by semester, by quarter, or by unit of study.

FIGURE 5.11. TEAM TIME SCHEDULE
FOR TEN-BLOCK SCHEDULE

	Day 1	Day 2
8:00–8:10	Homeroom	
Block I 8:15–9:25	Core Block 1	Core Block 5
Block II 9:30–10:40	Core Block 2	Core Block 6
Block III 10:45–11:55	Core Block 3	PE/Elective/Exploratory (Core Teachers Plan/Duty)
12:00–12:30	Lunch	
Block IV 12:35–1:45	PE/Elective/Exploratory (Core Teachers Plan)	PE/Elective/Exploratory (Core Teachers Plan)
Block V 1:50–3:00	Core Block 4	Core Block 7

FIGURE 5.12. TEAM ROTATION FOR 10-BLOCK SCHEDULE:
SAMPLE STUDENT SCHEDULE

	Day 1	Day 2	Day 3	Day 4	Day 5	Day 6	Day 7	Day 8
8:00–8:10	Homeroom							
Block I 8:15–9:25	LA	LA	SS	SS	SC	SC	M	M
Block II 9:30–10:40	M	M	LA	LA	SS	SS	SC	SC
Block III 10:45–11:55	SC	Spanish	M	Spanish	LA	Spanish	SS	Spanish
12:00–12:30	Lunch							
Block IV 12:35–1:45	PE/H	Band	PE/H	Band	PE/H	Band	PE/H	Band
Block V 1:50–3:00	SS	SC	SC	M	M	LA	LA	SS

Students attend each core class seven times over 8 days. Students leave the team to take PE/ health, band, and Spanish. PE/health meets opposite band (or some other elective or exploratory rotation) every other day. Spanish meets every other day opposite a core block. SC = Science; SS = Social Studies; M = Math; LA = Language Arts; PE/H = PE/health

FIGURE 5.13. TEAM ROTATION FOR 10-BLOCK SCHEDULE: TEACHER SCHEDULE A

	Day 1	Day 2	Day 3	Day 4	Day 5	Day 6	Day 7	Day 8
8:00–8:10	Homeroom							
Block I 8:15–9:25	Section 1	Section 1	Section 4	Section 4	Section 3	Section 3	Section 2	Section 2
Block II 9:30–10:40	Section 2	Section 2	Section 1	Section 1	Section 4	Section 4	Section 3	Section 3
Block III 10:45–11:55	Section 3	PLAN/ Duty	Section 2	PLAN/ Duty	Section 1	PLAN/ Duty	Section 4	PLAN/ Duty
12:00–12:30	Lunch							
Block IV 12:35–1:45	PLAN	PLAN	PLAN	PLAN	PLAN	PLAN	PLAN	PLAN
Block V 1:50–3:00	Section 4	Section 3	Section 3	Section 2	Section 2	Section 1	Section 1	Section 4

This schedule works for all the team teachers. Each of the core teachers instructs four sections; rotated over 8 days, they would see each section seven times in 8 days.

Block II, and either plan or perform a duty during Block III while students attend a PE/exploratory/elective class. After lunch, students attend a third PE/elective/exploratory course while teachers plan. Teachers complete the day with Section 3 in Block V. The rotation continues until classes have met seven times during the 8-day cycle.

Figure 5.14 is a possible master block schedule that coincides with the 10-block schedule described in Figures 5.11, 5.12 , and 5.13. Each grade level is assigned seven core blocks and three PE/exploratory/elective blocks over 2 days. This means that 9 of the available 10 PE/exploratory/elective blocks are assigned. Only one block (Day 1, Block I) is available for common planning time for the PE/exploratory/ elective teachers. To provide equivalent total planning time for these teachers it is necessary to add an additional planning block for each teacher spread throughout Day 2.

It also is possible to implement a different rotation than the 8-day rotation suggested by Figures 5.12 and 5.13. By dividing the time available for the two morning blocks into three shorter periods, we can meet each of the four classes daily. The three morning core classes are 45 minutes long,

FIGURE 5.14. 10-BLOCK MASTER SCHEDULE: GRADES 6, 7, AND 8

Times 8:00–8:10	Day	Block I 8:15–9:25	Block II 9:30–10:40	Block III 10:45–11:55	12:00–12:30	Block IV 12:35–1:45	Block V 1:50–3:00
Grade 6 — HR	Day 1	Core Block I	Core Block II	PE/Elective/Explor.*		Core Block III	PE/Elective/Explor.
	Day 2	Core Block IV	Core Block V	Core Block VI		Core Block VII	PE/Elective/Explor.
Grade 7 — HR	Day 1	Core Block I	Core Block II	Core Block III	L u n c h	PE/Elective/Explor.	Core Block IV
	Day 2	Core Block V	Core Block VI	PE/Elective/Explor.*		PE/Elective/Explor.	Core Block VII
Grade 8 — HR	Day 1	Core Block I	PE/Elective/Explor.	Core Block II		Core Block III	Core Block IV
	Day 2	PE/Elective/Explor.*	PE/Elective/Explor.	Core Block V		Core Block VI	Core Block VII
PE/Electives/Exploratory	Day 1	Plan	Grade 8	Grade 6		Grade 7	Grade 6
	Day 2	Grade 8	Grade 8	Grade 7		Grade 7	Grade 6

Obviously, it often is not possible to have lunch for the entire school during one 30-minute session. Figures 5.1 (p. 123), 5.2 (p. 124), and 5.3 (p. 125) offer other suggestions for lunch. For the PE/elective/exploratory teachers, Block I on Day 2 is common planning time. Additional planning time for each of these teachers must come from other blocks.

* On the day students have two PE/elective/exploratory classes (Day 1 for Grade 6; Day 2 for Grade 7; Day 2 for Grade 8), one of the four core classes is dropped. In an 8-day rotation (see Figure 5.10, p. 131), this means each core class meets for seven 70-minute classes, or an average of over 60 minutes per day.

with 5 minutes between classes for class changes. The afternoon core classes are 70 minutes long. To insure equality of instructional time it is necessary to rotate the classes. In Figure 5.15, on Day 1 teachers meet each of their four classes in 70-minute blocks and plan during Block IV. On Day 2 of the rotation, when students leave the team for two blocks, morning classes are shortened. Sections 1, 2, and 3 meet for 45 minutes; section 4 meets for 70 minutes. By rotating these classes over the next 6 days, instructional time is equalized.

FIGURE 5.15. TEAM ROTATION FOR 10-BLOCK SCHEDULE: TEACHER SCHEDULE B

	Day 1	Day 2	Day 3	Day 4	Day 5	Day 6	Day 7	Day 8
8:00–8:10	Homeroom							
Block I 8:15–9:25	Section 1	Section 1 / Section 2	Section 2	Section 2 / Section 3	Section 3	Section 3 / Section 4	Section 4	Section 4 / Section 1
Block II 9:30–10:40	Section 2	Section 3	Section 3	Section 4	Section 4	Section 1	Section 1	Section 2
Block III 10:45–11:55	Section 3	PLAN/ Duty	Section 4	PLAN/ Duty	Section 1	PLAN/ Duty	Section 2	PLAN/ Duty
12:00–12:30	Lunch							
Block IV 12:35–1:45	PLAN	PLAN	PLAN	PLAN	PLAN	PLAN	PLAN	PLAN
Block V 1:50–3:00	Section 4	Section 4	Section 1	Section 1	Section 2	Section 2	Section 3	Section 3

The advantages of the five-block middle school schedule include:

◆ Students have greater amounts of core time compared to many traditional middle school schedules, yet they have up to four scheduling slots for exploratories and electives.

◆ Sixty-five- or 70-minute blocks are easier than 90-minute blocks for many teachers to adapt to.

◆ The schedule adapts well to four-member teams.

♦ The schedule adapts well to schools with four grade levels.

A disadvantage, as compared with a four-block middle school schedule, is that both students and teachers are dealing with more classes throughout the school year.

6

SCHEDULING EXPLORATORY AND ELECTIVE CLASSES IN THE MIDDLE SCHOOL: EXPANDING THE POSSIBILITIES

This chapter offers various formats for scheduling middle school students in physical education, exploratory, and elective classes. In many ways, creating the elective and exploratory schedule is the most difficult aspect of middle school scheduling. We begin by defining elective and exploratory classes.

In essence, any course can be adapted to serve as either an exploratory or an elective; the major difference lies in the depth of knowledge or skill to be developed. Exploratory classes offer an appetizer; electives provide a full meal.

An elective class is a class chosen by the student that meets consistently over a period of at least one semester, and possibly for the entire school year, whose primary goal is to develop a high level of competence and/or performance that is appropriate for this age child. The student's progress is usually evaluated using traditional academic grades. Typical examples of a middle school elective class are foreign language, band, orchestra and chorus. Some elective classes are repeated, at higher skill levels, each year; for example, it is typical to offer sixth grade band, seventh grade band, and eighth grade band as sequential electives.

Some schools, however, do not organize electives by grade level. Beginning band, concert band, and symphonic band often include a mix of students in different grade levels who are placed in the appropriate performing group based on skill level. Of course mixed-grade-level electives bring a whole new complexity to the scheduling process.

An exploratory class is one that meets for less than a semester and whose major goal is to provide students with opportunities to *explore* a particular interest or content area to determine whether there is sufficient interest to continue study in the area. Such study may continue during the following middle school years and/or into high school. The original intent of exploratories in the middle school was to help students make better choices in high school; for example, do they want to take three or more years of a foreign language in high school? If so, which language? We believe the philosophy of exploratory classes for middle school students is best served if students are not assigned traditional academic grades in exploratory classes, at least in Grades 6 and 7.

Ideally, exploratories and electives are offered in a pyramid format, as shown in Figure 6.1. That is, in Grade 6 students may have opportunities to spend 6 weeks *exploring* each of these subjects: French, technology, Spanish, keyboarding, German, and art. During Grade 7, some students may choose to continue their exploration of Spanish for 9 weeks, technology for 9 weeks, and then add two other areas of exploration, such as guitar and family living. During Grade 8, students may continue to build on previous exploratories by taking a full semester of technology and art or a full year of a foreign language.

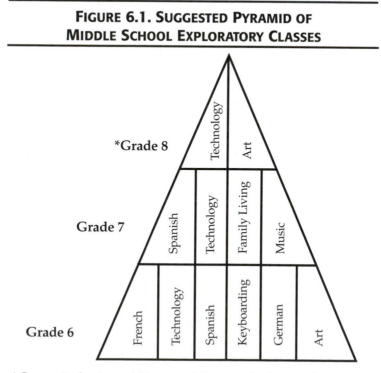

FIGURE 6.1. SUGGESTED PYRAMID OF MIDDLE SCHOOL EXPLORATORY CLASSES

* Some students could have a full year of a foreign language.

Middle schools can offer physical education, elective and exploratory classes in a rich variety of scheduling formats. Courses can be offered as daily periods, as periods on a rotational basis (every other day, every 4 days, etc.), as daily blocks, or as every-other-day blocks. Classes can be scheduled by single grade levels or by multigrade levels. Classes may be offered during nonteam time only—so that all team members are planning when students are attending noncore (encore) classes—or parallel to core classes. Each option presents a set of different issues.

Another consideration when building a schedule is the relative proportion of the day allocated to the basic core program versus that allocated to PE, elective, and exploratory courses. Some schools allot only one of six periods to these encore subjects; others allot four of eight periods to core and four to encore. Most schools fall somewhere between these two extremes. This chapter addresses these issues and offers a variety of different schedules as illustrations.

ONE PERIOD ALLOCATED FOR ENCORE

Almost all schools that provide only one period for PE, exploratory, and elective classes operate a six-period schedule. Students in these schools typically take five core classes: reading or foreign language, English, mathematics, science, and social studies. The sixth period must accommodate all other activities; it also is the time for the team teachers to plan. Figure 6.2 (p. 140) illustrates a typical master schedule for this situation.

The schedule shown in Figure 6.2 serves six teams, two at each grade level. One period per day is allocated for students to attend encore classes and for their team teachers to plan together. Specialists do not have common planning time; one or more of these specialists must plan each period of the day.

Figure 6.3 (p. 141) illustrates a number of different ways to use one daily period for encore. Example 1 illustrates a 2-day rotation; classes meet every other day. Students have PE/health every other day on Day 1 (left column) and an exploratory class every other day on Day 2 (right column). The exploratory class changes every 9 weeks, so that over the course of the year students are exposed to 9 weeks each of music, art, technology, and home and careers.

A 4-day rotation, which is often utilized in elementary schools, also is possible. Example 2 shows a 4-day cycle in which students attend one period of PE/health, art, music, and computers every 4 days; the rotation begins anew on day 5. In Example 3, PE/health is offered every other day and art and music are scheduled once every 4 days. In Example 4, PE/health is scheduled every other day; art and music classes meet once every 4 days during the first semester; family life and technology classes replace art and music in the schedule during the second semester.

FIGURE 6.2. SIX-PERIOD DAY: ONE PERIOD
PER TEAM FOR TEACHER PLANNING, PE,
ELECTIVES, AND EXPLORATORIES

Periods	1	2	3	4	5	6
Grade 6 Team 1	Core	Core	Core	Core	Core	Plan/* EEE
Grade 6 Team 2	Core	Core	Core	Core	Plan/ EEE	Core
Grade 7 Team 1	Core	Core	Core	Plan/ EEE	Core	Core
Grade 7 Team 2	Core	Core	Plan/ EEE	Core	Core	Core
Grade 8 Team 1	Core	Plan/ EEE	Core	Core	Core	Core
Grade 8 Team 2	Plan/ EEE	Core	Core	Core	Core	Core
PE/ Elective/ Exploratories	Grade 8 Team 2	Grade 8 Team 1	Grade 7 Team 2	Grade 7 Team 1	Grade 6 Team 2	Grade 6 Team 1

* One period is allocated for each team of students to attend either PE, elective, or exploratory classes. Core grade level teachers plan during this time. Specialists have no common planning time; one or more specialists must plan during each period, probably on a rotating basis.

A 6-day rotation occasionally is used in both elementary and middle schools. In Figure 6.3, Example 5 shows a 6-day rotation which provides students with two periods each of PE/health, music, and art every 6 days (actually it is a 3-day rotation). In Example 6, PE/health is provided every other day and one period each of music, art, and computers is scheduled every 6 days.

We make no comment here as to what exploratory areas should be scheduled for middle school students; this decision should be determined based on the district's or school's mission. The patterns shown in Figure 6.3 may be applied to any subjects.

One negative aspect of 4-day or 6-day rotations is that students see many teachers within each rotation. If 6 different classes are offered, students see 11 teachers each cycle, including the core team. It may not be

FIGURE 6.3. EXPLORATORY ROTATION POSSIBILITIES: ONE PERIOD—SAMPLE STUDENT SCHEDULES

2-, 4-, and 6-Day Rotations

Ex. 1 2-day	Day 1		Day 2	
	PE/H		Music (1st 9 weeks) Art (2nd 9 weeks) Technology (3rd 9 weeks) Home & Careers (4th 9 weeks)	

Ex. 2 4-day	Day 1	Day 2	Day 3	Day 4
	PE/H	Art	Music	Computers

Ex. 3 4-day	Day 1	Day 2	Day 3	Day 4
	PE/H	Art	PE/H	Music

Ex. 4 4-day	Day 1	Day 2	Day 3	Day 4
	PE/H	Art (Sem. 1) Fam. Life (Sem. 2)	PE/H	Music (Sem. 1) Tech. (Sem. 2)

Ex. 5 6-day	Day 1	Day 2	Day 3	Day 4	Day 5	Day 6
	PE/H	Music	Art	PE/H	Music	Art

Ex. 6 6-day	Day 1	Day 2	Day 3	Day 4	Day 5	Day 6
	PE/H	Music	PE/H	Art	PE/H	Computers

9-Week and 6-Week Rotations

Ex. 7 9 wks	1st 9 weeks	2nd 9 weeks	3rd 9 weeks	4th 9 weeks
	PE/H	Art	Music	Computers

Ex. 8 9 wks	1st 9 weeks	2nd 9 weeks	3rd 9 weeks	4th 9 weeks
	PE/H	Art	PE/H	Music

Ex. 9 6 wks	1st 6 weeks	2nd 6 weeks	3rd 6 weeks	4th 6 weeks	5th 6 weeks	6th 6 weeks
	PE/Health	Music	Art	Technology	Home & Careers	Drama

Ex. 10 6 wks	1st 6 weeks	2nd 6 weeks	3rd 6 weeks	4th 6 weeks	5th 6 weeks	6th 6 weeks
	PE/H	Music	PE/H	Art	Technology	Home & Careers

Ex. 11 6 wks	1st 6 weeks	2nd 6 weeks	3rd 6 weeks	4th 6 weeks	5th 6 weeks	6th 6 weeks
	PE/H	Music	PE/H	Art	PE/H	Computers

advisable for middle school students to have so many different adult contacts each week. Teachers also work with many different students each week, all year long. An exploratory teacher could easily see more than 500 students per rotation in a 6-day cycle.

Alternative scheduling rotations that reduce the number of different adult contacts per week are the 9-week rotation and the 6-week rotation (see Figure 6.3, p. 141). In Example 7, the sample student attends PE/health class every day for 9 weeks, followed by 9 weeks of art, 9 weeks of music, and 9 weeks of computers. Although students in this example (if they had five core teachers) could have nine different teachers during the year, they would only report to six different teachers each 9-week term.

A concern that many people have with this schedule is that middle school students do not receive any physical education class for three-fourths of the year. As an alternative, in Example 8, the first and third 9-week terms are devoted to PE/health. Art meets every day for 9 weeks second term, and music meets every day during the fourth 9-week term.

It also would be possible to operate a 6-week rotation, which would offer at least one more exploratory taste. Example 9 shows 6 weeks each of PE/health, music, art, technology, home and careers, and drama. Example 10 provides two 6-week terms of PE/health, and one 6-week term each of music, art, technology, and home and careers. Example 11 provides PE/health in three 6-week stints, interspersed with 6 weeks of music, art, and computers.

Figure 6.4 shows how 80 to 120 students could be scheduled in five different classes on a 5-day, or Monday-Friday, schedule. For example, a student in Group 1 has PE/health on Day 1, art on Day 2, music on Day 3, technology on Day 4, and home and careers on Day 5. Following this pattern, the art teacher works with Group 2 on Day 1, Group 1 on Day 2, Group 4 on Day 4, and Group 3 on Day 5. On Day 3, the art teacher is unassigned; this could be a planning or duty period. To ensure that such unassigned periods are distributed throughout the week, we would alter the pattern for different periods during the day. For example, if the schedule shown in Figure 6.4 were used in Period 2, we might move the rotation up to give the art teacher planning on Day 4 in Period 3.

Figure 6.5 illustrates a rotation similar to that in Figure 6.4, but with rotations every 7½ to 8 weeks.

Again this plan reduces the number of teachers each student encounters weekly. Instead of seeing five core and five encore teachers per week, as shown in Figure 6.4, students see only six teachers—five core and one encore—during each 8-week rotation. This also alleviates a major problem for encore teachers. In the schedule shown in Figure 6.4, each encore teacher serves four different groups of students in each teaching period. Assuming each teacher instructs 5 of the 6 periods, encore teachers then

FIGURE 6.4. DAILY EXPLORATORY ROTATION (ONE PERIOD) ELEMENTARY MODEL

	Day 1	Day 2	Day 3	Day 4	Day 5
Group 1	PE/H	Art	Music	Technology	Home & Careers
Group 2	Art	Music	Technology	Home & Careers	PE/H
Group 3	Music	Technology	Home & Careers	PE/H	Art
Group 4	Technology	Home & Careers	PE/H	Art	Music
Planning	Home & Careers Teacher	PE/Health Teacher	Art Teacher	Music Teacher	Technology Teacher

FIGURE 6.5. EXPLORATORY ROTATION (ONE PERIOD) 8-WEEK ROTATIONS (7½ WEEKS)

	1st 8 weeks	2nd 8 weeks	3rd 8 weeks	4th 8 weeks	5th 8 weeks
Group 1	PE/H	Art	Music	Technology	Home & Careers
Group 2	Art	Music	Technology	Home & Careers	PE/H
Group 3	Music	Technology	Home & Careers	PE/H	Art
Group 4	Technology	Home & Careers	PE/H	Art	Music
Planning	Home & Careers Teacher	PE/Health Teacher	Art Teacher	Music Teacher	Technology Teacher

work with at least 20 different groups of students weekly. This requires space to store all those ongoing projects—and a great memory for student names! In addition teachers must address the needs of 400 to 600 different students all year long—a formidable task.

In the schedule shown in Figure 6.5 (p. 143), each encore teacher sees only five or six different groups during each 8-week rotation. True, new groups are assigned every 8 weeks, but we argue that this situation is much more palatable than the 5-day rotation.

Figure 6.6 illustrates a 4-day rotational schedule serving four groups of students. PE/health classes meet every other day; art and music classes meet once every 4 days. The schedule requires two PE/health teachers, one music teacher, and one art teacher. The rotation begins anew after the fourth day. For example, Group 3 has art on Day 1, PE/health on Day 2, music on Day 3, and PE/health on Day 4. On Day 5 the rotation starts over with the art class.

FIGURE 6.6. DAILY EXPLORATORY ROTATION (ONE PERIOD): PE/HEALTH EVERY OTHER DAY OPPOSITE ART AND MUSIC

	Day 1	*Day 2*	*Day 3*	*Day 4*
Group 1	PE/H	Art	PE/H	Music
Group 2	PE/H	Music	PE/H	Art
Group 3	Art	PE/H	Music	PE/H
Group 4	Music	PE/H	Art	PE/H

Classes meet on a four-day rotation. After 4 days the rotation begins anew. Music and art could be replaced by other exploratories at the semester. A third exploratory could be added if the rotation were increased to 6 days.

The schedule illustrated in Figure 6.7 offers students PE/health every other day all year. On the opposite day students rotate through four different exploratory classes, each for 9 weeks. Thus, Group 1 has art, then music, then technology, and finally home and careers—each meeting every other day for 9 weeks. This schedule could serve between 80 and 120 students. As shown in Figure 6.7 the art and music teachers work with these four groups first semester; then they are replaced by the technology and home & careers teachers for the second semester. This practice allows the exploratory teachers to work with other groups of students during the opposite semester.

FIGURE 6.7. PE/HEALTH EVERY OTHER DAY (EOD): EXPLORATORY ROTATION EOD; CHANGE EVERY NINE WEEKS (ONE PERIOD, 80–120 STUDENTS)

	Day 1	Day 2
Group 1	PE/H	Art 1st 9 weeks Music 2nd 9 weeks Technology 3rd 9 weeks Home & Careers 4th 9 weeks
Group 2	PE/H	Music 1st 9 weeks Art 2nd 9 weeks Home & Careers 3rd 9 weeks Technology 4th 9 weeks
Group 3	Art 1st 9 weeks Music 2nd 9 weeks Technology 3rd 9 weeks Home & Careers 4th 9 weeks	PE/H
Group 4	Music 1st 9 weeks Art 2nd 9 weeks Home & Careers 3rd 9 weeks Technology 4th 9 weeks	PE/H

PE/health meets every other day opposite art, music, technology, or home and careers. During Semester 1, the technology and the home and careers teachers work with another team or at another school. During Semester 2, the art and music teachers work with another team or at another school. This plan requires two PE/health teachers.

It is not unusual to have larger class sizes for PE/health than for other encore subjects. The schedule shown in Figure 6.8 (p. 146) illustrates this possibility. Half of the team, Groups 1 to 3, has PE/health on Day 1 of the schedule. These 60 to 90 students are split between the two physical education teachers. On Day 2, Group 1 attends art class, Group 2 attends computers, and Group 3 attends music. Every 6 weeks the exploratory class changes. As shown, this group of 120 to 180 students receives 6 weeks each of art, music, and computers during the first semester. If necessary, these teachers then may be assigned to another team during this period. During the second semester students attend technology, home and careers, and drama for 6 weeks each, every other day opposite PE/health. Moving drama to the first semester and computers to the second semester would create an "Arts" semester and a "Technology" semester for students, which might increase the possibilities for integration. Each semester a minimum of two PE/health teachers and three encore teachers is required to staff this plan.

FIGURE 6.8. PE/HEALTH EVERY OTHER DAY (EOD): EXPLORATORY ROTATION EOD; CHANGE EVERY SIX WEEKS (ONE BLOCK, 120–180 STUDENTS)

	Day 1	*Day 2*
Group 1	PE/H Group 1 and ½ of group 2	Art 1st 6 weeks Music 2nd 6 weeks Computers 3rd 6 weeks Technology 4th 6 weeks Home & Careers 5th 6 weeks Drama 6th 6 weeks
Group 2		Computers 1st 6 weeks Art 2nd 6 weeks Music 3rd 6 weeks Drama 4th 6 weeks Technology 5th 6 weeks Home & Careers 6th 6 weeks
Group 3	PE/H Group 3 and ½ of Group 2	Music 1st 6 weeks Computer 2nd 6 weeks Art 3rd 6 weeks Home & Careers 4th 6 weeks Drama 5th 6 weeks Technology 6th 6 weeks
Group 4	Art 1st 6 weeks Music 2nd 6 weeks Computers 3rd 6 weeks Technology 4th 6 weeks Home & Careers 5th 6 weeks Drama 6th 6 weeks	PE/H Group 4 and ½ of Group 5
Group 5	Computers 1st 6 weeks Art 2nd 6 weeks Music 3rd 6 weeks Drama 4th 6 weeks Technology 5th 6 weeks Home & Careers 6th 6 weeks	
Group 6	Music 1st 6 weeks Computers 2nd 6 weeks Art 3rd 6 weeks Home & Careers 4th 6 weeks Drama 5th 6 weeks Technology 6th 6 weeks	PE/H Group 6 and ½ of Group 5

PE/health meets every other day opposite either art, music, technology, or home and careers. During Semester 1, the technology and the home and careers teachers work with another team or at another school. During Semester 2 the art and music teachers work with another team or at another school. This plan requires two PE/health teachers.

TWO PERIODS ALLOCATED FOR ENCORE

In most schools, two periods are allocated for noncore or encore classes. In the seven-period schedule, this leaves the equivalent of five periods for core; in the eight-period schedule, this leaves the equivalent of six periods for core.

Scheduling two periods for encore gives schedulers several options. The periods assigned to teams can be blocked together or they can be separated; both periods can provide common planning time, or one or no periods can be common planning time for the team teachers. Figure 6.9 is an example of a seven-period master schedule with two consecutive periods provided for encore classes.

FIGURE 6.9. SEVEN-PERIOD DAY: TWO PERIODS PER GRADE LEVEL FOR TEACHER PLANNING, PE, ELECTIVES, AND EXPLORATORIES

Periods	1	2	3	4	5	6	7
Grade 6	Core	Core	Core	Core	Core	Plan/ EEE	Plan/ EEE
Grade 7	Core	Core	Core	Plan/ EEE	Plan/ EEE	Core	Core
Grade 8	Core	Plan/ EEE	Plan/ EEE	Core	Core	Core	Core
PE/ Elective/ Exploratories*	Plan	Grade 8	Grade 8	Grade 7	Grade 7	Grade 6	Grade 6

* Two consecutive periods are allocated for students at each grade level to attend PE, elective, or exploratory classes. Core grade-level teachers plan during this time. Although only one planning period is shown for the encore teachers, the second planning periods for encore staff members are distributed throughout the day. For example, if there were 12 PE, elective, and exploratory teachers, all of them would receive their first planning period during Period 1, and two different teachers would plan during each of the next six periods.

When the periods are scheduled together consecutively for each grade or team, it is possible to block them together, as Figure 6.10 (p.148) illustrates. This arrangement permits encore teachers to block and alternate their classes if desired. A variety of possibilities for this alternation exists. For example, encore teachers may decide to alternate every other day or they may decide to meet both classes in the block in short periods on Monday, Tuesday, and Friday with one class meeting for the entire block on Wednesday and the other class meeting for the entire block on Thursday.

FIGURE 6.10. SEVEN-PERIOD DAY: TWO PERIODS BLOCKED TOGETHER PER GRADE LEVEL FOR TEACHER PLANNING, PE, ELECTIVES, AND EXPLORATORIES

Periods	1	2	3	4	5	6	7
Grade 6	Core	Core	Core	Core	Core	Plan/ EEE	
Grade 7	Core	Core	Core	Plan/ EEE		Core	Core
Grade 8	Core	Plan/ EEE		Core	Core	Core	Core
PE/ Elective/ Exploratories*	Plan	Grade 8		Grade 7		Grade 6	

* Two periods are blocked together for each grade level to attend PE, elective, or exploratory classes. Core grade-level teachers plan during this time. Encore classes can meet daily in periods or every other day in blocks. Although only one planning period is shown for the encore teachers, the second planning periods for encore staff members are distributed throughout the day. For example, if there were 12 PE, elective, and exploratory teachers, all of them would receive their first planning period during Period 1, and two different teachers would plan during each of the next six periods.

Some teachers prefer to have single planning periods, with one in the morning and one in the afternoon. This possibility is shown in Figure 6.11. While both periods offer common planning time, this arrangement eliminates the possibility of blocking for encore teachers. We also would argue that when teachers have a short planning period, even expeditious personal tasks leave little time for meaningful work.

FIGURE 6.11. SEVEN-PERIOD DAY: TWO SEPARATED PERIODS PER GRADE LEVEL FOR TEACHER PLANNING, PE, ELECTIVES, AND EXPLORATORIES

Periods	1	2	3	4	5	6	7
Grade 6	Core	Core	Core	Plan/ EEE	Core	Core	Plan/ EEE
Grade 7	Core	Plan/ EEE	Core	Core	Plan/ EEE	Core	Core
Grade 8	Core	Core	Plan/ EEE	Core	Core	Plan/ EEE	Core
PE/ Elective/ Exploratories*	Plan	Grade 7	Grade 8	Grade 6	Grade 7	Grade 8	Grade 6

* Two separate periods are allocated for each grade level to attend PE, elective, or exploratory classes. Core grade-level teachers plan during this time. Although only one planning period is shown for the encore teachers, the second planning periods for encore staff members are distributed throughout the day. For example, if there were 12 PE, elective, and exploratory teachers, all of them would receive their first planning period during Period 1, and two different teachers would plan during each of the next six periods.

To provide more flexibility for the scheduling of electives, some schools assign team teachers only one common planning period (each teacher's second planning period falls in a different period). As shown in Figure 6.12, this format allows one group of students to leave the team during periods 2– 6. By careful assignment, the scheduler can ensure that students who need the singleton orchestra class are available for that class, leaving the team during the appropriate period. Several problems, however, exist with this plan. During each period, except first period and during team planning time, 20 percent of the team's students are gone. This makes it virtually impossible to alter the team schedule; for example, the team could not block or schedule a special activity period without disrupting the elective schedule.

FIGURE 6.12. SEVEN-PERIOD DAY: TWO PERIODS FOR TEACHER PLANNING, PE ELECTIVES, AND EXPLORATORIES— ONE COMMON PLANNING PERIOD

Periods	1	2	3	4	5	6	7
English	Group 1	Group 2	Group 3	Plan/ EEE	Group 4	Group 5	Plan/ EEE
Reading	Group 2	Group 3	Plan/ EEE	Group 4	Group 5	Group 1	Plan/ EEE
Mathematics	Group 3	Plan/ EEE	Group 4	Group 5	Group 1	Group 2	Plan/ EEE
Social Studies	Group 4	Group 5	Group 1	Group 2	Group 3	Plan/ EEE	Plan/ EEE
Science	Group 5	Group 1	Group 2	Group 3	Plan/ EEE	Group 4	Plan/ EEE
PE/ Elective/ Exploratories*	Plan	Group 4	Group 5	Group 1	Group 2	Group 3	Groups 1–5

* Two separate periods are allocated for students to attend PE, elective or exploratory classes. Core grade-level teachers plan during this time; Period 7 provides common planning time. Although only one planning period is shown for the encore teachers, the second planning periods for encore staff members are distributed throughout the day. For example, if there were 12 PE, elective, and exploratory teachers, all of them would receive their first planning period during Period 1, and two different teachers would plan during each of the next six periods.

Figure 6.13 illustrates the master block schedule for an eight-period day with two planning periods for teachers and the equivalent of six periods for core. The two single periods are placed consecutively in this model. Again, as Figure 6.14 (p. 152) shows, the two periods can be blocked together; now encore classes can meet daily or alternately, in single periods or blocks. Obviously, by blocking the core periods together as shown in Figure 6.15 (p. 152), this master schedule becomes appropriate for the four-block schedule discussed in Chapter 4.

FIGURE 6.13. EIGHT-PERIOD DAY: TWO PERIODS PER GRADE LEVEL FOR TEACHER PLANNING, PE, ELECTIVES, AND EXPLORATORIES

Periods	1	2	3	4	5	6	7	8
Grade 6	Core	Core	Core	Core	Core	Core	Plan/ EEE	Plan/ EEE
Grade 7	Core	Core	Core	Core	Plan/ EEE	Plan/ EEE	Core	Core
Grade 8	Core	Core	Plan/ EEE	Plan/ EEE	Core	Core	Core	Core
PE/ Elective/ Exploratories*	Plan	Plan	Grade 8	Grade 8	Grade 7	Grade 7	Grade 6	Grade 6

* Two consecutive periods are allocated for students at each grade level to attend PE, elective, or exploratory classes. Core grade-level teachers plan during this time.

FIGURE 6.14. EIGHT-PERIOD DAY: TWO PERIODS BLOCKED TOGETHER PER GRADE LEVEL FOR TEACHER PLANNING, PE, ELECTIVES, AND EXPLORATORIES

Periods	1	2	3	4	5	6	7	8
Grade 6	Core	Core	Core	Core	Core	Core	Plan/ *EEE	
Grade 7	Core	Core	Core	Core	Plan/ EEE		Core	Core
Grade 8	Core	Core	Plan/ EEE		Core	Core	Core	Core
PE/ Elective/ Exploratories*	Plan		Grade 8	Grade 8	Grade 7	Grade 7	Grade 6	Grade 6

* Two periods are blocked together for students at each grade level to attend PE, elective, or exploratory classes. Core grade-level teachers plan during this time. Encore classes can meet daily in single periods or every other day in blocks.

FIGURE 6.15. FOUR-BLOCK MASTER SCHEDULE: ONE BLOCK PER GRADE LEVEL FOR TEACHER PLANNING, PE, ELECTIVES, AND EXPLORATORIES

Blocks	Block I	Block II	Block III	Block IV
Grade 6	Core	Core	Core	Plan/ EEE
Grade 7	Core	Core	Plan/ EEE	Core
Grade 8	Core	Plan/ EEE	Core	Core
PE/ Elective/ Exploratories*	Plan	Grade 8	Grade 7	Grade 6

* Two periods are blocked together for students at each grade level to attend PE, elective, or exploratory classes. Core grade-level teachers plan during this time. Encore classes can meet daily in single periods or every other day in blocks.

As shown previously for the seven-period day, the eight-period schedule also can be designed to offer two separate planning periods for the team with one in the morning and one in the afternoon (see Figure 6.16). Again, encore team blocking of these periods for PE, electives, or exploratories is not possible.

FIGURE 6.16. EIGHT-PERIOD DAY: TWO SEPARATE PERIODS PER GRADE LEVEL FOR TEACHER PLANNING, PE, ELECTIVES, AND EXPLORATORIES

Periods	1	2	3	4	5	6	7	8
Grade 6	Core	Core	Core	Plan/ EEE	Core	Core	Core	Plan/ EEE
Grade 7	Core	Plan/ EEE	Core	Core	Core	Plan/ EEE	Core	Core
Grade 8	Core	Core	Plan/ EEE	Core	Core	Core	Plan/ EEE	Core
PE/ Elective/ Exploratories*	Plan	Grade 7	Grade 8	Grade 6	Plan	Grade 7	Grade 8	Grade 6

* Two separate periods are allocated for students at each grade level to attend PE, elective, or exploratory classes. Core grade-level teachers plan during this time.

Also the eight-period day can be scheduled so that only one of the two planning periods assigned to team teachers is common. As shown in Figure 6.17 (p. 154), common planning time is provided during Period 8, and the second planning period for each teacher is distributed throughout the day to allow for more flexible scheduling of elective classes.

Figure 6.18 (p. 155) illustrates some of the possibilities available for scheduling encore classes in two periods. Examples 1 to 3 may be used for either consecutive or nonconsecutive periods; in examples 4 to 6, classes meet for a block every other day and must be scheduled in consecutive periods.

In Example 1, a daily period of PE/health and a daily elective period are offered. A student might take band every day for the year in Period 1 and PE/health every day for the year in Period 2. This schedule offers no room for exploration and only one period for an elective.

In Example 2, that daily period of PE/health is replaced by an exploratory wheel that includes PE/health (as in the rotations shown in Figures 6.4 (p. 143), 6.5 (p. 143), 6.6 (p. 144), 6.7 (p. 145) and 6.8 (p. 146)). A student could take orchestra every day in Period 1; in Period 2 the student might

FIGURE 6.17. EIGHT-PERIOD DAY: TWO PERIODS FOR TEACHER PLANNING, PE, ELECTIVES, AND EXPLORATORIES —ONE COMMON PLANNING PERIOD

Periods	1	2	3	4	5	6	7	8
Language Arts	Group 1	Group 1	Group 2	Group 2	Plan/ EEE	Group 3	Group 3	Plan/ EEE
Language Arts	Group 4	Group 4	Group 5	Group 5	Group 6	Group 6	Plan/ EEE	Plan/ EEE
Spanish	Group 2	Group 6	Group 3	Plan/ EEE	Group 4	Group 5	Group 1	Plan/ EEE
Mathematics	Group 3	Group 2	Group 4	Group 6	Group 1	Plan/ EEE	Group 5	Plan/ EEE
Social Studies	Group 5	Group 3	Plan/ EEE	Group 4	Group 2	Group 1	Group 6	Plan/ EEE
Science	Group 6	Plan/ EEE	Group 1	Group 3	Group 5	Group 4	Group 2	Plan/ EEE
PE/ Elective/ Exploratories	Plan	Group 5	Group 6	Group 1	Group 3	Group 2	Group 4	Groups 1–6

All students attend PE, elective, or exploratory classes during Period 8, which also provides common planning time for teachers. Teachers' second planning period and students' second period for PE, elective, or exploratory classes are scheduled throughout the day.

have 9 weeks each of PE, art, health, and computers. During each 9-week term these classes meet every day for a period. Thus, a student could complete one elective, the equivalent of a semester of PE/health, and two exploratory courses. Students are involved with only two encore teachers during each 9-week session.

Example 3 follows a similar pattern, but exploratory classes are provided on a 6-day rotation throughout the entire school year. Again a student could attend choir during Period 1 every day for the school year. In Period 2, the student could attend three exploratory classes on a 6-day rotation, such as the following: Day 1: PE/H; Day 2: art; Day 3: computers; Day 4: PE/H; Day 5: art; and Day 6: computers. This rotation does cause the problem mentioned previously: "hands-on" teachers are confronted with storing ongoing projects for many more students, and all exploratory teachers work with most of the school population all year long. (Some exploratory teachers, however, prefer this 6-day rotation because it allows them to benefit from the maturation that occurs during the school year.)

FIGURE 6.18. TWO-PERIOD ELECTIVE
AND EXPLORATORY POSSIBILITIES

Ex. 1	Per. 1	Elective meets daily for a period. Examples: Band, orchestra, choir, foreign language.	
	Per. 2	PE/Health meets daily for a period.	
Ex. 2	Per. 1	Elective meets daily for a period. Examples: Band, orchestra, choir, foreign language.	
	Per. 2	Exploratory classes meet daily for a period; exploratory classes change every 6, 9, 12, or 18 weeks. Examples: 9 weeks each of PE, art, health, and computers.	
Ex. 3	Per. 1	Elective meets daily for a period. Examples: Band, orchestra, choir, foreign language.	
	Per. 2	Exploratory classes meet daily for a period on a rotating cycle of 4 or 6 days. Example: In a 6-day cycle, 2 days each of art, music, and computers.	

		Day 1	*Day 2*
Ex. 4	Per. 1	Elective class meets for a block every other day.	Exploratory classes meet for a block every other day; exploratory classes change every 6, 9, 12, or 18 weeks.
	Per. 2		

		Day 1	*Day 2*
Ex. 5	Per. 1	Elective class meets for a block every other day.	PE/Health meets for a block every other day.
	Per. 2		

		Day 1	*Day 2*
Ex. 6	Per. 1	Exploratory classes meet for a block every other day; exploratory class changes every 6, 9, 12, or 18 weeks.	PE/Health meets for a block every other day.
	Per. 2		

In Example 4, students are scheduled exactly as in Example 2, but classes meet every other day in blocks. This practice allows "hands-on" teachers much more freedom in scheduling activities. Periods must be consecutive for this schedule to work. Example 5 is simply Example 1 scheduled every other day. The assignment of students is exactly the same; classes just meet on an alternate-block basis. Finally, Example 6 replaces the elective class with an exploratory rotation. PE/health meets every other day opposite, for example, 12 weeks of art, 12 weeks of home and careers, and 12 weeks of a technology class. A single-period version of this model also is possible.

SCHEDULING ITINERANT ELECTIVE TEACHERS

Blocking elective periods together for each grade level can cause a scheduling problem if itinerant teachers, such as band or orchestra, are available only certain periods of the day. For example, what if the band director only works in the middle school in the morning and the orchestra director only works in the middle school in the afternoon? If Figures 6.13 (p. 151) or 6.14 (p. 152) were used as the master block schedule, only eighth grade students could be in orchestra and only sixth and seventh grade students could be in band.

One way of approaching this problem is to give up the idea of scheduling teacher planning time in two consecutive periods. The master schedule shown in Figure 6.16 (p. 153) offers each grade level both a morning and an afternoon planning period and, therefore, access to the itinerants (i.e. band and orchestra in this case) who teach at those times. This technique does eliminate the possibility of any blocking of encore programs, because the periods are no longer consecutive.

How can we give students access to itinerants and still preserve the possibility of blocking encore classes? The schedules illustrated by Figures 6.19 and 6.20 illustrate two possibilities. In these schedules planning time for teachers is alternated every other day. For example, in Figure 6.19, sixth grade teachers plan in Periods 7 and 8 on Day 1 of the schedule; this is when the band director is available. If band were an every-other-day period, as is common in the Northeast, we would schedule band students during either Period 7 or 8. On Day 2 of the schedule the sixth grade teachers plan during Periods 3 and 4; the orchestra leader is available at this time. Again, orchestra could be offered every other day at this time for one period.

If encore teachers had decided to block and alternate their classes, the master schedule shown in Figure 6.20 (p. 158) could be employed. For example, on Day 1, Grade 8 teachers plan in Block II; orchestra students could be scheduled at this time. On Day 2, Grade 8 teachers plan during Block IV; band students can be scheduled at this time. By alternating the time each team plans and keeping constant the time itinerants come each day, we can provide all students access to these programs and keep blocks for teacher planning time and on core classes.

Perhaps an easier way to handle this problem is for a school to share itinerants on an every-other-day basis with another school. For example, if we keep the time for team planning constant every day as shown in Figure 6.15 (p. 152), and bring the orchestra teacher on Day 1 and the band director on Day 2, all students would have access to both programs. Students from all three grade levels could attend orchestra on Day 1 during their respective grade levels' planning blocks; similarly, students from all three grade levels could attend band on Day 2.

FIGURE 6.19. EIGHT-PERIOD DAY: TWO PERIODS PER GRADE LEVEL FOR TEACHER PLANNING, PE, ELECTIVES, AND EXPLORATORIES— ALTERNATING-DAY PLANNING TIMES TO ACCOMMODATE ITINERANT TEACHERS

Periods	1	2	3	4	5	6	7	8
Grade 6 Day 1	Core	Core	Core	Core	Core	Core	Plan/ EEE	Plan/ EEE
Grade 6 Day 2	Core	Core	Plan/ EEE	Plan/ EEE	Core	Core	Core	Core
Grade 7 Day 1	Core	Core	Core	Core	Plan/ EEE	Plan/ EEE	Core	Core
Grade 7 Day 2	Plan/ EEE	Plan/ EEE	Core	Core	Core	Core	Core	Core
Grade 8 Day 1	Core	Core	Plan/ EEE	Plan/ EEE	Core	Core	Core	Core
Grade 8 Day 2	Core	Core	Core	Core	Core	Core	Plan/ EEE	Plan/ EEE
PE/ Elective/ Exploratories Day 1	Plan	Plan	Grade 8	Grade 8	Grade 7	Grade 7	Grade 6	Grade 6
PE/ Elective/ Exploratories Day 2	Grade 7	Grade 7	Grade 6	Grade 6	Plan	Plan	Grade 8	Grade 8
Itinerants	Orchestra available only in morning.				Band available only in afternoon.			

Two periods are allocated for students at each grade level to attend either PE, elective, or exploratory classes. Core grade-level teachers plan during this time. Grade-level teachers plan one day in the morning and one day in the afternoon to give students access to the orchestra and band teachers, who are part-time morning and afternoon, respectively.

FIGURE 6.20. FOUR-BLOCK SCHEDULE: ONE BLOCK PER GRADE LEVEL FOR TEACHER PLANNING, PE, ELECTIVES, AND EXPLORATORIES—ALTERNATING-DAY PLANNING TIMES TO ACCOMMODATE ITINERANT TEACHERS

Blocks	Block I	Block II	Block III	Block IV
Grade 6 Day 1	Core	Core	Core	Plan/ EEE*
Grade 6 Day 2	Core	Plan/ EEE*	Core	Core
Grade 7 Day 1	Core	Core	Plan/ EEE*	Core
Grade 7 Day 2	Plan/ EEE*	Core	Core	Core
Grade 8 Day 1	Core	Plan/ EEE*	Core	Core
Grade 8 Day 2	Core	Core	Core	Plan/ EEE*
PE/ Elective/ Exploratories Day 1	Plan*	Grade 8	Grade 7	Grade 6
PE/ Elective/ Exploratories Day 2	Grade 7	Grade 6	Plan*	Grade 8
Itinerants	Orchestra available only in morning		Band available only in afternoon	

* One block is allocated for students at each grade level to attend PE, elective, or exploratory classes; classes can be offered on an alternating-day schedule. Core grade-level teachers plan during this time. Grade-level teachers plan one day in the morning and one day in the afternoon to give students access to the orchestra and band teachers, who are part-time morning and afternoon, respectively.

A major benefit of the alternating-day (A/B) schedule for school districts that utilize a large number of itinerant teachers and/or shared teaching spaces is that the A/B schedule makes the assignment of teachers and space more efficient (see Canady & Rettig, 1995b, Chap. 3 for more details). For example, what if two foreign language teachers, an art teacher, the band director, the orchestra leader, and a technology teacher are assigned to both the local middle and high school, and both schools have an A/B schedule? Three teachers can be assigned to the middle school on

"A" days, and three teachers assigned to the high school on "A" days. On "B" days the teachers switch schools. Consequently, no travel time is required mid-day to move from one school to the other. More than likely an instructional period is saved every day for each of the itinerant teachers. If one period per day is gained for each of the six teachers, essentially the schedule has provided "another teaching position" to augment the original six positions; this "position" could be used to add another class or to reduce the size of each of the classes already in the schedule. In addition to this savings, mileage costs also are eliminated.

If both the middle and high school were on the 4/4 block schedule, a similar plan could be implemented on a semester basis for selected subjects. For example, the Latin teacher might work at the high school during the fall semester, while the German teacher instructs at the middle school; for the spring semester they switch schools. Obviously, this plan only works for selected elective classes.

SCHEDULING ELECTIVES IN ALL FOUR BLOCKS

Another special situation that some schools face when scheduling PE, elective, and exploratory classes is the impossibility of serving all students' needs during just three of four blocks or six of eight periods. This often is the case when gymnasium space is limited; the gym must be used all day long. How, then, do we make sure that all students have access to the classes they need and all PE, elective, and exploratory teachers have planning time, while utilizing all encore teaching spaces every period or block of the day? The schedule illustrated in Figure 6.21 (p. 160) accomplishes this goal.

In the example shown, students attend PE/health every other day in a block opposite 9 weeks of music, 9 weeks of art, 9 weeks of technology, and 9 weeks of home and careers. We have four full-time PE/health teachers and full-time positions in art, music, technology, and home and careers. Six groups of students must be served in each block.

FIGURE 6.21. PE AND EXPLORATORY: NINE-WEEK DROP ONE ROTATION

	Block I		Block II		Block III		Block IV	
	Day 1	**Day 2**	**Day 1**	**Day 2**	**Day 1**	**Day 2**	**Day 1**	**Day 2**
1st 9 Weeks	Grp 1-Music Grp 2-Art Grp 3-Tech. Grp 4-PE A Grp 5-PE B Grp 6-PE C	Grp 1-PE A Grp 2-PE B Grp 3-PE C Grp 4-Music Grp 5-Art Grp 6-Tech.	Grp 7-Art Grp 8-Tech. Grp 9-HC Grp 10-PE B Grp 11-PE C Grp 12-PE D	Grp 7-PE B Grp 8-PE C Grp 9-PE D Grp 10-Art Grp 11-Tech. Grp 12-HC	Grp 13-Tech. Grp 14-HC Grp 15-Music Grp 16-PE C Grp 17-PE D Grp 18-PE A	Grp 13-PE C Grp 14-PE D Grp 15-PE A Grp 16-Tech. Grp 17-HC Grp 18-Music	Grp 19-HC Grp 20-Music Grp 21-Art Grp 22-PE D Grp 23-PE A Grp 24-PE B	Grp 19-PE D Grp 20-PE A Grp 21-PE B Grp 22-HC Grp 23-Music Grp 24-Art
Planning	PE D & HC		PE A & Music		PE B & Art		PE C & Tech.	
2nd 9 Weeks	Grp 1-HC Grp 2-Music Grp 3-Art Grp 4-PE A Grp 5-PE B Grp 6-PE C	Grp 1-PE A Grp 2-PE B Grp 3-PE C Grp 4-HC Grp 5-Music Grp 6-Art	Grp 7-Music Grp 8-Art Grp 9-Tech. Grp 10-PE B Grp 11-PE C Grp 12-PE D	Grp 7-PE B Grp 8-PE C Grp 9-PE D Grp 10-Music Grp 11-Art Grp 12-Tech.	Grp 13-Art Grp 14-Tech. Grp 15-HC Grp 16-PE C Grp 17-PE D Grp 18-PE A	Grp 13-PE C Grp 14-PE D Grp 15-PE A Grp 16-Art Grp 17-Tech. Grp 18-HC	Grp 19-Tech. Grp 20-HC Grp 21-Music Grp 22-PE D Grp 23-PE A Grp 24-PE B	Grp 19-PE D Grp 20-PE A Grp 21-PE B Grp 22-Tech. Grp 23-HC Grp 24-Music
Planning	PE D & Tech.		PE A & HC		PE B & Music		PE C & Art	
3rd 9 Weeks	Grp 1-Tech. Grp 2-HC Grp 3-Music Grp 4-PE A Grp 5-PE B Grp 6-PE C	Grp 1-PE A Grp 2-PE B Grp 3-PE C Grp 4-Tech. Grp 5-HC Grp 6-Music	Grp 7-HC Grp 8-Music Grp 9-Art Grp 10-PE B Grp 11-PE C Grp 12-PE D	Grp 7-PE B Grp 8-PE C Grp 9-PE D Grp 10-HC Grp 11-Music Grp 12-Art	Grp 13-Music Grp 14-Art Grp 15-Tech. Grp 16-PE C Grp 17-PE D Grp 18-PE A	Grp 13-PE C Grp 14-PE D Grp 15-PE A Grp 16-Music Grp 17-Art Grp 18-Tech.	Grp 19-Art Grp 20-Tech. Grp 21-HC Grp 22-PE D Grp 23-PE A Grp 24-PE B	Grp 19-PE D Grp 20-PE A Grp 21-PE B Grp 22-Art Grp 23-Tech. Grp 24-HC
Planning	PE D & Art		PE A & Tech.		PE B & HC		PE C & Music	
4th 9 Weeks	Grp 1-Art Grp 2-Tech. Grp 3-HC Grp 4-PE A Grp 5-PE B Grp 6-PE C	Grp 1-PE A Grp 2-PE B Grp 3-PE C Grp 4-Art Grp 5-Tech. Grp 6-HC	Grp 7-Tech. Grp 8-HC Grp 9-Music Grp 10-PE B Grp 11-PE C Grp 12-PE D	Grp 7-PE B Grp 8-PE C Grp 9-PE D Grp 10-Tech. Grp 11-HC Grp 12-Music	Grp 13-HC Grp 14-Music Grp 15-Art Grp 16-PE C Grp 17-PE D Grp 18-PE A	Grp 13-PE C Grp 14-PE D Grp 15-PE A Grp 16-HC Grp 17-Music Grp 18-Art	Grp 19-Music Grp 20-Art Grp 21-Tech. Grp 22-PE D Grp 23-PE A Grp 24-PE B	Grp 19-PE D Grp 20-PE A Grp 21-PE B Grp 22-Music Grp 23-Art Grp 24-Tech.
Planning	PE D & Music		PE A & Art		PE B & Tech.		PE C & HC	

Groups 1 to 6 receive their PE and exploratory classes during Block I, Groups 7 to 12 during Block II, Groups 13 to 18 during Block III, and Groups 19 to 24 during Block IV. PE is easy to schedule. Each teacher instructs three blocks and plans one block. Thus, one physical education teacher plans each block. PE Teacher D plans during Block I; PE Teacher A plans during Block II, PE Teacher B plans during Block III; and PE Teacher C plans during Block IV. The schedule for PE Teacher D is as follows:

Block I:	Plan
Block II:	Day 1, Group 12
	Day 2, Group 9
Block III:	Day 1, Group 17
	Day 2, Group 14
Block IV:	Day 1, Group 22
	Day 2, Group 19

The exploratory teachers' schedules shown in Figure 6.21 are a bit more complex because in order to serve all students, the planning time schedule must change every 9 weeks. For example, the technology teacher plans in Block IV during the first 9 weeks, in Block I during the second 9 weeks, in Block II during the third 9 weeks, and in Block III during the fourth 9 weeks. The technology teacher's schedule becomes the following:

		Block I	*Block II*	*Block III*	*Block IV*
1st 9 weeks	*Day 1*	Group 3	Group 8	Group 13	Plan
	Day 2	Group 6	Group 11	Group 16	Plan
2nd 9 weeks	*Day 1*	Plan	Group 9	Group 14	Group 19
	Day 2	Plan	Group 12	Group 17	Group 22
3rd 9 weeks	*Day 1*	Group 1	Plan	Group 15	Group 20
	Day 2	Group 4	Plan	Group 18	Group 23
4th 9 weeks	*Day 1*	Group 2	Group 7	Plan	Group 21
	Day 2	Group 5	Group 10	Plan	Group 24

Each of the four exploratory teachers works with six groups each 9-week term, three one day and three the next day. This same scheduling practice may be used in any period or block schedule.

THREE PERIODS ALLOCATED FOR ENCORE

Some schools (in affluent districts) offer the equivalent of three periods for encore classes. Figure 6.22 (p. 162) illustrates a master block schedule that provides three periods for encore and five periods for core. In the example shown, two of the three periods were placed consecutively for each grade level; one period is separate. In Figure 6.23, the two consecutive periods are blocked together. In both of these examples, core teachers work only five of eight periods, an expensive schedule to staff. Even more expensive, but not uncommon in the Northeast, is the nine-period day (Figure 6.24). Teachers instruct five periods and have one period for lunch and one period for a duty. Two periods are allocated for teacher planning time.

FIGURE 6.22. EIGHT-PERIOD DAY: THREE PERIODS PER GRADE LEVEL FOR TEACHER PLANNING, PE, ELECTIVES, AND EXPLORATORIES

Periods	1	2	3	4	5	6	7	8
Grade 6	Core	Plan/ EEE	Core	Core	Core	Core	Plan/ EEE	Plan/ EEE
Grade 7	Core	Plan/ EEE	Core	Core	Plan/ EEE	Plan/ EEE	Core	Core
Grade 8	Plan/ EEE	Core	Plan/ EEE	Plan/ EEE	Core	Core	Core	Core
PE/ Elective/ Exploratories *	Grade 8	Grades 6 & 7	Grade 8	Grade 8	Grade 7	Grade 7	Grade 6	Grade 6

* Three periods are allocated for students at each grade level to attend PE, elective, or exploratory classes. Core grade-level teachers plan or have duty during this time. Two of the three periods are blocked together. Lunch is a separate, shorter period.

If three periods are designated for encore classes, how can they be used? Figure 6.25 (p. 164) offers a variety of options. In Examples 1 to 3, single periods are maintained. In Example 1, one period is given to daily PE, one period to a daily elective, and one period is shared on a rotational cycle by several exploratories. For example, in a 6-day cycle, art could meet Days 1 and 4, general music Days 2 and 5, and the computer class Days 3 and 6. Each of these classes would meet two days out of every six for the entire school year. As an alternative, these classes could meet every day for a single period for 12 weeks each, as shown in Example 2. Example 3 replaces the exploratory rotation with a second elective.

In Examples 4 to 6, two classes are blocked and one class meets in a single period. Example 4 has PE and health blocked with an exploratory rotation. These classes meet every other day for a block. An elective class, such as band, orchestra, choir, or foreign language, is scheduled daily in the third, single period. Example 5 replaces the exploratory rotation with a second elective. In Example 6, PE/health meets every day in a period, while two electives meet every other day for a block.

FIGURE 6.23. EIGHT-PERIOD DAY: THREE PERIODS PER GRADE LEVEL FOR TEACHER PLANNING, PE, ELECTIVES, AND EXPLORATORIES—BLOCKED CORE TIME

Periods	1	2	3	4	5	6	7	8
Grade 6	Core	Plan/ EEE	Core				Plan/ EEE	
Grade 7	Core	Plan/ EEE	Core		Plan/ EEE		Core	
Grade 8	Plan/ EEE	Core	Plan/ EEE		Core			
PE/ Elective/ Exploratories*	Grade 8	Grade 6 & 7	Grade 8		Grade 7		Grade 6	

* Three periods are allocated for students at each grade level to attend PE, elective, or exploratory classes. Core grade-level teachers plan or have duty during this time. Two of the three periods are blocked together. Lunch is the same length as a period.

FIGURE 6.24. NINE-PERIOD DAY: THREE PERIODS PER GRADE LEVEL FOR TEACHER PLANNING, PE, ELECTIVES, AND EXPLORATORIES

Periods	1	2	3	4	5	6	7	8	9
Grade 6	Core	Core	Plan/ EEE	Lunch	Core	Core	Core	Plan/ EEE	Plan/ EEE
Grade 7	Core	Plan/ EEE	Core	Core	Lunch	Plan/ EEE	Plan/ EEE	Core	Core
Grade 8	Plan/ EEE	Core	Core	Plan/ EEE	Plan/ EEE	Lunch	Core	Core	Core
PE/ Elective/ Exploratories*	Grade 8	Grade 7	Grade 6	Grade 8	Grade 8	Grade 7	Grade 7	Grade 6	Grade 6

* Three periods are allocated for students at each grade level to attend PE, elective, or exploratory classes. Core grade-level teachers plan or have duty during this time. Two of the three periods are blocked together.

FIGURE 6.25. THREE-PERIOD ELECTIVE
AND EXPLORATORY POSSIBILITIES

Ex. 1	Per. 1	Elective meets daily for a period. Examples: Band, orchestra, choir, foreign language.	
	Per. 2	Exploratory classes meet daily for a period on a rotating cycle of 4 or 6 days. Example: In a 6-day cycle, two days each of art, music, and computers.	
	Per. 3	PE/Health meets daily for a period.	
Ex. 2	Per. 1	Elective meets daily for a period. Examples: Band, orchestra, choir, foreign language.	
	Per. 2	Exploratory classes meet daily for a period; exploratory classes change every 6, 9, 12, or 18 weeks. Example: 9 weeks each of PE, art, health, and computers.	
	Per. 3	PE/Health meets daily for a period.	
Ex. 3	Per. 1	Elective meets daily for a period. Examples: Band, orchestra, choir, foreign language.	
	Per. 2	Second elective meets daily for a period. Examples: Band, orchestra, choir, foreign language.	
	Per. 3	PE/Health meets daily for a period.	
Ex. 4	Per. 1	Elective meets daily for a period. Examples: Band, orchestra, choir, foreign language.	
		Day 1	*Day 2*
	Per. 2	PE/Health meets for a block every other day.	Exploratory classes meet for a block every other day; exploratory classes changs every 6, 9, 12, or 18 weeks.
	Per. 3		
Ex. 5	Per. 1	Elective meets daily for a period. Examples: Band, orchestra, choir, foreign language.	
		Day 1	*Day 2*
	Per. 2	PE/Health meets for a block every other day.	Second elective meets for a block every other day. Examples: Band, orchestra, choir, foreign language.
	Per. 3		
Ex. 6	Per. 1	PE/Health meets daily for a period.	
		Day 1	*Day 2*
	Per. 2	Elective meets for a block every other day. Examples: Band, or- chestra, choir, foreign language.	Second elective meets for a block every other day. Examples: Band, orchestra, choir, foreign language.
	Per. 3		

GUIDELINES FOR CHOOSING A SCHEDULE

In this chapter, we described and provided numerous charts and sample schedules to illustrate how middle schools can offer elective and exploratory classes in a variety of models. We essentially went from one end of the continuum of possibilities, where only one single period is available for scheduling elective and exploratory classes, to the other, where middle school students may spend up to 50 percent of the school day in such classes. We used a variety of formats to illustrate how electives and exploratories may be scheduled by including alternate-day, single periods; blocked periods; split-blocks; alternate-day blocks; rotational blocks; extended rotational blocks; quarter-on/quarter-off blocks; 3-day, 4-day, and 6-day rotational single and block periods; and 3-week, 6-week and 9-week rotational schedules. Furthermore, we provided these options within four types of scheduling models: modular, alternate-day, four-block and five-block.

Because we believe scheduling elective and exploratory classes is one of the most difficult aspects of middle school scheduling, we included numerous configurations for scheduling such classes; however, in light of what we know and believe about the nature of middle school students, several of the schedules offered do not earn our strong support. To address our dilemma, we decided not to express positive and negative feelings about each of the models; instead, we are returning to the premises developed in Chapter 1 and offering guidelines that will assist readers in deciding which of the proposed formats in this chapter should receive their attention. In making decisions about scheduling elective and exploratory classes, we believe these factors should be weighed:

- ♦ For students
    - How many teachers should students interact with during any one day, week, semester, year, or total years in the middle school?
    - How many assignments will students be responsible for during a particular period of time?
    - How many class changes and transitions are required each school day?
    - What are the possibilities for curriculum correlation and integration?
    - How balanced is a student's work load?
    - What level of choice do students have?
    - Can students build on exploratory content from the previous year?

- Is the amount of time in the instructional period appropriate to the nature of the subject content? (For example, can students be engaged sufficiently in classes such as art or technology in a 40- to 42-minute period?)

♦ For elective and exploratory teachers

- With the schedule being considered, how many students will I be expected to see during any one day, week, quarter, semester, year?
- Is the time being scheduled appropriate to the content and nature of my class?
- How many projects or class materials will I be expected to manage and store?
- Has continuity of my subject content been considered?
- Does the proposed schedule help or hinder my desire to integrate my content with core content?
- Does the schedule being considered permit me to plan and interact with other core teachers at least on a weekly basis?
- With the proposed schedule, how many grades and records will I be expected to determine and maintain?

Figures 6.2 through 6.25 show readers how to schedule from one to six elective and exploratory classes by using various types of middle school scheduling configurations. Although we know that the mechanics of scheduling such classes can be a major problem for school personnel, we urge readers not to start with the mechanics; instead, readers should begin with a clear statement of the major purpose of the elective and exploratory programs in their middle schools. Also, before deciding *how* to schedule such courses, consider what we know and believe about the nature of the middle school student. Guided by these deliberations, readers can best select from the many options illustrated in this chapter.

7

USING PRINCIPLES OF PARALLEL BLOCK SCHEDULING IN MIDDLE SCHOOL TO REDUCE CLASS SIZE

Middle school educators charged with the responsibility of creating the school schedule face the gargantuan task of integrating and balancing a dizzying array of programs, accommodating the choices of students and their parents, and meeting the teaching preferences of teachers. Middle schools serving a high number of at-risk students may find that none of the schedules offered in previous chapters truly provides the organizational structure that they need for students who must be scheduled in numerous types of extended or "pull-out" programs, often with a specialized teacher, such as an LD Resource, a Talented and Gifted (TAG), an English as a Second Language (ESL), or a remedial mathematics/reading teacher. Schools with extensive support services may need a schedule that can:

- ◆ Provide students with instructional support without having them miss teacher-directed instruction in other classes;
- ◆ Give students access to such programs without fragmenting the school day for themselves and other students; and
- ◆ Provide regular teachers, at least in reading/language arts and mathematics, smaller classes at various times during the school day and/or week.

We have adopted several elements of Parallel Block Scheduling (PBS), often used in elementary schools, to provide middle school personnel sample scheduling strategies that focus on providing smaller classes for regular teachers in reading/language arts and mathematics and still provide students access to support programs without fragmenting the school day for both teachers and students. We also offer scheduling strategies to help school personnel deal with the issue of homogeneous versus heterogeneous groupings in reading/language arts and mathematics.

First, we briefly share the basics of PBS with sample master and team schedules; second, we review the negative consequences of ability grouping and the scheduling of "pull-out" programs relative to the denial of educational opportunity; third, we propose a financially feasible restructuring plan for middle schools that reduces the need for strict tracking; and, finally, we share two specialized parallel block schedules that address specific instructional problem areas.

PARALLEL BLOCK SCHEDULING

Parallel block (PBS) scheduling is a set of strategies for elementary and middle school time organization developed by Canady and others during the past 30 years (Canady, 1988; Canady, 1990; Canady & Fogliani, 1989; Canady & Hotchkiss, 1984; Canady & Reina, 1993; Canady & Rettig, 1992; Canady & Rettig, 1995a; Hopkins & Canady, 1997; Rettig & Canady, 1995). The model incorporates opportunities for both small and large group instruction and provides an integrated plan for pull-out programs. With this plan, blocks of time for small group instruction run parallel to blocks of time for larger group instructional activities or support services. In elementary and middle schools, the reduced-size instructional groups usually are in the areas of reading/language arts and mathematics. By using the principles of PBS, middle school students and teachers reap these benefits:

- ◆ Equal teacher contact time allocations for all students regardless of ability;
- ◆ Smaller reading and/or mathematics instructional groups;
- ◆ Increased time for direct instruction in reading and mathematics;
- ◆ Less reliance on independent class work; and
- ◆ Uninterrupted time for instruction.

We begin with a basic nine-period master block schedule (Figure 7.1) with these features:

- ◆ Six teams of 150 to 180 students each, with 8 teachers per team;
- ◆ A 7-hour school day divided into nine 42-minute classes (some of which are blocked together), with 15 minutes for homeroom, 3 minutes between classes, and 3 minutes added to the last period for announcements; and

- Sufficient encore staff to provide two 42-minute periods (or one 85-minute block) of PE, electives or exploratory classes for students and planning for every teacher.[1]

FIGURE 7.1. MASTER PARALLEL BLOCK SCHEDULE

Time	8:00–8:15	8:15–8:57	9:00–9:42	9:45–10:27	10:30–11:12	11:15–11:57	12:00–12:42	12:45–1:27	1:30–2:12	2:15–3:00
Team 6-I	HR	LA/SS 1	LA/SS 2	LA/SS 3	L/R	M/SC 1	M/SC 2	M/SC 3	Plan	Plan
Team 6-II	HR	LA/SS 1	LA/SS 2	LA/SS 3	L/R	M/SC 1	M/SC 2	M/SC 3	Plan	Plan
Team 7-I	HR	LA/SS 1	LA/SS 2	LA/SS 3	M/SC 1	L/R	Plan	Plan	M/SC 2	M/SC 3
Team 7-II	HR	LA/SS 1	LA/SS 2	LA/SS 3	M/SC 1	L/R	Plan	Plan	M/SC 2	M/SC 3
Team 8-I	HR	LA/SS 1	LA/SS 2	Plan	Plan	LA/SS 3	L/R	M/SC 1	M/SC 2	M/SC 3
Team 8-II	HR	LA/SS 1	LA/SS 2	Plan	Plan	LA/SS 3	L/R	M/SC 1	M/SC 2	M/SC 3
PE/Exploratory/Elective	Duty	Plan	Plan	Grade 8	Grade 8	Lunch/Duty	Grade 7	Grade 7	Grade 6	Grade 6

THE MASTER SCHEDULE

As can be seen in the master schedule (Figure 7.1), the nine daily periods are allocated as follows:

- Three periods to language arts and social studies (labeled LA/SS 1, LA/SS 2, and LA/SS 3),
- Three periods to math and science (labeled M/SC 1, M/SC 2, and M/SC 3),

---

1 Do not be dismayed if our examples do not match your situation exactly. We acknowledge that resources differ from school to school. There are countless variations of this schedule, each idiosyncratic to the resources and needs of the individual school.

- ◆ Two periods to PE/exploratory/elective classes for students and planning for core teachers (labeled Plan), and
- ◆ One period to lunch and recess (labeled L/R).

ENCORE (PE/EXPLORATORY/ELECTIVE) AND LUNCH/RECESS

The encore team works with grade-level groups, as can be seen from the bottom line of Figure 7.1 (p. 169). After homeroom the related arts encore team plans, which allows all grade levels to begin the day in core instruction. From 9:45 to 11:12 eighth grade students attend encore (PE/exploratory/ elective). After lunch the seventh grade students attend encore classes from 12:00 to 1:27, and the sixth grade students attend encore classes from 1:30 until 3:00. The two-period block provides many possibilities for scheduling PE, exploratory, and elective classes (see Figure 6.18, p. 155, for a variety of options).

Lunch/recess is scheduled for sixth grade from 10:30 to 11:12, for seventh grade from 11:15 to 11:57, and for eighth grade from 12:00 to 12:42. If recess is provided, half of the grade level can begin lunch at the start of the period while the other half begins recess. After 15 minutes or so, the recess group can line up for lunch; after 25 minutes or so, the lunch group can leave for recess. Of course, this assumes room for the entire grade level in the cafeteria at one time. If this is not the case, the period can be divided exactly in half, creating, in essence, six lunch periods. In many schools, study periods are used to counterbalance lunch periods.

SAMPLE TEAM PARALLEL BLOCK SCHEDULE WITH LANGUAGE ARTS AND MATHEMATICS EXTENSIONS

We now turn our attention to the team schedule. As we look at the master schedule (Figure 7.1, p. 169) we can follow the time schedule allocated to Sixth Grade Team I. After homeroom (8:00 to 8:15), three LA/SS periods are provided (8:15 to 10:27). Following lunch/recess (10:30 to 11:12), three periods are allocated for math and science (11:15 to 1:27). The day ends with students in encore options and core teachers planning (1:30 to 3:00). Figure 7.2 details the schedule for each of the eight teachers on this team.

The team includes three language arts/reading/social studies teachers, three math/science teachers, one language arts/reading extension teacher, and one math extension teacher. Using the principles of parallel block scheduling, small group instruction in both language arts and mathematics is provided. In this schedule, each student receives the equivalent of two periods of language arts, two periods of mathematics, one period each of social studies and science, and two periods for PE, exploratories, and electives.

FIGURE 7.2. GRADE 6 TEAM I:
LANGUAGE ARTS EXTENSION AND MATH EXTENSION

Time	8:00–8:15	8:15–8:57	9:00–9:42	9:45–10:27	10:30–11:12	11:15–11:57	12:00–12:42	12:45–1:27	1:30–2:12	2:15–3:00
LA/SS Teacher 6A	HR	LA/SS 1,7	RWG 1	RWG 7	L/R	LA/SS 4,10	RWG 4	RWG 10	Plan	Plan
LA/SS Teacher 6B	HR	RWG 8	LA/SS 2,8	RWG 2	L/R	RWG 11	LA/SS 5,11	RWG 5	Plan	Plan
LA/SS Teacher 6C	HR	RWG 3	RWG 9	LA/SS 3,9	L/R	RWG 6	RWG 12	LA/SS 6,12	Plan	Plan
Math/ Science Teacher 6D	HR	M/Sci 4,10	RMG 4	RMG 10	L/R	M/Sci 1,7	RMG 1	RMG 7	Plan	Plan
Math/ Science Teacher 6E	HR	RMG 11	M/Sci 5,11	RMG 5	L/R	RMG 8	M/Sci 2,8	RMG 2	Plan	Plan
Math/ Science Teacher 6F	HR	RMG 6	RMG 12	M/Sci 6,12	L/R	RMG 3	RMG 9	M/Sci 3,9	Plan	Plan
LA / Exten. Teacher 6G	Duty	RWGs 2,9	RWGs 3,7	RWGs 1,8	L/R	RWGs 5,12	RWGs 6,10	RWGs 4,11	Plan	Plan
*Math/ Exten. Teacher 6H	Duty	RMGs 5,12	RMGs 6,10	RMGs 4,11	L/R	RMGs 2,9	RMGs 3,7	RMGs 1,8	Plan	Plan

Key: LA/SS = Language Arts and Social Studies; RWG = Reading-Writing Group; M/Sci = Mathematics and Science; RMG = Reduced Math Group.

* Could be a computer lab operated by a lab technician; teachers select appropriate software for various individuals and groups of students.

LANGUAGE ARTS/SOCIAL STUDIES SCHEDULE

Each language arts teacher is assigned two distinct reading-writing groups (RWGs); each of these groups is approximately one-half of a class, 12 to 15 students. Placing the two groups together forms the language arts class. As shown in Figure 7.2, Homeroom A consists of RWGs 1 and 7; Homeroom B (RWGs 2 and 8); Homeroom C (RWGs 3 and 9); Homeroom D (RWGs 4 and 10); Homeroom E (RWGs 5 and 11); and Homeroom F (RWGs 6 and 12). The composition of each RWG is important; we address the grouping issue in the next section of this chapter after the basic format of parallel block scheduling is presented.

We begin by detailing the schedule of one of the language arts/social studies instructors, Teacher 6A. Teacher 6A's morning begins with homeroom. After homeroom, the teacher works with a full class for total group language arts and social studies instruction; this group is composed of two reading-writing groups: RWG 1 and RWG 7. Next, the teacher works with RWG 1, which includes approximately 12 to 15 students, for 42 minutes, after which RWG 7 is taught by the teacher for a period. Following lunch, the teacher instructs a second large group in language arts and social studies (RWGs 4 and 10); this is math/science Teacher 6D's, the Teacher 6A's partner, homeroom. From 12:00 to 12:42 Teacher 6A meets with RWG 4, followed by RWG 10 (12:45 to 1:27). Teacher 6A completes the teaching day with individual and team planning from 1:30 to 3:00.

To summarize Teacher 6A's schedule: Teacher 6A instructs reading-writing groups of 15 or less for 4 periods; the teacher then instructs groups of 20 to 30 students in whole-group language arts and social studies for two periods; and Teacher 6A has individual planning, team planning, and lunch for one period each. During the school year Teacher 6A is only responsible for two classes of students; in some middle schools teachers work with as many as six groups of students daily.

GROUPING POSSIBILITIES FOR
PARALLEL BLOCK SCHEDULING

Before we look at Teacher 6A's partner's schedule, let's examine possible grouping arrangements for the construction of homerooms. If there are three language arts/social studies teachers and three mathematics/science teachers, then we want six homeroom groups. To form the homeroom groups, we establish 12 reading-writing groups (RWGs) and assign two of these groups to each teacher. There are a variety of ways to create and pair these groups. In the section that follows, we offer three different ways to form reading-writing groups and several different ways of combining groups to form homerooms.

GROUPING PLAN A

All Groups Heterogenous by Ability, Race, and Gender											
RWG 1	RWG 2	RWG 3	RWG 4	RWG 5	RWG 6	RWG 7	RWG 8	RWG 9	RWG 10	RWG 11	RWG 12

In Grouping Plan A, we create 12 groups that are balanced by ability, race, and gender; all groups are heterogeneous. Thus, if we pair any two groups together we achieve a heterogeneous homeroom.

GROUPING PLAN B

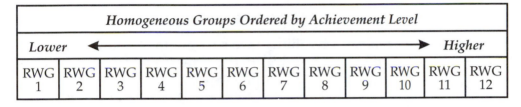

Homogeneous Groups Ordered by Achievement Level											
Lower ⟵————————————————————⟶ Higher											
RWG 1	RWG 2	RWG 3	RWG 4	RWG 5	RWG 6	RWG 7	RWG 8	RWG 9	RWG 10	RWG 11	RWG 12

Grouping Plan B establishes 12 ordered homogeneous groups (12 is the highest-achieving group; 1 is the lowest-achieving group) based upon performance in language arts. After determining the composition of the 12 instructional groups, a variety of pairings are possible to create homerooms.

PAIRING 1

We could pair groups 1 and 2, 3 and 4, 5 and 6, and so forth to create homerooms. These pairings obviously would result in severely tracked homerooms with the 11–12 combination creating the highest of the "high" homerooms and the 1–2 combination creating the lowest of the "low." While this grouping practice has been used in a variety of states for many years, it creates an economic and racial caste system that is insupportable in public schools. Many schools that have grouped in this manner found themselves facing Office of Civil Rights complaints for resegregating within the school.

PAIRING 2

Another possible format for combining RWGs to create homerooms is to pair Groups 1 and 12, 2 and 11, 3 and 10, 4 and 9, 5 and 8, and 6 and 7. There are several justifications for pairing this way. First, the pairing of groups 1 and 12, which on the surface seems irrational, does provide several benefits. Typically, the students who compose Group 12 have parents who write letters to the principal requesting placement for their child in the classroom of the perceived "best" teacher at the grade level. The students in Group 1 tend to have parents who rarely participate in their children's education; these students need the "best" teacher. By assigning each of these groups to the perceived "best teacher" we keep the parents of one group happy while serving the needs of the other group. This pairing also provides a set of role models for Group 1 to follow. Similarly, the pairing of groups 6 and 7 (the most "average" groups of the ranking) may be the perfect assignment for a new teacher; there will likely be few problem students and few "problem" parents in these middle groups. (While this discussion has been largely tongue-in-cheek, it does touch on issues about which educators often are uncomfortable discussing, and suggests the complexity of the grouping process and the need for careful planning and thought.)

PAIRING 3

Another more realistic possibility is to pair groups 1 and 7, 2 and 8, 3 and 9, 4 and 10, 5 and 11, and 6 and 12. In this arrangement, before we create any pairs, we suggest that all identified special education students be assigned to the lower-six subgroups, if appropriate for their reading level, and that all students exhibiting *severe* behavior problems be spread across all 12 groups. We then combine two of the groups to create each homeroom in such a way that the homerooms are relatively heterogeneous in composition, yet consist of two groups where each group has similar instructional characteristics; we refer to this pairing as "controlled heterogeneity." Our goal is to create homerooms that are diverse in gender, race, instructional needs, special education assignments, and behavior; we hope that no teacher would have a homeroom group without at least one of the two groups being able to work at or above grade level. In this pairing, although the homeroom composed of groups 1 and 7 obviously would be lower in ability than the homeroom composed of groups 6 and 12, the disparity is not nearly as great as in Pairing 1. Keep in mind that in parallel block schedules, teachers have at least one period to work alone with each reduced-size instructional group. To assist the teachers who are assigned RWGs 1 and 7 and RWGs 2 and 8, some schools operate an inclusion model in which the special education resource teacher is assigned to work with the base teacher when both groups are in the classroom.

GROUPING PLAN C

It is not necessary to strictly rank all groups as shown in the previous section. In Grouping Plan C, the top half of the grade level, groups 7 through 12, is divided into six *equal* groups that are balanced by ability, race, and gender. Students in these groups likely would be on or above grade level. The bottom half of the grade level is divided into six *ranked* groups. It might be that groups 4 to 6 are relatively equal and a year behind grade level. Groups 1 to 3 would be respectively lower.

Ranked Middle and Lower Groups						Heterogeneous High Groups					
Lower ⟷ Higher											
RWG 1	RWG 2	RWG 3	RWG 4	RWG 5	RWG 6	RWG 7	RWG 8	RWG 9	RWG 10	RWG 11	RWG 12

Now when we pair groups, each homeroom has one of the top groups, 7 to 12, containing students at or above grade level, and one of the lower groups which falls below grade level. All homerooms would have a few stars and would be relatively heterogeneous. (Regardless of the grouping strategy, we always try to ensure that all students have at least one friend in their homeroom.)

MATH/SCIENCE SCHEDULE

Teacher A's partner, math/science Teacher 6D, has a very similar schedule. If Teacher 6D's homeroom were constructed based on language arts achievement, we would regroup these students into two math groups based on mathematics achievement. These groups could be heterogeneous or homogeneous. We could use the "Concept Math" scheduling strategy for this time block (see below). In this example, shown in Figure 7.2 (p. 171), Teacher 6D begins the day working with a homeroom and "reduced math groups" (RMGs) 4 and 10 for math/science class. Following this class Teacher 6D instructs each group separately. After lunch and recess, Teacher 6A's homeroom is redivided into reduced math groups. Teacher 6D works with RMGs 1 and 7 together for math/science class from 11:15 to 11:57, after which each group receives separate instruction. The day ends with team and individual planning.

The labels we give to each period in the parallel block schedule are not carved in stone; they are negotiable based on what a school's students and curriculum require. In the next several sections, we explain our allocation of time and instruction in the schedule.

LANGUAGE ARTS AND SOCIAL STUDIES CLASS

At various times throughout this book we suggest schedules that combine language arts and social studies in a large block of time. In some cases, we pair teachers to teach these content areas; at other times, particularly at Grade 6, we schedule one teacher to teach both subjects to the same group of students. Our experience is that many middle school teachers often are experts at correlating and integrating these two fields of study. Occasionally, a teacher has majored in one subject and minored in the other. Often, students write position papers, debate, and engage in Socratic seminars about selected topics from the social studies, which reinforces many of the skills of the language arts area. In turn, the teacher can add depth to a piece of literature by providing students with the historical, political, or sociological background of a writer or text. We see blending these two areas of study as a way of making both more meaningful for students. The concept can be developed further by asking music and art teachers to enhance selected language art and social studies content through their programs. For example, if students are engaged in a unit of work related to the Westward Movement, literature, writing, art, and music of that period can be integrated into the entire unit of study.

READING-WRITING GROUPS

We suggest that teachers perform five major instructional activities with reading-writing groups (RWGs):

- ◆ Supervise extensive writing activities;
- ◆ Conduct brief reading-writing conferences with individual students;
- ◆ Coordinate the independent reading program;
- ◆ Model effective reading and speaking skills with oral and choral reading performances, debates and Socratic seminars (Ball & Brewer, 1996, 2000); and
- ◆ Most importantly, teach comprehension strategies, which include instructing students in how and where to locate information related to various levels of questions from multitexts (Sweet, 1993).

We believe that teachers can best supervise writing activities with 15 or fewer students. We hope that when classroom writing is occurring, teachers have access to a writing lab or, as a minimum, individual keyboards on a cart that can be wheeled from room to room. To manage these activities, we see teachers starting the class on a writing activity and then individually conferencing with students to address particular strengths or needs in writing or reading. In some cases, a student may need to read orally or be tutored on a special skill.

Because there are fewer students in RWGs, it seems to be a good time to supervise and coordinate the independent reading phase of a comprehensive middle school language arts program. We believe, however, that large amounts of RWG time should not be spent with students actually doing independent reading; this is better done during extension center time, whole-group language arts time, or at home. To encourage students to read independently, teachers might bring in various trade books and conduct "book talks," which are short, enticing introductions to the characters or events of a book. Teachers also might have classroom libraries from which students may select a book they enjoy reading. The rule might be that a student is never asked to read a book the student doesn't enjoy.

Students could be encouraged to write e-mail messages to the teacher or to another student about a special passage or idea in a book, and the receiving person could respond by e-mail. Small groups of three or four students might be encouraged to identify a common interest and then read the same book; this sometimes enhances their motivation to read, discuss, and write about the book's content.

It always is appropriate to model good reading and speaking. This is a time when the teacher might read to the students. If reading from Edgar Allen Poe, the teacher might turn off lights to add to the effects of the poem. Another strategy might to engage the RWG group in a choral reading activity. Students also might perform dramatic and/or humorous readings and engage in structured extemporaneous reading and speaking activities.

While teaching comprehension strategies, teachers provide students in RWGs with instructional strategies that they use to construct meaning before, during, and after reading (Sweet, 1993). These strategies include making inferences, identifying important information, monitoring, summarizing, and generating multilevel questions from a selected text. According to Sweet, when modeling these strategies, effective teachers treat them as a set of devices for constructing meaning instead of as independent activities that are isolated from the literacy context.

LANGUAGE ARTS EXTENSION

We propose that the language arts extension center serves these purposes:

- ◆ Permits individual and small groups of students needing traditional "pull-out" programs to attend them without missing any teacher-directed instruction;
- ◆ Provides an enrichment program for students who normally are denied such content unless they are identified as talented and/or gifted;
- ◆ Gives school personnel a plan for exposing students to extensive use of technology when the school has limited equipment, space, and/or staff training;
- ◆ Provide students with extended time for both instruction and supervised practice in selected content areas;
- ◆ Systematizes the scheduling of various support programs in schools so that individuals and small groups do not enter and leave classrooms randomly throughout the school day; and
- ◆ Provides students an opportunity to work in heterogeneous groupings with various support personnel without being graded and tested in traditional ways.

In our opinion, a great advantage of language arts extension is that it offers a way for school personnel to systematize pull-out programs in such a way as to reduce both fragmentation of the school day and the stigma attached to participation in such programs. Furthermore, proper use of extension programs makes it possible to reduce class size in reading-writing groups for core teachers. It also provides the opportunity for most support programs to become more integrated with the activities of the classroom teachers.

MATH/SCIENCE CLASS

As with language arts and social studies, we believe mathematics and science are a natural pairing. The content of each is relevant to the other, and often of interest to teachers of both subjects. Again, it is not unusual to find a middle school teacher who majored in one of the two subjects and minored in the other subject. A major advantage of scheduling math and science in the same block, where reduced groups are possible, is that teachers then have a choice of adapting the content of each subject to fit the particular group size. For example, the one whole-group period can be used for science or math, or both, when appropriate; if the plan is to engage students in a "hands-on" science experiment or laboratory activity, then the teacher may decide on those days to use the reduced groups for that special phase of science. On most days, however, the teacher-directed small groups involve students in mathematics. Again, we are trying to schedule in such a way that blending and delivering instruction of these content areas can be easier for teachers.

REDUCED MATH GROUPS (RMGs) AND MATH EXTENSION

Reduced groups in mathematics in middle schools typically are obtained through the use of a computer lab, often supervised by a paraprofessional lab technician. When a computer lab is not available, some schools use support persons (such as Title I math and a paraprofessional) to provide services that permit the reduced groups for the core teachers. In a few cases, we observed what we term "problem-based math labs"; possibly a support teacher and a paraprofessional, with a box of pocket calculators, supervise individuals, pairs and small groups of students working on rather complex math problems based on content appropriate for their age and interest levels. The idea is to get students actively engaged in thinking and performing mathematically and not passively watching the teacher solve problems and then trying to copy what the teacher did.

Although we believe these alternatives are valuable because they let core teachers work with small groups, we strongly recommend that middle schools try to provide a computer laboratory as an integral part of the math program. We recommend that the lab be supervised by a technician or a teacher other than a math teacher, because we believe that the best use of a math teacher is to have that teacher work with individuals and small groups of students, monitoring and adjusting instruction based on individual classroom assessments. Also, with the software that is now available in mathematics, schools can make mathematics more meaningful to students (Gilkey & Hunt, 1998, Appendix B). Through the computer students can easily go into an engineer's office and see how geometric measurements are used, or enter an architect's office and engage in real use of algebraic formulas to solve problems, or even, with the proper software, visit the lumber yard and use fractions to saw boards in building a new boat ramp or house!

TEAM SCHEDULE WITH SCIENCE AND SOCIAL STUDIES AS EXTENSION

When there are few pull-outs in a school, it often is advantageous to rethink the courses taught in each of the parallel blocks. The parallel block schedule with extension centers shown in Figure 7.2 (p. 171) may be more appropriate for Grades 5 or 6 (if Grade 5 is in the middle school), which often devote significantly more time to language arts and mathematics than to science and social studies. As discussed above, social studies shares the total-group language arts period and science shares the total-group math period. What if we wish to have the equivalent of a daily period of both social studies and science?

Figure 7.3 (p. 180) illustrates just such a possibility. For teachers 6A, 6B, and 6C, what had been a language arts and social studies class becomes only total-group language arts (LA), and for teachers D, E, and F, what had been a math *and* science class becomes only total group math class (TGM). Social studies replaces language arts extension on the team schedule, and science replaces math extension on the schedule. Thus, the team is now composed of three language arts/reading teachers, three math teachers, one social studies teacher, and one science teacher. Students receive 84 minutes of reading and language arts instruction (half in a small RWG and half in a large LA class), 84 minutes of math (half in a small RMG and half in a large TGM class), 42 minutes of social studies in a full-size class, 42 minutes of science in a full-size class, and two 42-minute periods (or one 87-minute block) for PE, electives, and exploratories.

FOUR-TEACHER TEAM

Similarly, we can construct a schedule for a four-teacher team. In Figure 7.4 (p. 181), three homeroom teachers are served by one extension teacher. Teacher 6B works with RWG 5 following homeroom. During Period 2, after RWG 2 returns to class from the extension center, Teacher 6B conducts the whole-group language arts and social studies lesson with

FIGURE 7.3. GRADE 6 TEAM I:
SCIENCE AND SOCIAL STUDIES EXTENSION CLASSES

Time	8:00–8:15	8:15–8:57	9:00–9:42	9:45–10:27	10:30–11:12	11:15–11:57	12:00–12:42	12:45–1:27	1:30–2:12	2:15–3:00
LA Teacher 6A	HR	LA 1,7	RWG 1	RWG 7	L/R	LA 4,10	RWG 4	RWG 10	Plan	Plan
LA Teacher 6B	HR	RWG 8	LA 2,8	RWG 2	L/R	RWG 11	LA 5,11	RWG 5	Plan	Plan
LA Teacher 6C	HR	RWG 3	RWG 9	LA 3,9	L/R	RWG 6	RWG 12	LA 6,12	Plan	Plan
Math Teacher 6D	HR	TGM 4,10	RMG 4	RMG 10	L/R	TGM 1,7	RMG 1	RMG 7	Plan	Plan
Math Teacher 6E	HR	RMG 11	TGM 5,11	RMG 5	L/R	RMG 8	TGM 2,8	RMG 2	Plan	Plan
Math Teacher 6F	HR	RMG 6	RMG 12	TGM 6,12	L/R	RMG 3	RMG 9	TGM 3,9	Plan	Plan
Social Studies Teacher 6G	Duty	SS RWGs 2,9	SS RWGs 3,7	SS RWGs 1,8	L/R	SS RWGs 5,12	SS RWGs 6,10	SS RWGs 4,11	Plan	Plan
Science Teacher 6H	Duty	SC RMGs 5,12	SC RMGs 6,10	SC RMGs 4,11	L/R	SC RMGs 2,9	SC RMGs 3,7	SC RMGs 1,8	Plan	Plan

Key: LA = Language Arts; RWG = Reading-Writing Group; TGM = Total Group Math; RMG = Reduced Math Group.

RWGs 2 and 5. Then RWG 2 receives small group instruction when RWG 5 goes to extension. After lunch, Teacher 6B becomes a math/science instructor. RMG 5 receives small-group instruction from 11:15 to 11:57. Both groups then come together for the total group math/science class after which RMG 2 receives small-group instruction. To conclude the day, Teacher 6B plans while students attend PE, exploratory, or elective classes. As with the schedule described in Figure 7.3, Teacher 6D could be assigned to teach social studies and science in place of language arts and mathematics extension.

FIGURE 7.4. GRADE 6 TEAM I: LANGUAGE ARTS EXTENSION AND MATH EXTENSION; FOUR TEACHERS

Time	8:00–8:15	8:15–8:57	9:00–9:42	9:45–10:27	10:30–11:12	11:15–11:57	12:00–12:42	12:45–1:27	1:30–2:12	2:15–3:00
Teacher 6A	HR	LA/SS 1,4	RWG 1	RWG 4	L/R	M/SC 1,4	RMG 4	RMG 4	Plan	Plan
Teacher 6B	HR	RWG 5	LA/SS 2,5	RWG 2	L/R	RMG 5	M/SC 2,5	RMG 2	Plan	Plan
Teacher 6C	HR	RWG 3	RWG 6	LA/SS 3,6	L/R	RMG 3	RMG 6	M/SC 3,6	Plan	Plan
		LA Extension (or Social Studies)				*Math Extension (or Science)				
Extension Teacher 6D	Duty	RWGs 2, 6	RWGs 3, 4	RWGs 1, 5	L/R	RMGs 2, 6	RMGs 3, 4	RMGs 1, 5	Plan	Plan

* This block also could be computer lab, foreign language for selected students, or pull-out resource for selected students.

DISCUSSION OF PARALLEL BLOCK SCHEDULING

The basic model of parallel block scheduling illustrated in Figures 7.1 (p. 169), 7.2 (p. 171), 7.3, and 7.4 provides a number of benefits:

- Class size is reduced for language arts and mathematics instruction;
- During the extension class, a re-teaching or enrichment time is provided for language arts and mathematics;
- While some homogeneous skill instruction is provided, the majority of a student's day is spent in a heterogeneous class; and
- Pull-out programs may be delivered during the extension time in a manner that is less disruptive to the basic instructional program.

A number of issues arise when implementing this model:

- How should the time be divided between whole-group instruction in language arts and social studies, as well as in math and science? Should three classes per week be allotted to social studies and two classes per week be allotted to language arts? What is the appropriate division of time? This must be decided based on curriculum requirements and the school's mission.

- ♦ What language arts objectives are covered by the base teacher and what language arts objectives are covered by the extension teacher? Does the extension teacher assign a grade for the class, contribute a grade to the base teacher's overall language arts grade, or not assign a grade at all? Of course these same issues exist between the math/science teacher and the math extension teacher.

In our second variation on this theme (Figure 7.3, p. 180), we substitute social studies for language arts extension and science for mathematics extension. While this plan maintains small groups in language arts and mathematics and solves the problem of time for social studies and science by allocating a period per day, no convenient time is left to provide pull-out programs, such as LD resource or ESL. We suggest that this version of PBS probably is most appropriate where few pull-outs exist or where inclusion is the predominant service model for special programs.

THE GROUPING PROBLEM IN MATHEMATICS

A variation of parallel block scheduling called the "Concept-Progress" Plan may be used to reduce dependence on strict homogeneous grouping. We illustrate the use of the scheduling format in mathematics, although it also is possible to apply it to language arts. First, we review the tracking problem in middle schools.

The practice of tracking often has been described as a response to the problems of educating diverse groups of students, as well as an attempt to address individual differences among students (Oakes, 1985, pp. 15–29). An unfortunate side effect of tracking, however, has been the denial of curricular access to many students. For example, students placed in lower tracks or ability groups receive fewer minutes of instruction from their teachers (Oakes, 1986, p. 16). Not only is less time spent in the active engagement of students in lower groups, these same students are presented a markedly different quality of content than are pupils in high ability tracks. Teachers of low-ability groups tend to focus on the "pedagogy of poverty" (Haberman, 1991), instructional methods that focus on the accomplishment of low-order skills such as memorization, while instruction in high-track classes includes the higher cognitive processes of analysis and critical thinking. Students in high groups are exposed to the "classics," while those considered less able languish in masses of worksheets and reading kits (Knapp & Shields, 1990, p. 754). In addition to "dumbing down" the content of curriculum for students in lower tracks, teachers also alter the rate of instruction. One study reported the pace of instruction slowed to such an extent that the higher-ability group progressed 15 times faster than did the lower-ability group (Shaverson, 1983). There also are indications that the quality of teaching is superior for students in higher-ability groups (Oakes, 1985, p. 16).

How pervasive is tracking in our nation's middle schools? In a 1990 survey of mathematics grouping practices in the middle grades, 57 percent of fifth grade, 77 percent of sixth grade, 84 percent of seventh grade, 88 percent of eighth grade, and 94 percent of ninth grade classes were organized by ability (Braddock, 1990). While it may seem obvious to say so, it is difficult for students to learn what they are not taught. And many children relegated to the lower tracks are taught far less than their upper-track peers. Different curricula, less actual instructional time, slower pacing, and a lower quality of instruction drastically alter what children receive in school. We believe there are compelling educational reasons for public school educators to create schedules that provide all students access to a full curriculum as well as assistance in mastering the critical elements on which high-stakes tests are based. In the section that follows, we suggest one scheduling practice that addresses this issue, the Concept-Progress model. Chapter 8 approaches the same issue with a different scheduling structure.

THE CONCEPT-PROGRESS MODEL

Figure 7.5 (p. 184) illustrates what we call the Concept-Progress model. The Concept-Progress model (Canady & Rettig, 1992) is a variation of PBS that has as its foundation the structured organization of the mathematics curriculum in distinct topics and the division of instructional time for mathematics in two different classes: Concept Math and Progress Math. First, we discuss this curriculum organization, which is called topical groupings. Second, we describe the two math periods. Third, we walk through a student's schedule. Finally, we review the merits of the plan in light of its goals and our initial discussion concerning curricular access.

TOPICAL GROUPINGS

There are several different ways to divide mathematics curricula into manageable units. Mathematics textbooks are divided conveniently in chapters that can serve as the basis for concept topics. Topics also can be created from the standards identified by the National Council of Teachers of Mathematics (1989). New state standards provide another framework for dividing the curriculum into assessable units. We propose that a dual system for the delivery of instruction be organized around these topics or

FIGURE 7.5. GRADE 6 TEAM I: CONCEPT-PROGRESS MODEL WITH COMPUTER LAB

Time	8:00–8:15	8:15–8:57	9:00–9:42	9:45–10:27	10:30–11:12	11:15–11:57	12:00–12:42	12:45–1:27	1:30–2:12	2:15–3:00
LA Teacher 6A	HR	LA 1,7	RWG 1	RWG 7	L/R	LA 4,10	RWG 4	RWG 10	Plan	Plan
LA Teacher 6B	HR	RWG 8	LA 2,8	RWG 2	L/R	RWG 11	LA 5,11	RWG 5	Plan	Plan
LA Teacher 6C	HR	RWG 3	RWG 9	LA 3,9	L/R	RWG 6	RWG 12	LA 6,12	Plan	Plan
Math/Science Teacher 6D	HR	SC 4,10	Concept Math 4,10	Progress Math D1 MPG 10 D2 MPG 4	L/R	SC 1,7	Concept Math 1,7	Progress Math D1 MPG 7 D2 MPG 1	Plan	Plan
Math/Science Teacher 6E	HR	SC 5,11	Concept Math 5,11	Progress Math D1 MPG 5 D2 MPG 11	L/R	SC 2,8	Concept Math 2,8	Progress Math D1 MPG 2 D2 MPG 8	Plan	Plan
Math/Science Teacher 6F	HR	SC 6,12	Concept Math 6,12	Progress Math D1 MPG 12 D2 MPG 6	L/R	SC 3,9	Concept Math 3,9	Progress Math D1 MPG 9 D2 MPG 3	Plan	Plan
Social Studies Teacher 6G	Duty	SS RWGs 2,9	SS RWGs 3,7	SS RWGs 1,8	L/R	SS RWGs 5,12	SS RWGs 6,10	SS RWGs 4,11	Plan	Plan
Mathematics Computer Lab	Duty	Grade 8	Grade 7	Day 1 MPGs 4,6,11 Day 2 MPGs 5,10,12	L/R	Grade 8	Grade 7	Day 1 MPGs 1,3,8 Day 2 MPGs 2,7,9	Plan	Plan

chapters. Units of 3 to 6 weeks duration are constructed around each topic (Dossey, 1989). Base instruction on the topic in the Concept class is followed by enrichment or re-teaching in a Progress class.

CONCEPT MATH

In the Concept Math class, the teacher works with a full class of heterogeneously grouped students. Membership in the class remains constant for the entire school year. The teacher's charge is to give basic on-grade-level instruction to all students. Children are introduced to material through a variety of teaching models; practice and reinforcement activities are conducted using a variety of instructional strategies. An instructional aide, volunteers, LD resource teacher, or peer tutors, if available, could assist students having difficulty. Because of the wide range of ability in this grouping, efforts are made to avoid self-esteem-defeating comparisons among students. No grades are given, and tests are administered only to provide the teacher with feedback for diagnostic purposes. A staff member skilled in whole-group teaching could be chosen to instruct all Concept Math classes.

PROGRESS MATH

In the model shown in Figure 7.5, students participate in the Concept class daily and the Progress class every other day. Each Concept class is divided into two Progress groups based on the results of a pretest on one of the topics; for example, Ratio and Proportion. At the end of a topic (3 to 6 weeks), another pretest is given and Progress groups are reconstituted accordingly.

Groups are smaller in Progress Math classes, ranging in size from about 10 to 15 students. Smaller classes encourage the use of "math manipulatives," problem-solving activities, computer-assisted instruction, guided practice, and individualized instruction. Depending on the performance-level placement for this topic, students could be working above grade level, on grade level, or below grade level. Appropriate homework and/or guided practice could be assigned and monitored. We recommend that students be evaluated for grades in the Progress Math class based on their improvement during the course of the topic. The task of this teacher is to push for the greatest possible progress towards mastery for each student during the time spent on the topic.

CONCEPT-PROGRESS SCHEDULE

To organize the Concept-Progress schedule, we utilize the same basic master schedule shown in Figure 7.1 (p. 169). Additionally, language arts, reading-writing groups, and social studies are provided in the same format as described with Figure 7.3 (p. 180). The math/science teachers provide science and both the Concept and the Progress classes. We offer two versions of the model, the first of which (Figure 7.5, p. 184) is probably more appropriate for sixth grade.

Let's follow a student who is in Reading-Writing Group 7 and Math Group 1. After homeroom with Teacher 6A, the student remains with Teacher 6A for language arts class, then attends social studies with Teacher 6G. The student returns to Teacher 6A for Reading-Writing Group 7 from 9:45 to 10:27; only 12 to 15 students are in this class. After lunch, the student has science with Teacher 6D followed by Concept Math with the same teacher. During the next period (12:45 to 1:27) our student travels to the computer lab on Day 1 and remains with Teacher 6D for Progress Math on Day 2. Appropriate software is used in the computer lab for practice, reinforcement, and enrichment of the mathematical concepts taught in class. Group 1 is combined with Groups 3 and 8 in the computer lab on Day 1. This means that there are between 36 and 45 students scheduled for the lab at this time. We realize that most middle school computer lab facilities do not have space for this many students, although it is arguable that with one professional and a technical aide, or perhaps even just two technical aides, a lab this size is appropriate. It may be necessary to divide the students into two different labs. Another way to reduce the numbers in the lab is to pull out students who receive special services (such as LD resource or ESL). Of course, if only two math teachers, rather than three, were feeding into the computer lab during this particular time period, a standard lab serving 30 students would suffice. The student's day ends with two periods allocated to PE, electives, and exploratory classes.

CONCEPT-PROGRESS MODEL DEPARTMENTALIZED VERSION

In the seventh and eighth grades, it may be more appropriate to departmentalize for science, concept math, and progress math. Figure 7.6 illustrates this schedule. Teacher 7D instructs only science. Teacher 7E, who is expert in whole-group presentation, instructs all Concept classes. Teacher 7F, who is expert in assessment and diagnosis, individual skill instruction, and enrichment, instructs all Progress classes.

Using the schedule illustrated in Figure 7.6 for seventh-grade team 7I (refer to Figure 7.1, p. 169, for master blocks), language arts, reading-writing groups, and social studies classes are scheduled similarly to the sixth grade. Our sample student (see shaded blocks in Figure 7.6), who is assigned to Reading-Writing Group (RWG) 7 and Math Progress Group (MPG) 1, attends language arts class with his or her homeroom Teacher 7A. The student then travels to Teacher 7G's social studies class, returning to his or her homeroom teacher for Reading-Writing Group 7. Science class with Teacher 7D follows. After lunch and PE, elective, or exploratory classes, the student travels with MPG 1 to Concept Math class with

Figure 7.6. Grade 7 Team I: Concept-Progress Model with Computer Lab; Departmentalized Science, Concept Math, and Progress Math

Time	8:00–8:15	8:15–8:57	9:00–9:42	9:45–10:27	10:30–11:12	11:15–11:57	12:00–12:42	12:45–1:27	1:30–2:12	2:15–3:00
LA Teacher 7A	HR	LA 1,7	RWG 1	RWG 7	LA 4,10	L/R	Plan	Plan	RWG 4	RWG 10
LA Teacher 7B	HR	RWG 8	LA 2,8	RWG 2	RWG 11	L/R	Plan	Plan	LA 5,11	RWG 5
LA Teacher 7C	HR	RWG 3	RWG 9	LA 3,9	RWG 6	L/R	Plan	Plan	RWG 12	LA 6,12
Science Teacher 7D	HR	SC 4,10	SC 5,11	SC 6,12	SC 1,7	L/R	Plan	Plan	SC 2,8	SC 3,9
Concept Math Teacher 7E	HR	Concept Math 6,12	Concept Math 4,10	Concept Math 5, 11	Concept Math 3,9	L/R	Plan	Plan	Concept Math 1,7	Concept Math 2,8
Progress Math Teacher 7F	HR	Progress Math D1 MPG 5 D2 MPG 11	Progress Math D1 MPG 6 D2 MPG 12	Progress Math D1 MPG 4 D2 MPG 10	Progress Math D1 MPG 2 D2 MPG 8	L/R	Plan	Plan	Progress Math D1 MPG 3 D2 MPG 9	Progress Math D1 MPG 1 D2 MPG 7
Social Studies Teacher 7G	Duty	SS RWGs 2,9	SS RWGs 3,7	SS RWGs 1,8	SS RWGs 5,12	L/R	Plan	Plan	SS RWGs 6,10	SS RWGs 5,11
Mathematics Computer Lab	Duty	Day 1 RMG 11 Day 2 RMG 5	Day 1 RMG 12 Day 2 RMG 6	Day 1 RMG 10 Day 2 RMG 4	Day 1 RMG 8 Day 2 RMG 2	L/R	Plan	Plan	Day 1 RMG 9 Day 2 RMG 3	Day 1 RMG 7 Day 2 RMG 1

Teacher 7E (1:30 to 2:12), and then moves on to Teacher 7F for Progress Math class on Day 1 and to the computer lab on Day 2.

Obviously, in this variation it is very important for the Concept Math, Progress Math, and computer lab instructors to coordinate efforts.

DISCUSSION OF THE CONCEPT-PROGRESS MODEL

Our primary goal in devising the scheduling structure described above is to increase curricular access for students. To accomplish this goal, we move toward greater use of heterogeneous instructional groupings while mitigating the negative effects of comparison grading in such classes. What improvements have we made?

The participation of students in Concept Math classes guarantees instruction of the entire grade-level math curriculum. Limiting grading of students to the performance-level Progress Math groupings cushions the self-esteem-defeating aspects of grading. We admit that the Progress Math placement smacks of ability grouping. How is it different? A criticism of tracking is the long-term nature of placements. As a matter of institutional policy, groups in tracked schools typically are reorganized only once a year. In our system, at the beginning of any given topic, a student can be reassigned to a new Progress group. This practice is supported by Slavin's (1987) admonition: "Grouping plans should frequently reassess student placements and should be flexible enough to allow for easy reassignments after initial placement" (p. 328). Care must be taken to ensure that pretesting and regrouping occur for each new topic. We estimate that there would be 9 to 12 opportunities each year for such reassessment. Regular regrouping becomes institutionalized. This regrouping of students is made possible because Concept Math and Progress Math classes are paced through each topic together (Slavin, 1987). While it does not totally remove the negative impact of tracking, we believe that our proposal represents a practical, politically acceptable, and research-supported plan, balancing heterogeneous groupings with temporary skill groupings (Knapp, Turnbull, & Shields, 1990).

Other benefits accrue from our proposal. Class size is reduced to 12 to 15 for reading groups and Progress Math instruction (Klein, 1985). Because teachers no longer juggle multiple groups, students aren't relegated to spending time with worksheets as they await their turn for instruction. Students' engaged time has been shown to be greater in schools that use parallel block scheduling (Fogliani, 1990). Discipline problems that often arise during independent practice are diminished. Additional behavior problems associated with long-term placement of students in lower groups are decreased.

The plan also enables school administrators to capitalize on the teaching strengths of a staff. Teachers who excel in large-group instruction can serve in this role; other teachers who are more expert in small-group instruction are able to perform in that capacity. Teaching assignments during the school year can be flexible. There is no need for a Progress Math teacher to instruct at the same performance level for the entire school year. As topics change, teachers' expertise also may vary. An instructor excited about providing enrichment and extension activities for a unit on geometry could also be expert at teaching the basics of subtraction with renaming. Both assignments could be arranged easily in the proposed schedule.

DESIGNING THE CONCEPT-PROGRESS MODEL IN THE FOUR-BLOCK SCHEDULE

The Concept-Progress model also can be scheduled in the four-block schedule (discussed in Chapter 4). Three blocks of instruction are allocated to language arts, science and social studies, and PE, electives, and exploratory classes. The fourth block is allocated to deliver the mathematics program through the Concept-Progress model. Again, the computer lab is utilized to reduce class size during the Progress class.

Using Figure 7.7 (p. 190), let's follow the schedule of an eighth grade student assigned to section 8-1, Group 8-1a.[2] After homeroom with Teacher 8A, the student attends math class with the same teacher. That is, on Day 1 of a 3-day cycle in Block I, the student attends Concept class for 90 minutes. On Day 2, 8-1 is divided to form two Progress groups (8-1a and 8-1b). Each group constitutes approximately half of the Concept class; however, students are placed in this grouping based on a pretest that measures their mastery of the particular concepts in the current topical unit (see above). So, on Day 2 our student spends the first 42 minutes of the block in Progress class with Teacher 8A, then goes to the computer lab for 42 minutes of practice, reinforcement, or enrichment. On Day 3, the student spends the entire block in Concept class with Teacher 8A. For instructional planning purposes, the eighth grade Concept-Progress rotation should start on Day 3. Thus, our student spends two consecutive days in Concept class (Days 3 and 1), followed by one day (Day 2) split between Progress class and the computer lab.

In Block II, the student attends a PE, exploratory, or elective class. In Block III, 8-1 is instructed by the social studies and science teachers on some alternating basis, for example alternate day, alternate quarter, alternate semester, or alternate unit. The last block of the day is spent in language arts class with Teacher 8C.

---

2   A clear understanding of the content of Chapter 4 is necessary to comprehend the notation used in Figure 7.7.

FIGURE 7.7. CONCEPT-PROGRESS MODEL IN THE FOUR-BLOCK SCHEDULE: PROVIDING REDUCED CLASS SIZE, REMEDIATION, AND ENRICHMENT IN MATHEMATICS

Teacher		Block I			Block II			Block III			Block IV		
		Day 1	Day 2	Day 3	Day 1	Day 2	Day 3	Day 1	Day 2	Day 3	Day 1	Day 2	Day 3
Grade 6	M 6A	6-1	6-1	6-1a / 6-1b	6-3	6-3	6-3a / 6-3b	6-5	6-5	6-5a / 6-5b	PE, Exploratory, or Elective Grade 6 Teachers Plan		
	M 6B	6-2	6-2	6-2a / 6-2b	6-4	6-4	6-4a / 6-4b	6-6	6-6	6-6a / 6-6b			
	LA 6C	6-3			6-5			6-1					
	LA 6D	6-4			6-6			6-2					
	SS 6E*	6-5			6-1			6-3					
	SC 6F*	6-6			6-2			6-4					
Grade 7	M 7A	7-1a / 7-1b	7-1	7-1	7-3a / 7-3b	7-3	7-3	PE, Exploratory, or Elective Grade 7 Teachers Plan			7-5a / 7-5b	7-5	7-5
	M 7B	7-2a / 7-2b	7-2	7-2	7-4a / 7-4b	7-4	7-4				7-6a / 7-6b	7-6	7-6
	LA 7C	7-3			7-5						7-1		
	LA 7D	7-4			7-6						7-2		
	SS 7E*	7-5			7-1						7-3		
	SC 7F*	7-6			7-2						7-4		

Teacher		Block I Day 1	Block I Day 2	Block I Day 3	Block II Day 1	Block II Day 2	Block II Day 3	Block III Day 1	Block III Day 2	Block III Day 3	Block IV Day 1	Block IV Day 2	Block IV Day 3
Grade 8	M 8A	8-1	8-1a / 8-1b	8-1	PE, Exploratory, or Elective — Grade 8 Teachers Plan			8-3	8-3a / 8-3b	8-3	8-5	8-5a / 8-5b	8-5
	M 8B	8-2	8-2a / 8-2b	8-2				8-4	8-4a / 8-4b	8-4	8-6	8-6a / 8-6b	8-6
	LA 8C	8-3						8-5			8-1		
	LA 8D	8-4						8-6			8-2		
	SS 8E*	8-5						8-1			8-3		
	SC 8F*	8-6						8-2			8-4		
Comp. Lab	42 mins.	7-1b / 7-2b	8-1b / 8-2b	6-1b / 6-2b	7-3b / 7-4b	P	6-3b / 6-4b	P	8-3b / 8-4b	6-5b / 6-6b	7-5b / 7-6b	8-5b / 8-6b	P
	42 mins.	7-1a / 7-2a	8-1a / 8-2a	6-1a / 6-2a	7-3a / 7-4a	P	6-3a / 6-4a	P	8-3a / 8-4a	6-5a / 6-6a	7-5a / 7-6a	8-5a / 8-6a	P
PE/EX/EL		Plan			Grade 8			Grade 7			Grade 6		

* Social studies and science teachers exchange groups on a rotational basis: every other day, every other week, every other unit, every other quarter, or every other semester.

As can be seen at the bottom of Figure 7.7 (p. 190), one computer lab is used to serve six math teachers and approximately 450 students. On Day 1 of the cycle, Grade 7 conducts Progress classes and computer lab; on Day 2 of the cycle, Grade 8 has Progress classes and computer lab; and on Day 3 the sixth grade has Progress classes and computer lab.

USING THE WRITING LAB TO REDUCE LANGUAGE ARTS CLASS SIZE IN THE FOUR-BLOCK SCHEDULE

Just as class size has been lowered in math during Progress classes (Figure 7.7, p. 190), class size can be reduced in language arts through the use of a writing lab. Figure 7.8 illustrates this possibility.[3]

Again, this schedule is built around the four-block plan. Four 90-minute instructional blocks are created: one for science and social studies; one for PE, elective, and exploratory classes; one for mathematics (perhaps the Concept-Progress model, as described above, or the math/algebra model described in Chapter 8); and one for language arts. We utilize a writing lab (preferably with computers) to reduce class size in language arts on 2 of every 6 days.[4]

Figure 7.8 depicts only the language arts program; mathematics, science/social studies, and the elective block are scheduled as shown in Figure 7.7 (p. 190). We use as an example language arts Teacher 6B. During Block I Teacher 6B works with section 6-2 for days 1 to 4. On Day 5 of the cycle, Teacher 6B's class is divided into two groups, 6-2a and 6-2b; Teacher 6B instructs group 6-2a for the entire block while 6-2b goes to writing lab.

On Day 6 of the schedule, the groups switch; 6-2b works with Teacher 6B for the block, while 6-2a travels to the writing lab. Similarly, seventh grade language arts teachers work with full-size groups on Days 5, 6, 1, and 2, and utilize the writing lab to split groups on Days 3 and 4. Eighth grade language arts teachers instruct full classes on Days 3, 4, 5, 6; classes are split on Days 1 and 2. Although we show this plan as part of a four-block schedule, it is possible to organize similarly in any schedule, either period or block.

---

3 Again, a thorough understanding of the four-block middle school schedule described in Chapter 4 is necessary to comprehend this model.

4 A variety of rotations might be used. Earlier we used a 3-day rotation for the Concept-Progress math schedule; in this model we show a 6-day rotation. There is no magic formula to determine the most appropriate rotation; instructional needs should dictate the cycle. For maximum efficiency, however, the number of teachers served by the computer lab or writing lab often implies a rotation.

FIGURE 7.8. USING THE WRITING LAB TO REDUCE CLASS SIZE FOR REMEDIATION AND ENRICHMENT IN LANGUAGE ARTS

Teacher	Block I Day 1	Day 2	Day 3	Day 4	Day 5	Day 6	Block II Day 1	Day 2	Day 3	Day 4	Day 5	Day 6	Block III Day 1	Day 2	Day 3	Day 4	Day 5	Day 6	Block IV Day 1	Day 2	Day 3	Day 4	Day 5	Day 6
Grade 6 — LA 6A	6-1	6-1	6-1	6-1	6-1a	6-1b	6-3	6-3	6-3	6-3	6-3a	6-3b	6-5	6-5	6-5	6-5	6-5a	6-5b	PE, Exploratory, or Elective, Grade 6 Teachers Plan					
Grade 6 — LA 6B	6-2	6-2	6-2	6-2	6-2a	6-2b	6-4	6-4	6-4	6-4	6-4a	6-4b	6-6	6-6	6-6	6-6	6-6a	6-6b	PE, Exploratory, or Elective, Grade 6 Teachers Plan					
Grade 7 — LA 7A	7-1	7-1	7-1a	7-1b	7-1	7-1	7-3	7-3	7-3a	7-3b	7-3	7-3	PE, Exploratory, or Elective, Grade 7 Teachers Plan						7-5	7-5	7-5a	7-5b	7-5	7-5
Grade 7 — LA 7B	7-2	7-2	7-2a	7-2b	7-2	7-2	7-4	7-4	7-4a	7-4b	7-4	7-4	PE, Exploratory, or Elective, Grade 7 Teachers Plan						7-6	7-6	7-6a	7-6b	7-6	7-6
Grade 8 — LA 8A	8-1a	8-1b	8-1	8-1	8-1	8-1	PE, Exploratory, or Elective, Grade 8 Teachers Plan						8-3a	8-3b	8-3	8-3	8-3	8-3	8-5a	8-5b	8-5	8-5	8-5	8-5
Grade 8 — LA 8B	8-2a	8-2b	8-2	8-2	8-2	8-2	PE, Exploratory, or Elective, Grade 8 Teachers Plan						8-4a	8-4b	8-4	8-4	8-4	8-4	8-6a	8-6b	8-6	8-6	8-6	8-6
Writing Lab	8-1a & 8-2b	8-1b & 8-2a	7-1a & 7-2b	7-1b & 7-2a	6-1a & 6-2b	6-1b & 6-2a	Plan	Plan	7-3b & 7-4b	7-3a & 7-4a	6-3b & 6-4b	6-3a & 6-4a	8-3a & 8-4a	8-3b & 8-4b	Plan	Plan	6-5b & 6-6b	6-5a & 6-6a	7-5b & 7-6b	7-5a & 7-6a	Plan	Plan	Plan	Plan

CONCLUSION

Parallel block scheduling is a powerful scheduling tool. This chapter only scratches the surface of its potential. We have, however, presented several models that provide a variety of possible benefits. Parallel block scheduling can help schools to accomplish these goals:

- ♦ Reducing class size during critical instructional periods;
- ♦ Integrating special programs with the basic instruction provided by core teachers;
- ♦ Offering an alternative to strict homogeneous grouping; and
- ♦ Offering a creative way to provide supplemental programs such as writing or math labs.

The possible applications of the principles of parallel block scheduling to the middle school are as unlimited as the creativity of the administrators and teachers designing the schedule.[5]

---

5 While a thorough examination of this topic is beyond the scope of this chapter, we encourage the reader to explore the reference section of this volume for related publications. In addition, our forthcoming book, tentatively titled *Parallel Block Scheduling in the Elementary School* (2001), will explore this topic in much greater detail.

8

SCHEDULING EXTENDED LEARNING TIME IN THE MIDDLE SCHOOL

Recent changes in state accountability systems have resulted in a growing number of statewide assessments designed to ensure a specified level of student learning. For years the attainment of locally awarded grades sufficed for students to graduate from high school or be promoted to the next grade level. New standards and "high-stakes" assessments measuring the attainment of these standards have altered this equation. Now, merely achieving a passing grade in a course may not suffice to graduate or to be promoted; in many states, a student now must "pass" a state test to earn the necessary credits. Concurrently, many schools across the nation have seen an increasing diversity in their student population, with increasing numbers of students with limited English proficiency (LEP). Many students cannot master the objectives necessary to pass the state tests in the time allotted. Often, the only alternative available for such students is to repeat a failed course. This chapter offers a variety of schedules that provide students with additional learning time so that it is not necessary to fail and repeat courses to attain the required mastery. We believe these options institutionalize sound practice.

Plan I shows how to provide additional learning time with periodic remedial interventions in mathematics. This plan has been adopted and implemented successfully at a number of middle and high schools across the nation. Plan II offers options to be applied when a large number of students fail a grade level. We show how a cohort of eighth or ninth grade students who have not met the standards for promotion to the next grade can complete the failed courses during the first semester and move to the next grade level for the second semester. In Plan III, we share a number of options in which we stop the regular schedule periodically to provide time for instructional interventions for students who are having difficulty keeping up, and to offer enrichment for students who are mastering the content in a timely fashion.

PLAN I: DESIGNING A MIDDLE SCHOOL SCHEDULE THAT PROVIDES VARIABLE LEARNING TIME FOR MATHEMATICS[1]

Successful completion of Algebra I has been identified as a key to further academic accomplishments in schooling. For years, Algebra I study in middle school has been limited to the select few students who maintained excellent grades in mathematics and performed well on a placement examination. In the past 10 years, a trend has developed to enlarge the pool of students taking Algebra I in middle school. While we applaud this increase in access to higher level mathematics, we worry that this new crop of algebra students will suffer the same consequences as older peers. Many high school students who first enroll in this demanding subject fall behind quickly and, because of the sequential nature of the subject, are unable to understand more advanced concepts later in the course. These students may receive failing grades early in the course, yet they must remain in the class for the remainder of the school year, often becoming attendance and behavior problems. After this unsuccessful experience, they are offered the opportunity to retake the course in summer school or during the next academic year.[2] We see this practice as an inflexible and punitive system that ignores an undeniable fact about students: some take longer to learn certain concepts than others. Given the diversity in public schools and the growing trend toward requiring the successful completion of Algebra I (and in some states, geometry) for graduation, we believe that a structure must be created that allows large numbers of students to complete this course successfully—as measured by an end-of-course test—but in different amounts of time. We contend that schools must consider scheduling that provides students varying amounts of time to complete the course, with institutionalized interventions occurring throughout the process.

The model has been designed for a middle school with the goal of having more than 75 percent of students successfully complete Algebra I by the end of eighth grade. To allow for variable amounts of learning time for

---

1 This section is adapted from Rettig, M. D. and Canady, R. L. (1998). High failure rates in required mathematics courses: Can a modified block schedule be part of the cure? *NASSP Bulletin, 82*(596), 56–65. This same scheduling twist can be applied to disciplines other than mathematics.

2 Algebra I is one of several courses which contributes to an unacceptably high failure-rate among ninth grade students in public schools throughout the United States. For example, in Virginia, during the 1995-96 school year 13.2% of all ninth grade students were retained, nearly double the rate of any other grade level (Virginia Department of Education, 1996).

students in mathematics, it is necessary to address four key issues: curriculum, instructional methods, assessment, and scheduling. Before addressing these key ideas in Plan I, we explain the overall master schedule.

MASTER SCHEDULE

Figure 8.1 (p. 199) is a full middle school four-block schedule (see Chapter 4 for more details). In this plan, all math teachers in the school—in this case there are six—work in a mathematics team across the three grade levels. Teachers of reading/language arts, science, and social studies work on team at each grade level. Teachers in this schedule never work with more than three groups of students at any one time; mathematics and reading/language arts teachers work with only three groups of students all year. This plan would be enhanced by the addition of a special-education resource teacher to teams.

To explain this middle school schedule, we describe first a teacher's schedule and then we write a sample student schedule. During Block I, sixth grade reading/language arts Teacher 6A works with Group 6-1; during Block II, Teacher 6A instructs Group 6-3; during Block III Group 6-5 receives instruction; and during Block IV—when all sixth grade students assigned to this team are with the total school mathematics team—Teacher 6A is planning with the other reading/language arts teacher (6B) plus the science, social studies, and resource teachers working on this team.

For a sample student schedule, we follow "Susan," who is assigned to the 6-1 reading/language arts group during Block I. During Block II, she could be assigned to a health and physical education class that meets for 90 minutes every other day for the entire quarter, semester, or year (depending on what the requirements are in the school district). On the days opposite PE/health, Susan may be scheduled for band, or she may take four to six exploratory classes on a rotating basis over the course of the year. Another option is for Susan to take a foreign language opposite PE/health. In some districts, she might attend sixth grade band for 90 minutes once every 3 days, a foreign language for 90 minutes once every 3 days, and an exploratory class following the same pattern.

Although we do not recommend it, the PE/health and exploratory block also could be divided into two 43-minute periods with 4 minutes for transition time. Susan then might attend PE/health for 43 minutes every day, and for the remaining 43 minutes attend band or exploratories on a rotating basis. We believe that students should be assigned a limited number of classes during any one time period during a school year; therefore, we recommend meeting PE/health and exploratories for 90 minutes daily on some rotational basis, such as every other day. We contend that this scheduling plan is in keeping with what we know about many middle school students and their lack of organizational skills.

Following Block II, Susan attends either social studies or science on an alternating basis. For example, these two classes could meet for 90 minutes every other day throughout the year, as shown in Figure 8.1, which would allocate the same time as if the class meets for 40 to 45 minutes every day for 180 days. Another option, which we prefer, is for one group of students to attend science while another group participates in social studies; after 4½ weeks, the teachers exchange the two groups. By following this pattern all year, Susan can receive grades in both science and social studies during each 9-week grading period, and she has been exposed to equal amounts of content in each subject. Also, if her school district requires standardized tests in the spring, she will have had recent contact in both subjects. If spring testing is not an issue, Susan may be assigned one semester of science and one full semester of social studies for 90 minutes each school day. During Block IV Susan is assigned to the math team. Throughout the year she may be assigned and reassigned to different teachers and groups depending on her performance in mathematics, as described in the following sections.

Figure 8.1a (p. 200) depicts an alternate form of this schedule for a situation in which fewer math teachers are available. In this model the math team of three teachers instructs half of the students in a grade level on Day 1 and the other half of the students on Day 2. For example, during Block I students in sections 8-1, 8-2, and 8-3 have math on Day 1, while students in sections 8-4, 8-5, and 8-6 are assigned to physical education, elective or exploratory classes. On Day 2 sections 8-1, 8-2, and 8-3 are assigned to the elective pool, while sections 8-4, 8-5, and 8-6 attend math.

If four teachers were available, it would be possible to create one, every-day section to address the same curriculum. During each math block we could then divide the 150 to 180 students at the grade level into seven sections. Three teachers would work with two sections each, every-other-day. The fourth teacher would instruct a single section every day. These students would have one less elective opportunity. If the every-other-day and everyday sections were paced through the curriculum similarly, membership in these sections could vary periodically based upon formative assessment results (see below).

MATHEMATICS CURRICULA—
ASSESSMENT AND SCHEDULING

We recommend that the Grade 6, Pre-algebra and Algebra I curricula each be divided into at least four distinct parts and that assessments be designed to measure students' mastery of each part. In addition, we suggest that a two-period block of time, of approximately 90 minutes, be allocated for mathematics in the school schedule. This could be considered two consecutive semester blocks in the four-block schedule as described above

FIGURE 8.1. MATH/ALGEBRA TEAM MIDDLE SCHOOL MASTER BLOCK SCHEDULE

	Block I				Block II				Block III				Block IV			
6th	LA 6A	LA 6B	SS 6	SC 6	LA 6A	LA 6B	SS 6	SC 6	LA 6A	LA 6B	SS 6	SC 6	LA 6A	LA 6B	SS 6	SC 6
D1	LA 6-1	LA 6-2	SS 6-3	SC 6-4	LA 6-3	LA 6-4	SS 6-5	SC 6-6	LA 6-5	LA 6-6	SS 6-1	SC 6-2	All 6th Grade Students in Math; Teacher Planning			
D2			SS 6-4	SC 6-3			SS 6-6	SC 6-5			SS 6-2	SC 6-1				
7th	LA 7A	LA 7B	SS 7	SC 7	LA 7A	LA 7B	SS 7	SC 7	LA 7A	LA 7B	SS 7	SC 7	LA 7A	LA 7B	SS 7	SC 7
D1	LA 7-1	LA 7-2	SS 7-3	SC 7-4	LA 7-3	LA 7-4	SS 7-5	SC 7-6	All 7th Grade Students in Math; Teacher Planning				LA 7-5	LA 7-6	SS 7-1	SC 7-2
D2			SS 7-4	SC 7-3			SS 7-6	SC 7-5							SS 7-2	SC 7-1
8th	LA 8A	LA 8B	SS 8	SC 8	LA 8A	LA 8B	SS 8	SC 8	LA 8A	LA 8B	SS 8	SC 8	LA 8A	LA 8B	SS 8	SC 8
D1	All 8th Grade Students in Math; Teacher Planning				LA 8-1	LA 8-2	SS 8-3	SC 8-4	LA 8-3	LA 8-4	SS 8-5	SC 8-6	LA 8-5	LA 8-6	SS 8-1	SC 8-2
D2							SS 8-4	SC 8-3			SS 8-6	SC 8-5			SS 8-2	SC 8-1
Math	8th Grade; 6 Teachers				Math Planning				7th Grade; 6 Teachers				6th Grade; 6 Teachers			
PE/Exp	6-5, 7-5, 6-6, 7-6				6-1, 7-1, 8-5, 6-2, 7-2, 8-6				6-3, 8-1, 6-4, 8-2				7-3, 8-3, 7-4, 8-4			

FIGURE 8.1A. MATH/ALGEBRA TEAM MIDDLE SCHOOL MASTER BLOCK SCHEDULE

	Block I				Block II				Block III				Block IV			
6th	LA 6A	LA 6B	SS6	SC6	LA 6A	LA 6B	SS6	SC6	LA 6A	LA 6B	SS6	SC6	LA 6A	LA 6B	SS6	SC6
D1	LA 6-1	SS 6-3	SC 6-4		LA 6-3	SS 6-5	SC 6-6		LA 6-5	SS 6-1	SC 6-2		Day 1 6-1, 6-2, 6-3 in Math			
D2	LA 6-2	SS 6-4	SC 6-3		LA 6-4	SS 6-6	SC 6-5		LA 6-6	SS 6-2	SC 6-1		Day 2 6-4, 6-5, 6-6 in Math			
7th	LA 7A	LA 7B	SS7	SC7	LA 7A	LA 7B	SS7	SC7	LA 7A	LA 7B	SS7	SC7	LA 7A	LA 7B	SS7	SC7
D1	LA 7-1	SS 7-3	SC 7-4		LA 7-3	SS 7-5	SC 7-6		Day 1 7-1, 7-2, 7-3 in Math				LA 7-5	SS 7-1	SC 7-2	
D2	LA 7-2	SS 7-4	SC 7-3		LA 7-4	SS 7-6	SC 7-5		Day 2 7-4, 7-5, 7-6 in Math				LA 7-6	SS 7-2	SC 7-1	
8th	LA 8A	LA 8B	SS8	SC8	LA 8A	LA 8B	SS8	SC8	LA 8A	LA 8B	SS8	SC8	LA 8A	LA 8B	SS8	SC8
D1	8-1, 8-2, 8-3 in Math				LA 8-1	SS 8-3	SC 8-4		LA 8-3	SS 8-5	SC 8-6		LA 8-5	SS 8-1	SC 8-2	
D2	8-4, 8-5, 8-6 in Math				LA 8-2	SS 8-4	SC 8-3		LA 8-4	SS 8-6	SC 8-5		LA 8-6	SS 8-2	SC 8-1	
MATH	8th Grade; 3-4 Teachers				Math Planning				7th Grade; 3-4 Teachers				6th Grade; 3-4 Teachers			
PE/Exp D1	6-5, 6-6, 7-5, 7-6, 8-4, 8-5, 8-6				6-1, 7-1, 8-5, 6-2, 7-2, 8-6				D1 6-3, 6-4, 7-1, 7-2, 7-3, 8-1, 8-2				D1 6-1, 6-2, 6-3, 7-3, 7-4, 8-3, 8-4			
PE/Exp D2	6-5, 6-6, 7-5, 7-6, 8-1, 8-2, 8-3								D2 6-3, 6-4, 7-4, 7-5, 7-6, 8-1, 8-2				D2 6-4, 6-5, 6-6, 7-3, 7-4, 8-3, 8-4			

(also see Chapter 4), a daily block in an A/B schedule (see Chapter 3), or two periods within a seven or eight single-period schedule. Math classes would meet for a block every day of the 36- to 40-week school year.

We developed two variations of this plan. In the first variation, Grade 6 students are kept in the same math course all year long, although the course offers periodic enrichment and/or remediation as warranted. All students begin taking Pre-algebra in the seventh grade. Based on their performance on assessments they are regrouped periodically into faster- or slower-moving sections. This practice continues into eighth grade. Our example shows some students venturing into Algebra II in the second semester of eighth grade. In the second variation, all students are kept together for both Grade 6 math and Grade 7 Pre-algebra. All students begin Algebra I in Grade 8, but are regrouped periodically into faster or slower sections. Some students will complete both Algebra I and geometry; other students may not finish Algebra I.

VARIATION 1

During the sixth grade math block, heterogeneous groups are assigned to all math teachers. The first assessment is administered after 40 days of instruction. Based on the results of the assessment, students are regrouped temporarily into classes in which specific remedial interventions or enrichment are provided. After 5 days of remediation and/or enrichment, students return to their original math classes for 40 days of new instruction, after which the second assessment is given and the second 5-day remediation and/or enrichment term occurs. The pattern continues for the 180-day school year (see Figure 8.2, p. 202). In our example, no effort is made to accelerate sixth grade students, although the model could be adapted to allow for this possibility.

During the seventh grade math block, a different procedure is initiated. All six of the school's math teachers are assigned heterogeneous sections of Pre-algebra during the same block. No section is designated as "honors." All sections are taught the same curriculum at the same pace. Each quarter of the course is taught in 20 to 25 days of double-period classes.[3] At the conclusion of each quarter, assessments are administered, and students are regrouped. Students who achieve sufficient mastery of

---

3 Because we suggest dividing the curriculum into at least four relatively equal segments, we have assigned equal time periods for each quarter. It certainly is possible to divide the available time unequally. For example, the first assessment might not be given until after 6 weeks of double blocks; the remaining curriculum, as well as the remaining 12 weeks of the semester, could be divided into three 4-week units. In any case, the school year is divided into eight "quarters"—four in each semester.

Part 1 proceed to Part 2. Students needing more time to master the concepts of Part 1 receive additional instructional time. Refer to the example illustrated in Figure 8.3.

FIGURE 8.2. PLAN I MATH TEAM SCHEDULE: GRADE 6 MATH—SIX TEACHERS

Days	40	5	40	5	40	5	40	5
Teacher A	Math 6 Part 1	Remedial Interventions	Math 6 Part 2	Enrichment	Math 6 Part 3	Remedial Interventions	Math 6 Part 4	Enrichment
Teacher B	Math 6 Part 1	Remedial Interventions	Math 6 Part 2	Enrichment	Math 6 Part 3	Remedial Interventions	Math 6 Part 4	Enrichment
Teacher C	Math 6 Part 1	Remedial Interventions	Math 6 Part 2	Enrichment	Math 6 Part 3	Remedial Interventions	Math 6 Part 4	Enrichment
Teacher D	Math 6 Part 1	Enrichment	Math 6 Part 2	Remedial Interventions	Math 6 Part 3	Enrichment	Math 6 Part 4	Remedial Interventions
Teacher E	Math 6 Part 1	Enrichment	Math 6 Part 2	Remedial Interventions	Math 6 Part 3	Enrichment	Math 6 Part 4	Remedial Interventions
Teacher F	Math 6 Part 1	Enrichment	Math 6 Part 2	Remedial Interventions	Math 6 Part 3	Enrichment	Math 6 Part 4	Remedial Interventions

FIGURE 8.3. PLAN I MATH TEAM SCHEDULE: GRADE 7 PRE-ALGEBRA AND ALGEBRA—SIX TEACHERS

	Q1	Q2	Q3	Q4	Q5	Q6	Q7	Q8
Teacher A	PreAlg Part 1	PreAlg Part 2	PreAlg Part 3	PreAlg Part 4	Alg Part 1	Alg Part 2	Alg Part 3	Alg Part 4
Teacher B	PreAlg Part 1	PreAlg Part 2	PreAlg Part 3	PreAlg Part 3	PreAlg Part 4	Alg Part 1	Alg Part 2	Alg Part 2
Teacher C	PreAlg Part 1	PreAlg Part 2	PreAlg Part 2	PreAlg Part 3	PreAlg Part 3	PreAlg Part 4	Alg Part 1	Alg Part 1
Teacher D	PreAlg Part 1	PreAlg Part 2	PreAlg Part 2	PreAlg Part 3	PreAlg Part 3	PreAlg Part 4	PreAlg Part 4	C. Lab*
Teacher E	PreAlg Part 1	PreAlg Part 1	PreAlg Part 1	PreAlg Part 2	PreAlg Part 2	PreAlg Part 3	PreAlg Part 3	PreAlg Part 4
Teacher F	PreAlg Part 1	PreAlg Part 1	PreAlg Part 2	PreAlg Part 2	PreAlg Part 3	PreAlg Part 3	PreAlg Part 4	PreAlg Part 4

Q1 stands for a quarter of the time it normally would take to complete a course within a double-block format, typically 4½ to 5 weeks. Also, math courses are divided into four distinct and assessable curriculum divisions. This chart is one example; the actual number of sections for each part of a course varies based on the assessment results.

* Could be Algebra, Part 1.

QUARTER 1

During Quarter 1 all students begin Pre-algebra together with teachers A–F. Classes are grouped heterogeneously; teachers have developed pacing guides and teach the first quarter of the curriculum in 20 to 25 days, depending on the school calendar. Assessments are administered, and depending on a student's level of mastery, the student either moves on to Part 2 or remains in Part 1 for extended learning time.

QUARTER 2

Figure 8.3 (p. 202) is an example in which two-thirds of the students are able to proceed to Part 2; these students are regrouped with teachers A to D. Those students needing additional time in Part 1 are assigned to teachers E and F. Several decades of research tells us that simply failing students and having them repeat courses (or in this case, parts of courses) does not "fix" them. We also know the social and academic problems that come with tracking; therefore, we must be careful how we organize and conduct the "repeat" sections or quarters of this model.

We propose that students recommended for extended learning time be given a grade such as "I" (Incomplete); "E" (Extended learning time required); or "WIP" (Work in progress). In addition, a Mathematics Learning Plan (MLP) should be prepared by the referring teacher, explaining the areas in which the student needs academic assistance (e.g., factoring, word problems, etc.). If good assessments have been developed before beginning the program, preparing MLPs should not be a major problem.

For this scheduling model to work optimally, we believe that there must be a computer lab and technician made available just for these students during this block of "intensive care" time. Students are stationed in the computer lab using appropriate software selected to address their needs as specified in their MLP. Pulling students from the lab, Teachers E and F then have the flexibility to group and regroup students with similar needs as identified in the MLP to provide focused direct instruction. During this extended time, we recommend that selected other teachers in the school also be assigned to assist. For example, if English is not the primary language of some students, then an ESL teacher should be available for assistance. Special education resource teachers and Title I teachers, if available, also could assist with the extended learning sections.

Students needing extended learning time generally can be assigned to several possible classes (see Figure 8.3, p. 202). This is an important feature of this model. We hope to avoid a "repeaters' section" for as long as possible.[4] Such grouping assignments traditionally have not worked well.

QUARTER 3

At the end of Quarter 2 another regrouping may occur, if necessary. Students who need more learning time for Part 2 may be reassigned to Part 2 again. We show one-third of the original group moving to Part 3, half the group now in Part 2, and one group still in Part 1 (Teacher E).

QUARTER 4

At the end of Quarter 3 any students who have been working with Teachers A or B on Part 3 of the course may be regrouped to Teachers B, C, or D to repeat Part 3 if their mastery is not sufficient. Students who have mastered the concepts of Part 2 by the end of Quarter 3 may move on with Teacher B, C, or D while those students who need more learning time for Part 2 are instructed by Teacher E or F, who at this point may be assisted by one or more learning resource personnel, such as ESL or LD teachers.

QUARTER 5

At the end of Quarter 4 we show one-sixth of the students completing Pre-algebra; any student with a grade of B or better is said to have completed Pre-algebra "with honors." Completers may move on to take a new course; Teacher A becomes available to teach other math courses as well. Students from Teacher A who have not mastered Part 4 are regrouped with Teacher B during Quarter 5. Students from Teachers B, C, and D who have mastered Part 3 are regrouped with Teacher B to take Part 4 during Quarter 5. Students who need more learning time for Part 3 work with Teachers C, D, or F. Teacher E instructs a repeat of Part 2.

QUARTER 6

At the end of Quarter 5 we show students needing more time in Part 4 regrouped with Teachers C or D. Those who have completed Part 4 may begin taking Algebra with Teacher B during Quarter 6. Students from Teachers C, D, E, or F who need more time in Part 3 or are just beginning Part 3 are regrouped with Teachers E and F.

QUARTER 7

At the end of Quarter 6, students from Teachers C and D who have mastered Part 4 are regrouped with Teacher C to begin Algebra; students

---

4 We also wish to avoid creating "repeater teachers." Although we have specified the teaching assignments of various teachers for this model, within any quarter (Q5 for example), teachers' roles may be exchanged.

who need more time in Part 4 are regrouped with Teachers D or F. Teacher E works with those students who need more time in Part 3.

QUARTER 8

In Quarter 8, students mastering Part 1 of Algebra move on to Part 2 with Teacher B; those who need more time regroup with Teacher C. Students finishing Pre-algebra, Part 4, are assigned to the computer lab for the next 4½ to 5 weeks; it may be too late in the school year to begin another course. Students who need more time in Part 4 work with Teachers E and F. Any student who has not mastered Part 4 by the end of Quarter 8 is advised to attend summer school.

Figure 8.4 extrapolates a possible scenario for the eighth grade if our seventh grade groups progressed as shown in Figure 8.3 (p. 202). Admittedly, the picture drawn in these two figures is very optimistic. We have visited very few schools in which all middle-school-aged children finish Algebra I and half of the eighth grade class completes significant work in geometry and Algebra II. The situation described in Variation II may be more realistic for the majority of schools.

VARIATION 2

The schedule shown in Figure 8.5 (p. 207) suggests that similarly to sixth grade, seventh grade students are kept together in heterogeneous groups instructed in Pre-algebra for 40-day terms followed by 5-day terms for remedial interventions and/or enrichment. At the beginning of the eighth grade, all students are assigned to heterogeneous groups for Part 1 of Algebra I. Figure 8.6 (p. 207) shows one possible progression of groupings given this scenario. As described earlier, when students need to repeat a section, an effort is made to provide additional support resources.

Figure 8.7 (p. 208) illustrates a similar Pre-algebra plan when only four mathematics teachers are available. Figure 8.8 (p. 208) suggests a possible format for three mathematics teachers.

We realize that the progressive regroupings described in Figures 8.2 to 8.8 are but one of many permutations possible, and that the number of sections of each "part" is dependent on students' performance on the assessments. We contend, however, that this plan allows for systematic and timely instructional support, and that it helps to institutionalize what we know to be good practice. We often are asked why this plan is better than simply dividing the Algebra I curriculum into Algebra, Part 1, and Algebra I, Part 2, and then spending a school year on each part. The more traditional approach is designed to teach the material more slowly for a select group of students.

We suggest that we can develop a stronger student, as well as deal with grouping issues more creatively, by initially teaching a selected section of content at a regular pace. Following this initial instruction, our plan requires that an assessment be administered. Students who have mastered material sufficiently progress to the next part; they are not held back. Students not mastering the content at an acceptable level receive extended learning time; however, they now have an overview or "map" of what they have to learn and an individual diagnosis of what concepts still require mastery. With the Mathematics Learning Plan, specific focused groups, based on individual needs, can be formed to assist with these individual deficits. We contend that this format will result in stronger students than simply identifying a body of content and teaching it more slowly.

(Text continues on page 209, following Figure 8.8.)

FIGURE 8.4. PLAN I MATH TEAM SCHEDULE: GRADE 8 ALGEBRA, GEOMETRY, AND ALGEBRA II—SIX TEACHERS

	Q1	Q2	Q3	Q4	Q5	Q6	Q7	Q8
Teacher A	Geom Part 1	Geom Part 2	Geom Part 3	Geom Part 4	Algebra II			
Teacher B	Alg Part 3	Alg Part 3	Alg Part 4	Alg Part 4	Geom Part 1	Geom Part 2	Geom Part 2	Geom Part 3
Teacher C	Alg Part 2	Alg Part 2	Alg Part 3	Alg Part 4	Alg Part 4	Geom Part 1	Geom Part 2	Geom Part 2
Teacher D	Alg Part 1	Alg Part 1	Alg Part 2	Alg Part 3	Alg Part 3	Alg Part 4	Alg Part 4	C. Lab*
Teacher E	Alg Part 1	Alg Part 1	Alg Part 2	Alg Part 2	Alg Part 3	Alg Part 3	Alg Part 4	Alg Part 4
Teacher F	Alg Part 1	Alg Part 1	Alg Part 2	Alg Part 2	Alg Part 3	Alg Part 3	Alg Part 4	Alg Part 4

Q1 stands for a quarter of the time it normally would take to complete a course within a double-block format, typically 4½ to 5 weeks. Also, math courses are divided into four distinct and assessable curriculum divisions. This chart is one example; the actual number of sections for each part of each course varies based on the assessment results.

* Could be Geometry, Part 1.

FIGURE 8.5. PLAN I MATH TEAM SCHEDULE:
GRADE 7 PRE-ALGEBRA—SIX TEACHERS

Days	40	5	40	5	40	5	40	5
Teacher A	PreAlg Part 1	Remedial Interventions	PreAlg Part 2	Enrichment	PreAlg Part 3	Remedial Interventions	PreAlg Part 4	Enrichment
Teacher B	PreAlg Part 1	Remedial Interventions	PreAlg Part 2	Enrichment	PreAlg Part 3	Remedial Interventions	PreAlg Part 4	Enrichment
Teacher C	PreAlg Part 1	Remedial Interventions	PreAlg Part 2	Enrichment	PreAlg Part 3	Remedial Interventions	PreAlg Part 4	Enrichment
Teacher D	PreAlg Part 1	Enrichment	PreAlg Part 2	Remedial Interventions	PreAlg Part 3	Enrichment	PreAlg Part 4	Remedial Interventions
Teacher E	PreAlg Part 1	Enrichment	PreAlg Part 2	Remedial Interventions	PreAlg Part 3	Enrichment	PreAlg Part 4	Remedial Interventions
Teacher F	PreAlg Part 1	Enrichment	PreAlg Part 2	Remedial Interventions	PreAlg Part 3	Enrichment	PreAlg Part 4	Remedial Interventions

FIGURE 8.6. PLAN I MATH TEAM SCHEDULE:
GRADE 8 ALGEBRA AND GEOMETRY

	Q1	Q2	Q3	Q4	Q5	Q6	Q7	Q8
Teacher A	Alg Part 1	Alg Part 2	Alg Part 3	Alg Part 4	Geom Part 1	Geom Part 2	Geom Part 3	Geom Part 4
Teacher B	Alg Part 1	Alg Part 2	Alg Part 2	Alg Part 3	Alg Part 3	Alg Part 4	Geom Part 1	Geom Part 2
Teacher C	Alg Part 1	Alg Part 2	Alg Part 2	Alg Part 3	Alg Part 3	Alg Part 4	Alg Part 4	C. Lab*
Teacher D	Alg Part 1	Alg Part 1	Alg Part 2	Alg Part 2	Alg Part 3	Alg Part 4	Alg Part 4	C. Lab*
Teacher E	Alg Part 1	Alg Part 1	Alg Part 2	Alg Part 3	Alg Part 3	Alg Part 3	Alg Part 4	Alg Part 4
Teacher F	Alg Part 1	Alg Part 1	Alg Part 2	Alg Part 2	Alg Part 3	Alg Part 3	Alg Part 4	Alg Part 4

Q1 stands for a quarter of the time it normally would take to complete a course within a double-block format, typically 4½ to 5 weeks. Also, math courses are divided into four distinct and assessable curriculum divisions. This chart is one example; the actual number of sections for each part of a course varies based on the assessment results.

* Could be Geometry, Part 1.

FIGURE 8.7. PLAN I MATH TEAM SCHEDULE: FOUR TEACHERS

	Q1	Q2	Q3	Q4	Q5	Q6	Q7	Q8
Teacher A	Part 1	Part 2	Part 3	Part 4	Start Next Sequential Course			
Teacher B	Part 1	Part 2	Part 3	Part 3	Part 4	Part 4	Start Next Course	
Teacher C	Part 1	Part 1	Part 2	Part 2	Part 3	Part 4	Part 4	C. Lab*
Teacher D	Part 1	Part 1	Part 2	Part 2	Part 3	Part 3	Part 4	Part 4

Q1 stands for a quarter of the time it normally would take to complete a course. In a single-period or A/B schedule, this is 9 weeks; in a four-block schedule this is 4½ weeks. The curriculum is divided into four parts.

* Could start next sequential course.

FIGURE 8.8. PLAN I MATH TEAM SCHEDULE: THREE TEACHERS

	Term 1 9–10 weeks	Term 2 9–10 weeks	Term 3 9–10 weeks	Term 4 9–10 weeks
Teacher A	Part 1 & 2	Part 3 & 4	Start Next Sequential Course	
Teacher B	Part 1 & 2	Part 2 & 3	Part 3 & 4	Start Next Course
Teacher C	Part 1 & 2	Part 1 & 2	Part 2 & 3	Part 3 & 4

This schedule also could be divided into 4½- to 5-week sections similar to the plans shown in Figures 8.3 (p. 202), 8.4 (p. 206), 8.6, and 8.7.

BENEFITS OF PLAN I

- ◆ All students are treated equally. Movement to the next part of the course is based on objective assessments of learning goals.

- ◆ Remediation is more immediate than in current schedules. Students who need it can receive re-teaching at least every 4½ to 5 weeks. Intervention strategies are institutionalized, rather than being dependent on each teacher's desire and ability. Students falling behind do not flounder for the balance of the year, waiting for summer school or the next school year to try again.

- ◆ Content mastery is based on the achievement of specific curricular goals, not the number of minutes spent in a seat.

- ◆ A variety of placements is available for transfer students.

- ◆ Honors credit is conferred based on performance, not on *prediction of performance.*

- ◆ There are incentives to finish expeditiously; the sooner students finish, the more time they have for other course options.

- ◆ Math teachers work as a team to reconstruct curriculum, design innovative instructional methods, create objective assessments, and regroup students within the scheduling format.

CONCERNS AND ISSUES RELATED TO PLAN I

- ◆ Multiple math teachers are pulled from their traditional middle school teams and must teach at all three grade levels; this change may increase the number of preparations some math teachers have, although in the middle school schedule shown, teachers would prepare for three classes at most.

- ◆ Professional staff development time will be necessary to decide on curriculum "parts" and to design assessments. *It is critical that this important task be completed and institutionalized before implementation of this plan.*

- ◆ Staff development time also is needed to address instructional practices in longer class periods (Canady & Rettig, 1996; Gilkey & Hunt, 1998).

- ◆ It may be necessary to adapt the grading system. We suggest that no "F"s be given to students who need additional learning time. A grade of "E" (Extended learning time required) could be assigned instead. If it is unrealistic to create a new letter grade, schools could use the commonly available "I" (Incomplete), although in many school districts, this grade connotes unfinished required work, not the need for more time to learn.

♦ "Honors" parents initially may resist the lack of "honors" sections.

♦ There is no guarantee that section sizes after each regrouping will remain equal. Depending on the number of students assigned to each part of the course after assessments, some sections may be larger than others. If initial class sizes are at or near the maximum allowable numbers (by accreditation standards, union contract, or district policy), it may be difficult to maintain this balance. It may be possible to serve larger sections if additional resources can be provided. For example, if students in the repeat section were assigned to the computer lab as a base, and small groups were served by the math teacher as well as other resource personnel, it may be possible to assign a larger number of students to this section.

♦ Some will argue that regrouping is simply another form of tracking. We contend that the regrouping is based on achievement and that multiple opportunities exist to complete the course in a timely fashion. Groupings are temporary; regrouping based on the attainment of learning goals is institutionalized.

♦ Students finishing in the seventh quarter must be assigned to a computer lab or study hall for the next 4½ to 5 weeks; staff must be assigned similarly. Although this may not be optimal use of students' time or instructional personnel, software is available that could reinforce and advance students' skills in mathematics. Teachers who become available at these times could assist with students in repeat sections.

PLAN II: DESIGNING A SCHEDULE THAT OFFERS THE "SECOND-CHANCE SEMESTER"

For schools unable to organize their mathematics and/or language arts program with intervention steps scheduled throughout each semester, as proposed in Plan I, we suggest modifying the traditional 4/4 block schedule to create what we call the "Second-Chance Semester Plan."

VARIATION 1

We begin by describing the Plan of Assistance for 38 hypothetical students in Grade 8 who did not complete a sufficient number of credits to be promoted to Grade 9, which is housed in the local high school. In our example, many of the 38 retained students had multiple absences and had put forth little effort in their classes. Although several of the middle school teachers were of the opinion that retention would not "fix" the many problems of the 38 students, the teachers felt that they could not in good conscience send the students on to high school. The teachers also believed that having the retained students repeat their failed classes along with other students would be unlikely to produce any better results than those seen the previous year; therefore, the Second-Chance Semester Plan was proposed.

The retained students were treated as a cohort group and placed in four core classes scheduled in a modified 4/4 scheduling format during the fall semester. As shown in Figure 8.9, two of the core classes, Language Arts 8 and Mathematics 8 or Pre-algebra, are scheduled for the full 90-minute block for the entire semester. Repeats of science and social studies are scheduled during Block III on an alternating-day basis.

Two questions may arise. First, why is more time given to language arts and mathematics than to science and social studies? This reflects the regular time allocation; the eighth grade operates a four-block schedule, with two year-long blocks devoted to language arts and mathematics and one year-long block shared by science and social studies. Second, why allow less time (one semester instead of two) to repeat the course? We assume students learned at least some of the material presented in the original class. In many states, this practice is permitted for all repeated courses; a student repeating a class does not have to spend as much time to earn a credit as a student who is taking the class for the first time. In an ideal situation, we would customize the repeat sections as much as possible based on the percentage of objectives mastered during the student's first attempt.

During the remaining 90-minute block (Block IV), these students are regrouped with other students in Grade 8 and provided a physical education/health class and an elective class scheduled on an alternating-day basis; that is, the students attend a PE/health class every other day for the entire semester. Opposite the PE/health class, students may enroll in an elective, such as band, follow an exploratory rotation wheel, receive extended instructional time in selected subjects, or be assigned a supervised study hall period.

Any students in this cohort group who pass a sufficient number of their fall classes to meet the district's requirement for eighth grade completion are permitted to go to the high school and enter Grade 9 at the beginning of the spring semester. This plan is possible if the high school were also on a 4/4 schedule.

If 22 of the 38 students completed eighth grade and moved to the high school in January, they could enroll in four high-school credit classes and ultimately maintain the possibility of graduating with their original class. Keeping alive the possibility that students can graduate with their age-

FIGURE 8.9. PLAN II, VARIATION 1: SAMPLE MODIFIED FOUR-BLOCK MIDDLE SCHOOL SCHEDULE FOR RETAINED GRADE 8 STUDENTS

Periods	Fall Semester	Spring Semester
1	Language Arts 8 (Repeat Course)	English 9* (New Course)
2		
3	Math 8 or Pre-algebra (Repeat Course)	Algebra I, Part 1* or Other Math (New Course)
4		
Lunch	(30 minutes)	(30 minutes)
5	Social Studies (Repeat Course)	World Geography* or Spanish I* (New Course)
6	Science (Repeat Course)	
7	Exploratory or Elective	Exploratory or Elective
8	PE/Health	PE/Health

* If a student still needs to omplete 8th grade courses during the semester, they may be scheduled in place of these high school courses.

group peers seems to be a critical factor in reducing the number of students who leave high school.

During the second semester the 16 students remaining at the middle school would be given yet another opportunity to pass the courses that they had failed first semester. It would be possible, however, to begin earning some high school credit. If a student passed Mathematics 8 first semester, why not let the student try to earn a high school credit for Pre-algebra or Algebra I? One block of PE/health, paired with art, music, band, or an exploratory, also would continue to be offered on an alternating-day basis.

If the students earn at least some high school credit during the spring semester of their repeat of Grade 8, and if they attend a high school offering the possibility of at least seven credits per year, they still might graduate with members of their original class. We believe that schools must keep providing incentives to stay in school and opportunities for students to succeed.

VARIATION 2

For middle schools operating a 4/4 schedule in which almost all courses meet every day for 90 minutes for one semester, the following plan could be considered. Students who failed one or more courses during the fall semester could be regrouped into a cohort. During the second semester, two of the four 90-minute blocks could be redivided into three 60-minute periods to accommodate up to three repeat classes for students. One block of 90 minutes would remain for a new course and one block would continue to be allocated to PE/health, exploratories, and electives (see Figure 8.10).

If a student needs to repeat only one course during the spring semester, the student would spend 60 minutes of a regularly scheduled 90-minute block in the repeat class; the remaining 30 minutes could be used for supervised study time, or the student could spend time in the library or in a computer lab. This student would be able to take two new courses in addition to the repeat. If a student must repeat two courses, two of the 60-minute periods are assigned for this purpose. One 60-minute period is scheduled for supervised study, tutoring, library, or computer lab. A student also could repeat three classes, although no additional time would be available for supervised study, computer lab, or the like.

FIGURE 8.10. PLAN II, VARIATION 2:
ADAPTATION DESIGNED TO ACCOMMODATE FIRST-SEMESTER
FAILURES IN MIDDLE SCHOOLS USING THE 4/4 SCHEDULE

Periods	Fall Semester	Spring Semester
1	Course 1 (90 minutes)	Repeat Course 1 (60 minutes)
2		Repeat Course 2 (60 minutes)
3	Course 2 (90 minutes)	
4		Repeat Course 3 (60 minutes)
Lunch	*(30 minutes)*	*(30 minutes)*
5	Course 3 (90 minutes)	New Course 5 (90 minutes)
6		
7	Course 4 (90 minutes)	New Course 6 (90 minutes)
8		

VARIATION 3

Another version of the above plan is for those students who cannot or will not do any schoolwork outside of school. In Figure 8.11, we suggest that students repeat failed fall semester courses during the spring semester in a different format. Again, the regular school day is organized around the 4/4 block schedule, but for those students repeating courses, teachers would plan to teach during approximately one-half of the block and then supervise all homework and follow-up study during the remainder of the block. If students do not have word processors at home, they should be permitted to do their written work at school. If students need access to calculators or computer labs, then let's provide them with *supervised work time* at school. We base this recommendation on the fact that sometimes a student fails simply because the student did not *turn in* sufficient work to earn credit. Students who have strong support systems at home tend to be better at meeting out-of-school requirements. Having designated time at school with supervised assistance should increase the odds that a greater number of students will be successful in their courses.

FIGURE 8.11. PLAN II, VARIATION 3: ADAPTATION DESIGNED TO ACCOMMODATE FIRST SEMESTER FAILURES IN MIDDLE SCHOOLS USING THE 4/4 SCHEDULE

Periods	Fall Semester	Spring Semester
1	Course 1 (90 minutes)	Repeat Course 1 (45 minutes)
2		Support for Repeat Course 1
3	Course 2 (90 minutes)	Repeat Course 2 (45 minutes)
4		Support for Repeat Course 2
Lunch	(30 minutes)	(30 minutes)
5	Course 3 (90 minutes)	New Course 5 (90 minutes)
6		
7	Course 4 (90 minutes)	New Course 6 (90 minutes)
8		

PLAN III:
DESIGNING A SCHEDULE THAT INSTITUTIONALIZES PERIODIC INTENSIVE REMEDIAL INTERVENTIONS AND/OR ENRICHMENT

In Plan III, temporary focused groups are formed for specific instructional needs of students. The plan is useful primarily for students who lack support from outside of the school and, for various reasons, often fail because they do not complete necessary work. These students need teacher/adult guidance at school to complete assignments successfully. Often such students have difficulty dealing with these out-of-school requirements: completing a research paper, retaking a major test, making up work after a lengthy absence, and completing projects for a Science Fair or Parent Night at school.

In Plan III, we suggest building into the school schedule designated days throughout the year that provide extended learning time for *specific purposes*. Again, we use the school schedule as a resource to institutionalize what we believe to be a good practice—ensuring extended periods of time when students have access to the materials and labs they need to complete important assignments. The plan also provides time for teachers to regroup students on a temporary basis in order to give assistance to students when extra help is needed.

We begin by offering four examples that adapt the middle school four-block schedule or 4/4 block schedule. The plan illustrated in Figure 8.12 shows how teachers can have 1 day every 20 school days to work with each of their classes all day. The schedule also permits each teacher or each team of teachers to have a full day for personal and team planning every 20 days.

This example shows a middle school on a four-block or 4/4 schedule in which a teaching team has Block IV for planning. Core teachers instruct during Blocks I, II, and III on Monday, Tuesday, Thursday, and Friday. On Wednesday of Week 1, all teachers having Block IV for planning teach their Block I courses and students all day; on Wednesday of Week 2, they work with students in Block II courses all day; on Wednesday of Week 3, they have students in Block III all day; and on Wednesday of Week 4, this particular team of teachers has the full day for planning. Of course, the particular day that a team has for planning and for full-day instruction depends on which block is that team's planning block. If the team plans during Block I, then the first Wednesday of the cycle is a planning day. The team works with Course 2 students on the second Wednesday, Course 3 students on the third Wednesday, and Course 4 students on the fourth Wednesday. During the days when a teacher has a class all day, it is suggested that the time be spent primarily in helping students complete

FIGURE 8.12. EXTENDED CLASS TIME AND TEACHER PLANNING BLOCKS IN THE FOUR-BLOCK OR 4/4 SEMESTER PLAN: ONE DAY FOR TEACHER PLANNING EVERY 20 SCHOOL DAYS

	Mon.	Tues.	Wed.				Thurs.	Fri.
			W1	W2	W3	W4		
Block I	Course 1	Course 1	C1	C2	C3	C4	Course 1	Course 1
Block II	Course 2	Course 2	C1	C2	C3	C4	Course 2	Course 2
Lunch	Lunch							
Block III	Course 3	Course 3	C1	C2	C3	C4	Course 3	Course 3
Block IV	Course 4	Course 4	C1	C2	C3	C4	Course 4	Course 4

This plan provides one full day for individual teachers and/or teams of teachers to work with groups of students once every 20 days.

delayed assignments or assignments requiring special materials, support, and supervision.

The situation shown in Figure 8.12 involves the entire school. What if only one team wants to create a schedule in which they have extended class periods with each of their sections on some kind of rotational basis? Figure 8.13 (p. 217) offers this possibility. Block IV is designated for team planning; all students on the team attend PE, exploratory classes, or electives during this time. This block remains constant. During Blocks I through III all students are in core classes. On each of three consecutive Wednesdays, teachers could work with one of their three classes for the entire core block.

In this situation, it also would be possible to group and regroup students within teams to complete specific tasks or to provide remedial assistance; other students may be provided enrichment and/or additional exploratory opportunities. For example, members of one team might decide that on the first Wednesday of the cycle, all students would be regrouped as follows: (a) one of the teachers would work with enrichment groups; (b) one would work with math students needing extra help on a particular topic; c) one teacher would assist students in language arts, for example, on specific writing skills identified during the past 15 days as needing work; and (d) one teacher would be responsible for working with all students assigned to the team who needed help with their research projects and test make-ups.

**FIGURE 8.13. EXTENDED CLASS TIME FOR CORE CLASSES IN
THE FOUR-BLOCK OR 4/4 SEMESTER PLAN: ONE DAY FOR
EXTENDED CLASSES EVERY 15 SCHOOL DAYS**

	Mon.	Tues.	Wed.			Thurs.	Fri.
			W1	W2	W3		
Block I	Course 1	Course 1	C1	C2	C3	Course 1	Course 1
Block II	Course 2	Course 2	C1	C2	C3	Course 2	Course 2
Lunch	Lunch						
Block III	Course 3	Course 3	C1	C2	C3	Course 3	Course 3
Block IV	PE/Electives/Exploratories; Teacher Planning						

This plan provides one full day for individual teachers and/or teams of teachers to work with groups of students once every 15 days.

Figure 8.14 illustrates another variation; teachers and students complete the rotation in one 5-day week. In this example, this group of teachers meets all of their classes in regular-length blocks on Monday. Then on Tuesday of the same week, they work with students in Course 1 all day; on Wednesday, Course 2; on Thursday, Course 3; and on Friday they have a full day for planning.

**FIGURE 8.14. EXTENDED TEACHER TEACHING TIME AND PLANNING
BLOCKS IN THE FOUR-BLOCK OR 4/4 SEMESTER PLAN: ONE FULL DAY
FOR TEACHER PLANNING AND CLASS MEETINGS IN A SELECTED 4-DAY CYCLE**

	Mon.	Tues.	Wed.	Thurs.	Fri.
Block I	Course 1	Course 1	Course 2	Course 3	Course 4
Block II	Course 2	Course 1	Course 2	Course 3	Course 4
Block III	Course 3	Course 1	Course 2	Course 3	Course 4
Block IV	Course 4	Course 1	Course 2	Course 3	Course 4

Teachers in schools on the four-block or 4/4 block might prefer just a half-day for the activities described above; in which event, the modified schedule shown in Figure 8.15 (p. 218) is appropriate. Again, we show a teacher's schedule with Block IV for planning. This teacher has a half-day with each of her three classes on Days 1 to 3 and a half-day for planning on Day 4.

FIGURE 8.15. EXTENDED TEACHER PLANNING BLOCKS IN THE 4/4 SEMESTER PLAN: ONE HALF-DAY FOR EXTENDED CLASS TIME FOR STUDENT SUPPORT ON A 4-DAY CYCLE

	Day 1	*Day 2*	*Day 3*	*Day 4*
Block I *90 min.*	Course 1	Course 2	Course 3	**Course 4**
Block II *90 min.*	Course 1	Course 2	Course 3	**Course 4**
Lunch	Lunch			
Block III *90 min.*	Course 2	Course 1	Course 1	Course 2
Block IV *90 min.*	Course 3	**Course 4**	**Course 4**	Course 3

For a school with an alternating-day or A/B schedule, Plan III is an option (see Figure 8.16, p. 219). The A/B schedule in this example is based on a seven-period school day with Period 5 remaining a single period. On Mondays and Thursdays Periods 1, 3, and 7 are blocked and on Tuesdays and Fridays Periods 2, 4, and 6 are blocked, which explains why this particular alternating schedule sometimes is referred to as an Odd/Even schedule. On Wednesdays the schedule is rotated so that on the first Wednesday of the cycle, classes scheduled during Period 1 meet all day, on the second Wednesday of the cycle, Period 2 classes meet all day, and so on. Teachers have the full day for planning depending on their assigned planning period. For example, if a teacher's planning periods are 3 and 6, then the teacher's full planning days are W3, the third Wednesday of the cycle, and W6, the sixth Wednesday of the cycle.

For a school that employs a traditional, daily single-period schedule this same idea can be utilized as illustrated in Figure 8.17 (p. 219). All seven classes meet as single periods on Mondays, Tuesdays, Thursdays, and Fridays. During the first Wednesday, all students and teachers having assignments during Period 1 meet; those having classes during Period 2 meet the second Wednesday, and so on. Again, teacher full-day planning days vary according to the periods they are assigned for planning.

FIGURE 8.16. EXTENDED BLOCKS FOR STUDENT SUPPORT AND TEACHER PLANNING (BASED ON A 7-COURSE ALTERNATING-DAY SCHEDULE)

Mon.	Tues.	Wed. 1	Wed. 2	Wed. 3	Wed. 4	Wed. 5	Wed. 6	Wed. 7	Thurs.	Fri.
1	2	1	2	3	4	5	6	7	1	2
1	2	1	2	3	4	5	6	7	1	2
3	4	1	2	3	4	5	6	7	3	4
3	4	1	2	3	4	5	6	7	3	4
5	5	1	2	3	4	5	6	7	5	5
7	6	1	2	3	4	5	6	7	7	6
7	6	1	2	3	4	5	6	7	7	6

A different class meets for the entire day every Wednesday; the cycle completes over a 7-week period.

FIGURE 8.17. EXTENDED BLOCKS FOR STUDENT SUPPORT AND TEACHER PLANNING (BASED ON A 7-PERIOD-DAY SCHEDULE)

Mon.	Tues.	Wed. 1	Wed. 2	Wed. 3	Wed. 4	Wed. 5	Wed. 6	Wed. 7	Thurs.	Fri.
1	1	1	2	3	4	5	6	7	1	1
2	2	1	2	3	4	5	6	7	2	2
3	3	1	2	3	4	5	6	7	3	3
4	4	1	2	3	4	5	6	7	4	4
5	5	1	2	3	4	5	6	7	5	5
6	6	1	2	3	4	5	6	7	6	6
7	7	1	2	3	4	5	6	7	7	7

A different class meets for the entire day every Wednesday; the cycle completes over a 7-week period.

CONCLUSION

Educators know that all students do not learn at the same rate. Typical middle school and high school schedules are not designed to address this truth; in most schools, all students are allotted equal time for learning. For some students, the time provided is too long; boredom sets in. For other students, insufficient time is provided; when critical skills and content are not mastered, frustration and failure result. If all students are to master Algebra I and other higher level mathematics courses successfully, schedules must be devised in which *time,* rather than *achievement,* becomes the variable.

9

TEACHING IN THE MIDDLE SCHOOL BLOCK SCHEDULE

Our experience in working with middle and high schools in over 40 states, and our talking with hundreds of teachers, students, and school administrators, convinces us that a major need that must be addressed with full implementation of block scheduling in middle and high schools is helping teachers gain the necessary strategies and skills to teach successfully in a large block of time. Although we have found that adapting to "teaching in the block" is easier for middle school teachers than for high school teachers, we fear that if all teachers do not alter techniques to utilize extended blocks of time effectively and efficiently, many of the benefits of block scheduling will be missed and students will not experience the full potential of block scheduling.

We must remember that we have several generations of teachers in our schools who "grew up" working in traditional single-period schedules in which they were expected to see five or six groups of students each for 40 to 50 minutes daily. We contend that such a scheduling format almost forces teachers into a mode of instruction in which a typical class begins with "Come on students, let's get quiet!" Then comes roll call, followed by a review of what was taught the previous day. Next, some new information is introduced, typically by the teacher, who may use a chalkboard or an overhead transparency. After this "teacher talk," a few questions are asked, with a few class members responding. Finally, independent work might be assigned, which if unfinished in class often becomes homework. Those students with strong support systems at home typically are the only ones who complete such assignments on a regular basis.

We believe that it is unreasonable to expect teachers to adapt to large blocks of instructional time with either enthusiasm or success if school districts do not offer both generic and subject-specific staff development and support during both pre-block and the first two years of implementation. New teachers coming into the school also must be provided intensive staff development and support.

A critical question for persons involved with block scheduling is this: *Do teachers in America truly want the time to teach?* We find that the majority of teachers do! We argue that a change to block scheduling can become a catalyst for teachers to seek different teaching strategies—many teachers are quick to perceive this need and to ask for help.

We urge school personnel *not* to move to any form of block scheduling if teachers are not provided with a *minimum* of 5, and hopefully 10 days, of staff development that is both generic and subject-specific. These workshop days must be designed to allow teachers to participate in activities with a high degree of engagement; it would be most inappropriate to just "talk to" teachers. In these workshops, strategies must be modeled for teachers who later must design instruction for students in large blocks of time. Later in this chapter, we offer specific suggestions for the content we recommend for 5-day and 10-day workshops to assist teachers in *surviving* and then *thriving* in the block! We begin, however, by describing a lesson-planning format designed for long instructional blocks. We follow this with a discussion about teaching techniques that we believe can help teachers to utilize blocks effectively.

THREE-PART LESSON DESIGN: EXPLANATION, APPLICATION, AND SYNTHESIS[1]

We have observed that teachers who are most successful in block scheduling typically plan lessons in three parts. We have "borrowed" the terms explanation, application, and synthesis to describe these parts (Hunter, 1976, 1982; Bloom, 1956).

EXPLANATION

Depending on the length of the block and the nature of the lesson or topic, teachers spend 25 to 40 minutes in what we call explanation. To some extent, during explanation, teachers do what many teachers have done for years. They are "on stage," usually in front of the class. They may or may not call on students for various responses, but, for the most part, they use chalkboards, overhead projectors, and various types of materials to explain what students are to learn. During this instructional phase of the lesson, teachers often do what some call direct instruction and may include the steps described as Hunter's lesson design (Hunter, 1976). During explanation the focus is on what is to be learned, appreciated, constructed, dissected, prepared, developed, located, discussed, written, or performed. This step includes identifying objectives, specifying tasks to

---

1 Adapted from Canady and Rettig, 1995b, Chapter 8.

be completed and demonstrating to students how to meet the learning expectations successfully. During the explanation phase teachers may, for example, illustrate how to solve a particular math problem, write a succinct thesis statement, construct or read a time line in history, or store and retrieve computer data.

APPLICATION

Following 25 to 40 minutes of explanation, experienced block teachers usually move into a phase that we call "application," which extends for 30 to 60 minutes. Here students become more active learners, and teachers become more like coaches and facilitators. Students are assisted in applying what the teacher has been explaining; some call this phase of the lesson "hands-on" time. We define the application phase of a lesson broadly; as a minimum students need to become less passive and more active. Ideally, some physical movement may occur; the teacher might direct students to "stand up and discuss these three points with your lab partner," or to rearrange their chairs in preparation for a Socratic seminar. Even a trip to the media center or to a writing lab may be part of this lesson phase. We believe that, as a minimum, the application phase must include some form of "structured talk" with time for feedback and an opportunity to respond to lingering questions on the part of students.

We have noted that it is the application phase that is most difficult for teachers to implement. Apparently, many teachers do not possess sufficient strategies and/or have the classroom management skills to plan and implement active-learning activities that give students opportunities to use and apply what was taught during the explanation phase. We suggest that staff development efforts preceding the implementation of a block schedule focus primarily on helping teachers gain skills and confidence in preparing lessons that involve students and move them toward applying what they are expected to learn. Too often, teaching, learning, and testing never move beyond regurgitating "what the teacher said." *As long as the application phase of a lesson is short-changed or eliminated, retention of learning will be limited.*

Some practical examples of activities used during the application phase of a lesson include:

♦ *A language arts teacher* engages students in the writing process or simply allows students to use computers for word processing to correct their papers based on feedback from the teacher and/or writers' workshop group. Another teacher accompanies the class to the library to assist students with some specific research to help them begin a research paper (see Strzepek, Newton, & Walker, 2000).

♦ *A social studies teacher* conducts a Paideia seminar (see Ball &
Brewer, 2000); the following day students prepare position papers individually, in pairs, or in teams based on the seminar
topic discussed during the previous class meeting. Later, during the unit of work, the teacher provides opportunities for
students to experience how a historian goes about the task of
locating, discovering, identifying, classifying, and writing history by assigning students to become a historian for a period
of time in their community. They might develop guides for interviewing selected community members, or they might decide to invite guests to come to school for class or small group
interviews. Students might start by visiting a local cemetery to
collect information relative to a particular period of history,
such as the years 1941 to 1945. Do they know any of the fami-
lies who had sons or daughters die during World War II?
Would they want to interview any of those family members?
In what theater of operations (Europe or the Pacific) did their
family member die? Do they know how he/she died? What
was it like living in their local community during that war?
What was rationing? How did it work? The goal is to help students make history real and alive, not just something that occurred in the past that we now need to memorize. (For additional application-phase ideas for history teachers, see Cohen,
1995.)

♦ *A science teacher* moves to a laboratory activity during the application phase or conducts a Paideia seminar on a topic such
as the ethics of genetic engineering. Or, at the beginning of a
unit, the teacher involves the class in a concept-development
lesson; students brainstorm what they know about the proposed topic of study and then, with teacher assistance, begin
to classify and categorize their information into useful concepts. Utilizing a KWL chart (What do we Know? What do we
Want to learn? What have we Learned?) might be an appropriate application strategy; students complete the chart at the end
of each lesson for several days throughout the unit.

♦ *A mathematics teacher* accompanies students to the computer
laboratory for work on their current topic, or the students
work in pairs in the commons area of the school applying specific principles of measurement that were explained earlier in
the block. (For additional ideas for multiapplication strategies
in mathematics see Gilkey & Hunt, 1998.)

♦ *A foreign language teacher* takes the class to the language lab as
part of the lesson or brings in a native speaker of the language

to provide practice to students. (For additional ideas for the application phase of a lesson in a foreign language, see Blaz, 1998.)

- If the school were following one of the schedules proposed in Chapter 8, which gives teachers one full day per month with each of their classes, a middle school class might spend all or part of that day visiting a museum, attending a concert, observing in a courtroom or police station, or shadowing a hospital emergency room nurse. Later, students could use the application time in the block recording their observations, perhaps using a computer. Or students might watch a tape of court proceedings and develop a story from a segment of the trial.

We found that many teachers, especially in physical education, the vocational arts, and some of the performing arts, such as theater, dance, and drama, often welcome longer blocks of instructional time and have no difficulty designing application activities. Our experience is that staff development in appropriate active learning strategies is more critical for teachers of mathematics, social sciences, English, health, and foreign languages.

SYNTHESIS

The third instructional phase in lessons designed for block teaching is similar to Bloom's (1956) concept of "synthesis," but also includes some elements of what Madeline Hunter (1976, 1982) termed "closure." This part of the lesson usually consumes 15 to 30 minutes, depending on the content of the lesson and the length of the block. During the synthesis phase of the lesson, the teacher involves the students in connecting the explanation part of the lesson with the application phase. It is a time for reflection, review, and sometimes reteaching; as one teacher said to us: "It is a critical phase when the teacher, hopefully by leading the students, helps give meaning to the lesson." Sometimes, when appropriate, it may be a time to help answer the student's question: "Why are we learning this stuff? What can we ever do with it?" The relevance of the day's learning should be reaffirmed during the synthesis phase. It also is a time to clarify critical elements of the lesson, to complete student note taking, and to suggest what is planned for the next class session.

Depending on the concept to be taught, the basic building blocks of this lesson format might be rearranged. It may be appropriate, at times, to conduct the application phase of the lesson first, especially when the teacher's goal is for students to "discover" the concept. For example, a science teacher might purposefully conduct a demonstration or have students perform an experiment prior to any "explanation." The "explanation" phase then becomes an analysis of what students observed and an attempt to have them infer the scientific concepts illustrated by the demonstration or experiment. Such a lesson follows the format Application, Explanation, Synthesis, rather than the Explanation, Application, Synthesis order described above.

We do not mean to be excessively critical of teachers. Collectively we have spent over seven decades teaching both in rural and urban public schools and in college and university classrooms. To a large extent we are expressing and admitting our own frustrations and deficits. We also have worked in hundreds of middle and high schools across America conducting workshops and making presentations. It is our conclusion that for years teachers were trained and expected to teach in short, fragmented, daily periods of time, and that they developed teaching practices that "fit the schedule" given them! If teachers must plan to teach in 40 to 50 minutes of time, do all the administrative work expected of them during each class period, see 100 to 180 students per day, and prepare 3 to 6 preparations each day, no wonder we see so much unenthusiastic lecturing as we walk through school hallways throughout America! What else should we expect?

We have found the three-part lesson design—Explanation, Application, Synthesis—to be simple and easy to explain to teachers; however, we believe the following design, which draws from Hunter and other direct-instruction models and which was reconfigured by Hotchkiss (1996, p. 24), also offers a valuable format for designing lessons be delivered in an extended block of time.

The Hotchkiss model (see Figure 9.1) starts with an opportunity for homework review and feedback; she suggests that teachers might take the first 10 to 12 minutes of a 90-minute block for this. One or more of the interactive strategies offered by Kagan (1990) could be used to engage students and allow the teacher an opportunity to move about the room to monitor and give individual and small group assistance where needed. It seems to us that teachers of mathematics and foreign languages particularly could use the ideas suggested.

Following homework check, Hotchkiss suggests that the teacher determine what is the best way to present the material for today's lesson. Do I use some type of technology, such as Powerpoint presentation software? Do I engage the students in a Socratic seminar? Do I use a lecture format with some built-in interactive strategies? Do I use an inquiry model in presenting the lesson? Do I use a cooperative learning strategy? This decision is a critical step in formulating the lesson plan. It seems to us that the appropriate format should be based on the following:

♦ What is the primary goal of the lesson?

♦ What are students in this class expected to be able to do at the close of the class?

FIGURE 9.1. DESIGNING LESSONS FOR THE BLOCK SCHEDULE WITH ACTIVE-LEARNING STRATEGIES

Homework Review (10–15 Minutes)

Inside-Outside Circles (Kagan, 1990)   Roundtable (Ch. 3)

Pairs-Check (Kagan, 1990)   Think-Pair-Share (Ch. 3)

Team Interview (Kagan, 1990)   Mix-Freeze-Group (Kagan, 1990)

Graffiti (Kagan, 1990)   Send-a-Problem (Ch. 9)

Presentation (20–25 Minutes)

Interactive Lecture (Ch. 3)   Demonstration

CD ROM (Ch. 7)   Inductive Thinking (Ch. 4)

Video Disc (Ch. 7)   Directed Reading/Thinking Activity (Ch. 8)

Videotape (Ch. 7)   Concept Attainment (Ch. 4)

Socratic Seminars (Ch. 2)   Concept Formation (Ch. 4)

Inquiry (Gunter et al., 1995)   Synectics (Ch. 4)

Direct Instruction (Ch. 9)   Memory Model (Ch. 4)

Activity (30–35 Minutes)

Role Play (Gunter et al., 1995)   Team Review

Simulation (Ch. 5)   Graffiti (Kagan, 1990)

Synectics (Ch. 4)   Roundtable (Ch. 3)

Science Laboratory   Pair-Share (Ch. 2)

Computer Reinforcement   Learning Centers (Ch. 6)

Mix-Freeze-Group (Kagan, 1990)   Send-a-Problem (Ch. 9)

Inside-Outside Circles (Kagan, 1990)   Pairs-Check (Kagan, 1990)

Writing Lab (Ch. 8)   Jigsaw (Slavin, 1986)

Teams Games Tournaments (TGT) (Slavin, 1986)   Student Teams Achievement Divisions (STAD) (Slavin, 1986; Ch. 3)

Guided Practice (10–15 Minutes)

Reteach (10–15 Minutes)

Closure (5–10 Minutes)

Adapted from Phyllis R. Hotchkiss, Hotchkiss Educational Consulting Services, Richmond, Virginia. All chapter references are from Canady, R. L. & Rettig, M. D. (1996). *Teaching in the Block*. Larchmont, NY: Eye on Education.

♦ What level of knowledge or skill is expected of students today?

♦ Will they simply be asked to recall some information, or will students solve a problem or construct a product?

♦ Must they interact or react with the material or lecture in some way? Will students analyze or synthesize and create something new?

♦ Is this class of students difficult to manage? If so, that may establish some limits on how I present a particular lesson.

These are just a few of the factors that should be considered in deciding presentation format as well as the activity to follow.

The activity section of the lesson is designed to increase the odds for retention by having the students become more engaged with the content. Hotchkiss offers several strategies, along with numerous references, that can be considered in providing students with opportunities to master the material or skill in greater depth.

After completing "homework check," "presentation," and "activity," Hotchkiss ends her format for teaching in the block by essentially following the final steps of Hunter's lesson design: First, when appropriate, offer some type of "guided practice" to determine whether and where additional teaching may be needed, and, in some cases, to give students a chance to get started on their independent practice or homework. Second, if students are experiencing difficulties during guided practice, the teacher has an opportunity to "reteach." Third, provide "closure;" the teacher might summarize the day's lesson, discuss the essential elements of the lesson and give students a chance to complete notes for the day's lesson. Closure also may include a time for the teacher to respond to student questions, to discuss the homework assignment, and to provide a brief explanation of how today's lesson connects with past and future class sessions. (For additional ideas for lessons designed for teaching in the block, see Ball & Brewer, 2000; Blaz, 1998; Canady & Rettig, 1996; Gilkey & Hunt, 1998; Strzepek, Newton, & Walker, 2000.)

INSTRUCTIONAL STRATEGIES
FOR THE BLOCK SCHEDULE

In the sections that follow, we discuss several teaching models that we believe can assist teachers in creating more active classrooms, thereby engaging the interests and efforts of their students. Each of the strategies discussed is appropriate for any kind of schedule, single-period or block; however, variety and activity undoubtedly are more critical for instruction in extended class periods. Included in this discussion are these techniques: cooperative learning, Paideia seminars, and other models of teaching such as synectics, concept development, concept attainment, and inquiry. Also, we briefly describe the possibilities for simulations, learning centers, and the use of technology. Finally, although we have stated consistently that the lecture is overused and cannot continue to be the only instructional strategy employed by teachers—especially in block scheduling—we do recognize the utility of this strategy. We conclude this section by revisiting the lecture format and offering tips for its improvement and inclusion as one of the many instructional tools of the professional educator.

COOPERATIVE LEARNING

Cooperative learning[2] is a model of teaching that has received considerable attention in recent years. Research suggests that it is an effective active teaching model for use with heterogeneous groups of students (Slavin, 1980, 1988, 1990). It is important for practitioners to learn both the theoretical basis for cooperative learning and its practical application in the classroom. While discussion in sufficient detail to enable true implementation of cooperative learning is beyond the scope of this chapter, we offer an introduction and a reference list of useful resources for those who wish to pursue this topic in greater depth. The basic formula (admittedly gross oversimplification) for the implementation of cooperative learning includes these six steps:[3]

CLASS BUILDING

In this step of the process, it is critical for students in a class to bond together as a cohesive group, *before* they are placed in smaller cooperative learning teams. All too often we leave this step to chance—hoping that the class will develop into a "good group." A variety of proactive techniques can be utilized to facilitate a positive classroom environment and esprit de corps. Basically, three kinds of strategies encourage such bonding: get-to-know-you activities, service activities, and group successes (such as working on a common problem).

We frequently have been in school classrooms in which the students barely know each other. It is unreasonable to expect students to work together cooperatively on content if no level of trust exists. Thus, activities are needed that enable students to learn each others' names, interests, likes and dislikes, to help develop a level of comfort among students which will make the success of cooperative teams more likely. Two

---

2 For additional cooperative learning strategies, we suggest these references: Strebe, 1996, Chapter 3; Kagan, 1990; and Lanzoni, 1997.
3 Adapted from Kagan (1990).

sources of such activities are *Community Building in the Classroom* (Shaw, 1992) and *Schools without Fear: Group Activities for Building Community* (Lehr & Martin, 1994).

In addition to get-to-know-you activities, class members tend to bond together when groups provide service to others. We see evidence of this truth every day as people struggling with natural disasters work together in a selfless pursuit of community good. Providing classes with opportunities to be of service to the school, individuals, or outside groups also is an effective means of class building.

Finally, any time a group meets with success, or for that matter cohesively weathers a failure, the group members become closer. Thus, challenging groups to achieve a certain attainable level of excellence and then helping the groups meet that challenge will draw the members closer together.

TEAM FORMATION

Cooperative learning teams can be composed in three different manners: teacher selection, student selection, or random selection. Most often teachers create cooperative learning teams by dividing students into groups of four or five students. We generally recommend that each team be heterogenous in composition based primarily on the most important abilities or skills in a particular subject area, especially if the teacher plans to have the teams compete against each other. Thus, teams in mathematics might be organized based upon quiz scores or the results of a unit pretest, while physical education teams could be based upon speed, strength, and agility. Regardless, an effort is usually made to create teams that also are heterogeneous based on gender, racial or ethnic background, socioeconomic status, and/or a variety of other student characteristics.

Student-selected teams occasionally are used, especially when the focus of the teams' efforts is a project requiring substantial effort outside school. We have seen one creative way in which a high school teacher in Virginia enlisted the aid of students in forming balanced cooperative learning teams. In his class of 24 students, the teacher selected 6 students to be the "team formation" committee. These students were challenged by the teacher to meet privately and create six balanced three-person teams from among the remaining students in the class. The teacher then assigned one member of the committee to each team, thus creating six four-member teams. This procedure encouraged the committee to form fair and equal teams. Different students composed the committee each time teams were reformed.

Finally, teachers occasionally create teams through random procedures such as line-ups and numbering-off (Kagan, 1990). These groups typically are formed for the sole purpose of class building and stay together only a short time.

In general, we recommend that teams be kept together approximately 4½ to 6 weeks; that should be long enough for students to form a close working relationship, but short enough that social issues do not override the academic benefits. By keeping teams together for this duration, teachers can limit the amount of time students with personality conflicts are kept together and also guarantee friends that at some point during the school year they will be on the same team. In any case, we suggest that teachers inform students in advance of the number of weeks teams will stay together; if not, students will lobby either to disband early if they are unhappy with their teams, or to stay together for eternity, if the opposite is true.

TEAM BUILDING AND TEAM IDENTITY

Similar to the step of class building, which is designed to draw the entire group together, the steps of team building and team identity are utilized to bond a four- or five-person cooperative learning team together. Typically, for team building, get-to-know-you activities are employed that facilitate positive student interaction. For example, the three-step interview (Kagan, 1990) is a useful cooperative learning structure that helps students get to know each other. In this simple activity, students within a four-person team pair off, one in each pair becoming the interviewer and one the interviewee. A set of generic questions is created, such as these:

- What's your name?
- Tell me something about your family.
- Tell me about your school career.
- What are your hobbies and interests?
- Tell me something interesting about yourself that others might not know.

Students in both pairs interview each other with these questions, write down the responses, and then, in a round-robin format, introduce their partners to the other pair within the team.

Another simple team-building strategy attempts to have all students on the team agree on likes and dislikes. For example, they may attempt to agree on a food, a movie, an actress, a political leader, a place, and an activity that they all like, as well as ones they dislike. The teams then share these commonalities with the rest of the class. Discovering these common likes and dislikes begins to bond the team members together. (See Canady & Rettig, 1996, Chapter 3, for several examples of "Things-in-Common" sheets.)

As with team building, allowing teams to develop an identity brings the members together. Once students become familiar with each other they are asked to create a team name, design a team sign, and develop a team handshake. Signs are posted and handshakes are demonstrated to the other teams. Often team pictures are taken with an instant camera. Each of these activities takes time, but theoretically the time lost to team building and the development of a team identity is recouped later because of the close and efficient working relationships that become established.

COOPERATIVE LEARNING STRUCTURES

In the parlance of cooperative learning, "structures" are generic activities that may be utilized and adapted to any grade level and any subject matter. Cooperative learning is far more complex than simply throwing an activity at a group of students and saying: "Work together on this task." We know what happens when this occurs. Certain students take over, either through force of their personality, or because no one else exhibits much interest in the task. Other students become "free-riders," do nothing, and create animosity because of their refusal to participate. Thus, structuring activities carefully is an important aspect of the successful cooperative learning classroom. To be effective, cooperative learning structures, as a minimum, must meet these four criteria:

1. The structure must have a *group goal*. A task must be created for students that results in a group product or group evaluation of some sort. For example, in the three-step interview, described previously, the group goal is for the team to get to know each other better.

2. The group goal must be met through the *face-to-face interaction* of all team members. In well-designed structures, team members do not toil in total independence. At least part of the work must be completed through discussion and interaction among members. Again, in the three-step interview students are required to interact while interviewing their partners, and again when they introduce their partners to the other pair in the team.

3. The face-to-face interaction must result in a state of *positive interdependence* in which all student contributions are necessary and no one student's contribution is sufficient. This is the idea that the participation of all team members is necessary for success. If even one member does not pull his or her weight, the team cannot be successful. We sink or swim together. During the three-step interview, if a team member decides not to cooperate, it is impossible for the partner to complete his or her job and thus the activity falls apart.

4. Finally, and perhaps most often overlooked, although students are somewhat dependent on each other, *individual ac-*

countability is emphasized and carefully orchestrated. The essence of cooperative learning is that *we work together, we learn together, but we are held individually accountable for our own learning.* Thus, in the interview, each team member is held accountable because he or she is asked to write answers to the questions and to introduce his or her partner. These activities can be checked by the teacher, thereby providing the necessary individual accountability.

GROUP PROCESSING AND EVALUATION

The final step of the process of implementing cooperative learning in the classroom is for team members and the teacher to debrief regarding students' contributions to group efforts. Students are encouraged to self-evaluate and peer evaluate. Often, as part of this step, group rewards and recognition are provided, although much controversy exists regarding the appropriateness and effectiveness of extrinsic rewards in the cooperative learning classroom (Kohn, 1991).

Cooperative learning techniques can be adapted to work with students of all ages. Experts in the field include Robert Slavin (1990), David and Roger Johnson (1987, 1990), and Spencer Kagan (1990). Common structures include Roundtable, Pairs Check, Jigsaw, Numbered Heads Together, Think-Pair-Share, Corners, Send-a-Problem, Inside-Outside Circles, Student Teams Achievement Divisions (STAD), as well as others. This discussion is merely a brief introduction to the potential of cooperative learning. Readers desiring more information should consult the reference list and consider attending one of the various training sessions offered around the country each year.

One strategy that we find to be particularly useful was developed by John Strebe, a mathematics teacher from Mt. Hebron High School in Howard County, Maryland. *1, 2, 4* is a great technique for enhancing the learning that occurs when using a worksheet. After a worksheet is distributed, students are told to enter the *1* mode. They are instructed to turn away from their teammates and to work silently on the worksheet for a fixed amount of time (such as 5 minutes). The operative word during *1* mode is *Respect*; students are to respect other students' right to work in a quiet, distraction-free environment. When time is up the teacher directs students to enter 2 mode, in which students meet with preassigned partners to discuss their responses. The operative word during this phase is *Defend*; students are to defend their responses, trying to come to agreement. After a fixed period of time in 2 mode, the teacher calls out *4*. Two pairs come together to try and achieve *Consensus*. Following this step groups may be asked to share their responses with the entire class. *1, 2, 4* allows a teacher to get much greater mileage from a simple worksheet by engaging students with both the material and each other.

We believe that the proper application of cooperative learning techniques is the single most effective means of providing active learning strategies for a wide variety of teachers and students during the application stage of lessons designed for extended blocks of time. We end with a few ideas to get teachers started:

SEVENTEEN QUICK COOPERATIVE STARTERS[4]

1. Turn to Your Neighbor: 3 to 5 minutes. Ask the students to turn to a neighbor and ask something about the lesson; for example, to explain a concept you've just taught; to explain the assignment; to explain how to do what you've just taught; to summarize the three most important points of the discussion; or whatever fits the lesson.

2. Reading Groups: Students read material together and answer the questions. One person is the Reader, another the Recorder, and the third the Checker (who checks to make certain everyone understands and agrees with the answers). They must come up with three possible answers to each question and circle their favorite one. When finished, they sign the paper to certify that they all understand and agree on the answers.

3. Jigsaw: Each person reads and studies part of a selection, then teaches what he or she has learned to the other members of the group. Each then quizzes the group members until satisfied that everyone knows his or her part thoroughly.

4. Focus Trios: Before a film, lecture, or reading, have students summarize together what they already know about the subject and come up with questions they have about it. Afterwards, the trios answer questions, discuss new information, and formulate new questions.

5. Drill Partners: Have students drill each other on the facts they need to know until they are certain both partners know and can remember them all. This works for spelling, vocabulary, math, grammar, test review, and other fact-centered exercises. Give bonus points on the test if all members score above a certain percentage.

6. Worksheet Checkmates: Have two students, each with different jobs, do one worksheet. The Reader reads, then suggests an answer; the Writer either agrees or comes up with another

---

4 Developed from Johnson, D., Johnson, R., & Holubec, E. (1990). *Circles of Learning: Cooperation in the Classroom.* Edina, MN: Interaction Book.

answer. When they both understand and agree on an answer, the Writer can write it. Then students switch roles.

7. Homework Checkers: Have students compare homework answers, discuss any they have not answered similarly, then correct their papers and add the reason they changed an answer. They make certain everyone's answers agree, then staple the papers together. The teacher grades one paper from each group and gives group members that grade.

8. Test Reviewers: Have students prepare each other for a test. They get bonus points if every group member scores above a preset level.

9. Composition Pairs: Student A explains what he or she plans to write, while Student B takes notes or makes an outline. Together they plan the opening or thesis statement. Then Student B explains while Student A writes. They exchange outlines, and use them in writing their papers.

10. Problem Solvers: Give groups a problem to solve. Each student must contribute to part of the solution. Groups can decide who does what, but they must show where all members contributed. Or, they can come up with the solution together, but each must be able to explain how to solve the problem.

11. Computer Groups: Students work together on the computer. They must agree on the input before it is entered. One person is the Keyboard Operator, another the Monitor Reader, a third the Verifier (who collects opinions on the input from the other two and makes the final decision). Roles are rotated daily so everyone gets experience at all three jobs.

12. Book or News Report Pairs: Students interview each other on the books or news item they read; then they report on their partner's materials.

13. Writing Response Groups: Students read and respond to each other's papers three times:

a. They mark what they like with a star and put a question mark anywhere there is something they don't understand or think is weak. Then they discuss the paper as a whole with the writer.

b. They mark problems with grammar, usage, punctuation, spelling, or format and discuss them with the author.

c. They proofread the final draft and point out any errors for the author to correct.

Teachers can assign questions for students to answer about their group members' papers to help them focus on certain problems or skills.

14. Skill Teachers/Concept Clarifiers: Students work in pairs on skills (such as identifying adjectives in sentences or completing a proof in geometry) and/or concepts (such as "ecology" or "economics") until both can perform the operation or explain the content easily.

15. Group Reports: Students research a topic together. Each is responsible for checking at least one different source and writing at least three notecards of information. They write the report together; each is responsible for seeing that his or her information is included. For oral reports, each must take a part and help the others rehearse until they are all at ease.

16. Summary Pairs: Have students alternate reading and orally summarizing paragraphs. One reads and summarizes while the other checks the paragraph for accuracy and adds anything left out. They alternate roles with each paragraph.

17. Elaborating and Relating Pairs: Have students elaborate on what they are reading and learning by relating it to what they already know about the subject. This can be done before and after a reading selection, listening to a lecture, or seeing a film.

PAIDEIA SEMINAR TEACHING[5]

The Paideia seminar is a group discussion technique developed by Mortimer Adler (1982) and first discussed in his book *The Paideia Proposal*. This Socratic teaching method focuses on a selection of text or a specific material, such as a video, that all participants must review and examine prior to the seminar. Very specific rules govern the participation of both teachers and students; it is distinctively different from a "typical" class discussion. For example, often in a class discussion, students may see the discussion as a "frill" just for a "participation" grade; if you miss class, "so what; it was just a discussion!"

The Paideia seminar is most frequently utilized in English, the social sciences, and the humanities, but it can be adapted for use in any discipline. Its use requires specific intensive instruction by skilled trainers. The following description of this strategy, sometimes referred to as a Socratic

---

5 For additional information on Paideia seminars, the reader is encouraged to see Ball & Brewer, 2000; and Canady & Rettig, 1996, Chap. 2.

seminar, may be helpful in demonstrating how teachers might employ the seminar during the application phase of a lesson in a block schedule.

THE SEMINAR[6]

The Socratic seminar is a strategy for creating active learners as students engage in the exploration and evaluation of ideas. In a Socratic seminar, the students and teacher examine a text as partners. The effectiveness of the seminar depends primarily upon the text being reviewed, the questions asked, the teacher who leads the seminar, and the students who participate. Considering each of these four components of a seminar helps explain its unique character and format.

THE STUDENTS

In a Socratic seminar, the students share with the teacher the responsibility for the quality of the seminar. Good seminars occur when the students read the text before the seminar occurs, listen courteously and attentively, share their ideas and questions in response to the ideas and questions of others, and search for evidence in the text to support their ideas.

Students acquire these seminar behaviors in at least three ways. First, the students hear the teacher explain before the initial seminar its purposes and the behaviors appropriate to these purposes. Second, the students and teacher evaluate the first few seminars and identify how the seminar process could be improved. Third, when the students realize that the teacher is really not looking for right answers but is encouraging the exchange of their opinions and ideas, they discover the excitement of exploring the important questions raised in serious writing. This excitement contributes to the development of willing readers eager to discuss ideas in a courteous manner.

THE TEACHER

In a Socratic seminar, the teacher plays the dual role of leader and participant. As the seminar leader, the teacher keeps the discussion focused on the text, asks follow-up questions, helps clarify positions when arguments become confused, and involves reluctant students while controlling their more vocal peers.

As a seminar participant, the teacher joins with the students in the examination of the seminar reading; however, the teacher is not permitted to express his or her interpretation of the text. This requires the teacher to know the text sufficiently to recognize the potential of varied interpreta-

---

6 The following descriptions are based on materials provided for workshops by Patricia A. Ciabotti, Coordinator of Coalition of Essential Schools, Broward County Public Schools, Fort Lauderdale, Florida 33301.

tions, to design questions that elicit differing interpretations, to be patient enough to allow the students' understandings to evolve, and to be willing to explore the untraditional insights that adolescent minds may produce.

A key aspect of the teacher's role during the seminar is to avoid any evaluative statements. If students perceive that the teacher is affirming a particular point of view or position, students will be less likely to support conflicting positions and the discussion will come to a grinding halt. This may be the most difficult part for the teacher, who undoubtedly has his or her own opinion.

Obviously, assuming the dual role of seminar leader and participant is easier for the teacher if the opening question is one which truly interests the teacher as well as the students.

THE QUESTIONS

The discussion in a Socratic seminar includes three types of questions: opening, core, and closing. The *opening* question may be asked by the teacher or solicited from students when the class becomes experienced with seminars. Subsequent questions in a Socratic seminar arise from discussion of the opening question. These questions also may be asked by the teacher or by a student in response to the comments of participants. Opening questions should have no right or wrong answers; instead, the questions should require the seminar participants to evaluate, judge, speculate, or apply a definition or principle. The questions may relate to the whole text or to only a selected portion of the text; however, both the initial question and those asked subsequently should lead the seminar participants into a close examination of the text. By following this format, the line of inquiry in a Socratic seminar *evolves* rather than having been predetermined by the teacher. In general, a good opening question is one that inspires at least 20 minutes of discussion without it being necessary for the teacher to formulate new questions to encourage further exchange. *Core* questions are directed at specific issues. The *closing* question attempts to have students relate the text and to their lives.

THE TEXT

The reading examined in a Socratic seminar is from a primary source rather than a summary or a review. It can be a complete work, an excerpt of a work, or even two or three short works. Reading from a primary source ensures that the participants are engaged in discovering the author's ideas rather than deciphering someone else's interpretation.

The main consideration when choosing a seminar reading is its ability to provoke and sustain discussion and inquiry. A stimulating seminar text will raise questions in the minds of the participants. The text also may raise questions which may never be answered satisfactorily. (Is it true that many of life's most important questions may not have absolute answers for all of us?) Successful seminars, therefore, frequently end with the participants leaving the seminar with more questions than they brought to the seminar.

Middle school teachers utilizing Socratic seminars do not necessarily conduct seminars on a scheduled basis; instead they make certain that they are have content that truly lends itself to the seminar format. For example, in language arts the content might be a particular literature selection that "invites" in-depth discussion, or it may be an ethical issue in science or history that requires close examination from several perspectives. It is important that seminar content correlates with requirements of the curriculum and is not simply an "add-on" for purposes of motivation. Ball (as cited in Canady & Rettig, 1995b) states that "the seminar allows me to require independent readings of novels without the 'busy work' of study questions. When the students discuss the novel in seminar and explore the possible interpretations of the work, it is then that I know how thoroughly they have read and prepared." Ball further states that, as a teacher, she has clear objectives in mind because she must maintain the focus on the learning process while appearing to give up control to the students. She reports that her students have grown tremendously by engaging in the seminar process; for example, my students "now know how to disagree with one another respectfully; yet they also know how to develop and to support their own ideas without fear of reprisal" (Canady & Rettig, 1995b, p. 223).

Teachers with experience in conducting Socratic seminars report that although the seminar is a marvelous teaching tool, it is not useful for all topics; therefore, they still must utilize other teaching strategies, such as those suggested in this chapter. Some teachers find that it is difficult to get the majority of students to prepare adequately before a seminar begins; therefore, it is important that seminar teachers build preseminar tasks into their lesson plans to insure adequate preparation before the seminar is conducted.

As with cooperative learning, it is difficult to capture the essence and practice of Paideia seminars through reading. We suggest that training in this exciting teaching strategy is an appropriate part of any staff development effort in preparation for, or during the implementation of, block scheduling.

THE "OTHER" MODELS OF TEACHING

Every form of instruction is in some manner a "model of teaching." Traditionally, our schools have overused the model of teaching we call "lecture/discussion." This model is characterized by a preponderance of "teacher-talk" accompanied by a few questions, for which students are to provide correct answers. "Direct instruction" is another commonly used model of teaching, which Madeline Hunter popularized during the past 15 years. It is primarily used to teach basic skills, knowledge, and facts.

"Cooperative learning," a third model of instruction, which we discussed earlier, has gained many followers in the past 20 years.

Each of these models has its place in the professional teachers' instructional repertoire, as do a host of other "models of teaching" that have received far less exposure. Several of these "other" models of instruction have been described in the work of Bruce Joyce (1992), *Models of Teaching*, and Mary Alice Gunter, Thomas Estes, and Jan Schwab (1990). *Instruction: A Models Approach*. Included in this chapter are the models of "concept development," "concept attainment," "inquiry," and "synectics." A brief description of each of these models follows.[7]

CONCEPT DEVELOPMENT

This model, which was originated by Hilda Taba, teaches students to organize data based on perceived similarities and then to categorize and label the data, producing a conceptual map. Students explore their own thinking and begin to understand how concepts are formed. This model is appropriate for use with teaching objectives related to contrasting, applying, categorizing, and analyzing data.

The first step of concept development is *listing*. In some manner a database of knowledge regarding a particular topic must be created. The teacher may ask students to compose two sentences related to a topic, for example, "democracy." Students then are encouraged to underline the most important words or phrases in their two sentences. Through student participation, each of these words or phrases is listed on chart paper or the chalkboard.

In the second step of concept development, *grouping or categorizing*, students are asked to choose five or six of the words or phrases that seem to be connected in some manner. They are asked to suggest, without labeling, the connection among the items chosen. Again, in our example for democracy, a student might see the relationship between "speech, assembly, religion, and privacy" as having to do with "freedoms." After several examples are shared, students then are asked to group or categorize all data on the list. This task can be accomplished in cooperative learning groups, in pairs, or individually; markers and chart paper or blank overhead transparencies and transparency pens are useful display media.

During the third step, *labeling and defining relationships*, students name their categories and suggest conceptual connections among the different groupings. Lines, arrows, boxes, diagrams, and other visual graphic organizers are useful techniques for depicting such relationships. At this point,

---

7 Sections on concept development, concept attainment, inquiry, and synectics have evolved from our use of Gunter, Estes, and Swabb's 1990 work, *Instruction: A Models Approach*.

it is effective to have several individuals, pairs, or groups present their conceptual maps to the class.

In the fourth step, students are asked to refine their concept map by *re-grouping, reanalyzing relationships, and subsuming categories* if necessary. In this manner they use ideas from the previous student presentations to assist in improving their understanding of the concept. Finally, students are asked to *synthesize and/or summarize* their understanding of the concept, usually through oral presentation or written work.

Concept development is an especially effective strategy when used as an alternative assessment (i.e., pretest) of students' knowledge and understanding as part of the introduction of a unit or to provide closure and synthesis at the end of a unit.

CONCEPT ATTAINMENT

By providing a series of positive and negative examples, a teacher leads students to a definition of a concept and determination of its essential attributes. This model is especially effective during the explanation phase of a lesson when attempting to teach objectives related to comprehension, comparison, discrimination, and recall.

In the first step of concept attainment, the teacher must *choose a concept, carefully define it, and identify the essential attributes of the definition*. For example, a teacher might attempt to bring students to *Webster's* definition of the concept of "research"—"careful, systematic, patient study and investigation in some field of knowledge, undertaken to discover or establish facts or principles" (Guralnik, 1974, p. 1208). With regard to the essential attributes, the teacher might decide that the definition she or he wants the students to arrive at must include the notions of "careful," "systematic," "investigation," "knowledge," and "purpose."

The teacher *creates or selects both positive and negative examples of the concept* as the second step of concept attainment. For example, "George Seifert, the coach of football's San Francisco 49ers, watched many game films to learn the offensive propensities of the Dallas Cowboys prior to Sunday's big game."[8] This example contains all of the essential attributes for the definition of "research." In contrast, "Mary enjoyed reading about the Wild West; it made her yearn to live during that era," while perhaps fulfilling the requirement for "knowledge," does not contain the other necessary attributes of the definition.

The third step of the process involves *introducing the lesson to the students*. The concept to be defined is *not* shared with students. The teacher should explain that positive examples of an idea will be given, as will ex-

---

8 The idea for this lesson came from Kathy Pierce of the Louisa County Public Schools in Mineral, Virginia.

amples which do not meet the requirements of the definition. Students will be trying both to discover the concept and to define it.

Next the *teacher presents the examples*. When the first positive example is presented, all of its attributes are brainstormed by the students and listed on the board by the teacher. For example, with regard to our previous example about "research," other potential attributes of the example were "football," "George Seifert," "games," "films," "Dallas," and so forth. These would have been listed. When a second, and different, positive example is given, the group should eliminate those attributes which are not common to all positive examples. Negative examples are given to emphasize the necessary qualities of the definition, but they cannot be used to eliminate attributes. Through this process the definition is pared down to its essentials.

In the fourth step, students are asked to *compose a definition* for the concept by using the remaining "essential attributes." Finally, *the definition is tested by using it to evaluate several new positive and negative examples*.

While the process of concept attainment certainly is more circuitous than "Here's the definition; memorize it!," it leads students to a much deeper understanding of concepts. In addition, the process by which the definition was developed offers numerous memory cues that will assist students in retaining their new knowledge.

INQUIRY

Given a puzzling situation, students follow a scientific process to formulate hypotheses. This problem-solving model emphasizes careful and logical procedures, the tentative nature of knowledge, and the need for group cooperation in solving problems. Learners are encouraged to seek multiple answers. The inquiry model can be utilized to meet objectives related to problem solving, analyzing, hypothesizing, and evaluating.

Inquiry requires that the teacher possess thorough knowledge of the chosen topic. Thus, the first step of this process is for the teacher to *select and research the problem*. A puzzling situation or event which is related to the content of the subject often is intrinsically motivating for students to discover the answer. For example, the following situation has been presented to classes: Two men go into a bar and order drinks. An hour later, one of them dies. What was the cause of death? The goal of the lesson is for students to discover the cause of death through a systematic process of inquiry. The second step involves a careful *introduction of the process to the students*. Students are presented with the puzzling situation and given a means for recording data (chart paper, etc.).

Students gather relevant data during the third step of the process. The teacher is the "fount of all wisdom"; students are encouraged to pose clearly articulated "yes/no" questions. No student discussion during the questioning is permitted. Occasionally, groups are permitted to "caucus" to discuss their ideas. The teacher records relevant data on chart paper, overhead transparencies, or the chalkboard. For example, given the puzzling situation described above, a student might ask any of these questions:

- "Was the dead man shot by the other man?" Answer: No.
- "Did the dead man die of natural causes?" Answer: No.
- "Do the drinks have something to do with the death?" Answer: Yes.
- "Was the dead man poisoned?" Answer: Yes.
- "Did the men have the same drink?" Answer: Yes.

In the fourth step of the model, when students begin to think that they have the answer to the puzzling situation, they are encouraged to *develop a theory and describe causal relationships*. This explanation is written on the board and evaluated by the class. If it is rejected, alternate theories can be posed. During the fifth step, when a theory is accepted by the class, *the theory's rules and effects are detailed and tested*. Students' questions of the teacher continue to be the primary means of verifying theories and their rules during steps four and five. Finally, the class and the teacher *discuss the process and possible improvements*.

Inquiry is useful for exploring the mysteries of literature and social studies, as well as science. It can be used in any phase of the three-part lesson design: during explanation as a means of developing an anticipatory set, and during application or synthesis to test students' understanding of principles taught and, hopefully, learned.

SYNECTICS

This model stimulates creative thought and problem solving through the development of metaphorical analogies. Just as the outsider can sometimes "see" more clearly than the insider who is blinded by his or her closeness to a problem or situation, these analogies distance students from the commonplace reality of a topic, encouraging creative thinking and new insights. The synectics model is particularly effective for the creative exploration of topics, for problem solving, and as a prewriting activity.

In step one of the synectics model, students are asked to describe the topic, either orally or through writing. Much as in the first step of concept development, the most important words and phrases generated are listed by the teacher. For example, in using this model with a group during a workshop, the topic was "computer technology." Each participant was asked to write a short paragraph on the topic, and then to underline the most important words and phrases, which were shared with the entire group on chart paper (Figure 9.2).

FIGURE 9.2. STEP 1: DESCRIBE THE TOPIC

*What are the most important words and phrases
in your short paragraph about technology?*

efficiency	programming	necessity	time-saving
education	knowledge	dependent	user-friendly
specialist	money-saving	analysis	everyday life
helpless	facilitates	outdated	life-saving
frightening	problems	reliability	

In the second step students are asked to read over the list and to propose items from a general category—such as plants, machines, places, appliances, and automobiles—that capture the essence of the list. In the example described, using the list generated from the topic of computer technology (Figure 9.2), the group was asked to propose "vehicles" that came to mind. This yielded another list (Figure 9.3). (One student suggested a "rollercoaster" because computer technology was "frightening—it makes me feel helpless and dependent.")

FIGURE 9.3. STEP 2: CREATE DIRECT ANALOGIES

What vehicle does the list in Step 1 bring to mind? Why?

cruise ship	sports car	bike	roller coaster
jet	train	monorail	UFO
motorcycle	monorail	skateboard	bobsled/luge
rollerblades	go-cart	unicycle	elevator

A vote was held to select the vehicle that the group thought most nearly captured the sense of the words generated in Step 1; "jet" was chosen. Participants then were asked to close their eyes and imagine how it would feel to be a jet. A list of these "feelings" was created (Figure 9.4).

FIGURE 9.4. STEP 3: CREATE PERSONAL ANALOGIES

How does it feel to be a...? (Jet)			
power	sense of unknown	cold	organized
weighted down	marvel	amazement	dependent on pilot
strong	invincible	inflexible	fast
protected	rusty	exhausted	intelligent
blinded	anticipating	shaky	superior
helpless	secure	ready to land	

The next step was to identify words from among these feelings that constituted a pair of opposites; these pairs, called "compressed conflicts," formed another list (Figure 9.5). Again, the group voted, this time to select the most representative word pair; they chose *"invincible-helpless."*

FIGURE 9.5. STEP 4: IDENTIFY COMPRESSED CONFLICTS

What pairs of feelings seem to be in opposition to each other?		
strong-rusty	strong-helpless	invincible-rusty
secure-helpless	superior-shaky	power-exhausted
invincible-helpless	invincible-blinded	unknown-secure
inflexible-organized	rusty-protected	cold-protected
blind-intelligent	strong-exhausted	

Next, the group reflected on the compressed conflict "invincible-helpless," naming any creatures this brought to mind. From the list generated (Figure 9.6), a final vote was taken and *human* was chosen as the creature that came closest to capturing the conflicts expressed by this pair.

FIGURE 9.6. STEP 5: CREATE NEW ANALOGIES

What creature comes to mind when you think of the compressed conflict invincible-helpless?			
whale	bald eagle	elephant	dinosaur
cow	piranha	*human*	spore
yellow jacket	woman	man	jellyfish
tick			

Finally, in the sixth step of the process students were asked to re-describe the original topic of computer technology by orally stating how computer technology and being "human" were similar. Each person was asked to write a second paragraph using either "human" or another crea-ture from the list in Figure 9.6 as a basis for a discussion of the topic. In-sights into the nature of computer technology were far more sophisticated and moving than the original paragraphs used to begin the lesson.

Synectics is a creative means for examining and reexamining topics. It probably is most useful in social studies and English, although occasion-ally it may be used with science, math, and health to explore the ethical and affective aspects of these subjects. Several other models of teaching are illustrated in detail in Chapter 4 of Canady and Rettig (1996).

SIMULATIONS[9]

Simulations are structured activities that attempt to create the appear-ance or effect of a real environment or situation. The intent is to have stu-dents experience a process or event in a manner closely resembling reality, but without the dangers and risks. These activities often have been uti-lized in social studies and science classrooms to simulate economic, politi-cal, and environmental situations. Middle school students particularly re-spond enthusiastically to this form of instruction. The use of computer simulations has grown dramatically in recent years. Advantages[10] of sim-ulations include:

- Participants receive an experience similar to that in the real world.
- Participants have opportunities to solve complex problems and to observe others solving problems.
- Simulations provide greater possibilities for transfer to real life situations.
- Simulations provide a responsive environment with immedi-ate feedback.
- Simulations foster an understanding of events of extended du-ration in compressed time.
- Simulations are psychologically engaging and motivating.
- Simulations are safe.

Issues that must be addressed regarding simulations include:

---

9 For a more detailed description, see Canady and Rettig, 1996, Chapter 5.
10 Advantages, issues, and steps are based on Cruickshank (1980).

- Many faculty are unfamiliar with simulations and require training.
- Simulations require extended blocks of time; they fit nicely in block schedules.
- Simulations tend to be less available than other teaching materials; few teachers know they exist.
- Simulations can be expensive.
- Because they require active and vocal participation, simulations can be noisy.
- Just as with any other instructional strategy, simulations can be applied only to certain teaching objectives.

Cruickshank's (1980) research in the field of educational games and simulations suggests these six steps for their use:

1. Prepare thoroughly. Choose a simulation that closely matches the instructional objectives and takes into account students' previous experience with both the content and process of the simulation.

2. Plan an introduction that motivates students' participation and includes a careful outline of the rules of play. Do not attempt to cover every detail of the game; get started as soon as possible.

3. Carefully assign students' roles. How will high-status roles be assigned for this simulation and for other games over time?

4. If teams are utilized, make sure they are heterogeneous.

5. Remove yourself from control of the simulation as much as possible. Facilitate and advise; avoid directing the action.

6. When the simulation is completed, encourage students to reflect on the process, its relationship to the objectives of the lesson, and improvements that could be made.

We believe that simulations can be stimulating activities that are utilized most appropriately during the application stage of lessons. Because of the length of time required to engage in such activities, they are a natural addition to the repertoire of instructional strategies for teachers (especially social studies and science teachers) operating in block schedules.

TECHNOLOGY

A lengthy discussion of the potential for the use of technology in instruction is beyond the scope of this book. Longer blocks of time, however, offer a number of possibilities for greater use of computer labs and, perhaps more importantly, offer innumerable opportunities for the integration of technology with classroom instructional models. For specific suggestions for involving technology in instruction designed for the block, see Chapter 7 of Canady and Rettig (1996).

LEARNING CENTERS OR STATIONS

For decades, learning centers have been a basic part of the elementary teacher's classroom structure. Some middle school teachers include them in their classrooms, but we found very few high school teachers who utilize learning centers on any regular basis. We believe the longer teaching block may offer an opportunity for middle school teachers to consider including centers as one of their many teaching tools.

Learning centers can be designed to provide for varied interests and competencies of students; they can add interest and motivation to a topic; they may provide for student independence, responsibility and individualization; and they can be a way to permit students to *apply* skills and information in a meaningful context.

Materials for middle school learning centers could include some of the following, adapted to the appropriate specific subject:

♦ Various media such as newspapers, audio- and videotapes, magazines, selected library books, and/or computer software;

♦ task cards;

♦ Activity packets;

♦ Case studies to analyze;

♦ Equipment, such as a microscope in science or jump ropes at a particular physical education station;

♦ Tools, ingredients, or materials required to complete a particular task in a home economics or electronics classroom;

♦ Paints, tools, and possibly directions for completing a particular art or crafts project;

♦ Devices for measuring or completing various tasks in a geometry class;

♦ Short science experiments at stations; and

♦ Listening centers in a language class.

If teachers have prepared students to utilize various types of cooperative learning strategies, tasks requiring cooperative learning work groups can be included in various centers. Several of the cooperative learning "starters" suggested previously may be useful as center activities for students during the application phase of a lesson.

If centers are to work successfully, teachers must organize and implement them cautiously, realizing that it is easy for a classroom to get out of control. In fact, learning centers may not be appropriate for some teachers and some classrooms. Before beginning work in the centers, discuss the rules and procedures that must be followed; and have this information posted at each center. As part of the organizational structure for a classroom with centers/stations, it is helpful to have a display area in each classroom, or possibly in the hallway outside the classroom, to show work accomplished.

For more information on learning centers see Canady and Rettig (1996), Chapter 6.

IMPROVING LECTURES

In various forms, the lecture historically has been the most widely used teaching model in high school classrooms throughout the country. Although in recent years the lecture has come under attack, we believe that the lecture, well done and under appropriate circumstances, can be effective and should be utilized. Cashin (1985) defines lecture as "teaching by the spoken word with emphasis on one-way communication; the teacher talks, and (hopefully) the students listen," (p. 2), and, we might add, hopefully the students learn! In the above definition, we accept that in many lectures some two-way communication may occur, usually in a question and answer format, with the teacher asking most of the questions and the students trying to feed back the responses they think the teacher wants.

Because "lecture success" is so dependent on the person presenting the lecture, the following material, based on Henry Ellington's paper "Some Hints on How to be an Effective Lecturer" (1984, pp. 1–4), focuses on ways to make the lecture model more effective.

- ◆ To plan for a successful lecture, we suggest that the teacher first determine the purpose of the lecture. In some cases, the purpose may be fairly obvious; in other cases, the teacher will need to determine the objectives of the particular lesson. Keep in mind that the lecture is best suited to objectives of the lower cognitive type.
- ◆ Next select the content of the lecture. What is it the teacher expects the students to learn that best fits the lecture mode? Basic structures that can be adapted to the lecture format are these:
    - • Providing a simple list of topics, which, in turn, are examined and discussed;
    - • Showing classification hierarchies that indicate the relationship between the various topics, subgroups, and topics being examined;

- Illustrating chained structures, in which students are led through the various stages of an argument, proof, or derivation in a logical sequence;
- Examining inductive structures, which begin by looking at specific cases or examples of an "as-yet-unstated" general principle or rule and then use selected processes to arrive at the principle or rule by a process of induction;
- Focusing on problem-centered structures, which begin with a statement of the problem, then a presentation of various possible approaches, and finally a possible solution, which may be determined by involving the students in discussion;
- Examining comparative structures, in which two or more points of view are compared under a series of headings;
- Illustrating a variation of information and the relationship of the information by using a matrix structure;
- Explaining linked structures to help students see linked patterns, concepts or topics, moving from one to another along lines of association or logical relation; and
- Illustrating networks to show how concepts and subsystems are interrelated.

Most lectures also will be enhanced if the teacher includes some form of visual aid such as transparencies, printed handouts, or graphic organizers, visual charts, and diagrams to help students understand the relationship of various components in a selected body of information.

Visuals are most critical when the primary purpose of the lecture is to assist students in "untangling" complicated concepts or ideas. For example, an empty diagram or flow chart is a useful graphic organizer as a history teacher explains the branches of government and how each branch is related or the sequence of events through which a bill becomes a law in the United States. A science teacher could use the lecture model with visual organizers during the explanation phase of the lesson, to demonstrate a particular genetic pattern that students will examine under a microscope later, during the application phase of the lesson.

Like visual aids, selected periods of structured talk and/or review at appropriate intervals enhance the lecture model. We developed the review activity shown in Figure 9.7, which we call "the 5-minute pause that refreshes the memory." If teachers follow these steps on a regular basis when lecturing, students will be more attentive, take better notes, and be more alert throughout the lecture; they will not need to ask the teacher as many questions, and they are likely to retain the information for a longer period of time.

**FIGURE 9.7. THE 5-MINUTE PAUSE THAT REFRESHES
THE MEMORY (AND INCREASES THE ODDS FOR RETENTION!)**

Following a brief* lecture or part of a lecture:

1. Have students review the notes from the presentation independently.

2. Have students meet in pairs or in groups of four or five:
   - To review their notes;
   - To identify/highlight the critical points made during the presentation; and
   - To discuss and clarify any misunderstandings (students may ask the teacher for clarification, but only if members of the pair and/or group disagree or can not answer).

3. Have students in teams accomplish one or more of the following:
   - Complete a Pluses, Minuses, and Interesting Points (PMI) chart regarding the content; and/or
   - Similarly, note one point they agree with, one point they disagree with, and one point that they find interesting or unusual; and/or
   - Similarly, list comments that support, refute, clarify, or question the material; and/or
   - Formulate two good test questions regarding the content.

When students come to expect this pattern on a regular basis, they will take better notes and the entire process can occur in about 5 minutes. It may be advantageous to repeat "the 5-minute pause that refreshes the memory" two or three times during a block.

> * We define brief as somewhere between 15 and 30 minutes, depending on the age and maturity of the students and the complexity of the content being presented.

One way to enhance the 5-minute pause strategy is for the teacher to determine the desired student outcome for the particular lesson *before* the lesson is presented. Most student outcomes belong to one of the following three categories: (a) I expect students to be able to recall some specific information or material as a result of being engaged in this lesson; or (b) I expect the students to interact with the content, lecture or material in some way; or (c) I expect the students to be able to analyze, synthesize, and create new material based on what has been studied (during this day's lesson and possibly from the content of the entire unit of study as well).

If the goal for the lesson is simply to have students recall information, then it is very important that during Step 3 of the 5-minute pause, clarification of any misunderstandings occurs, critical elements of the lesson are emphasized, and correct notes are recorded. Sometimes reteaching occurs and new explanations are offered following the pause session.

If the outcome of the lesson is for students to react and/or interact with the lecture or materials being presented, then the elements of Step 3 are different. Students would be asked, for example, to state: What do you agree with? What do you disagree with? What did you find interesting? The task is not to regurgitate the information, but instead respond to the material in some way. The students might be given a Venn diagram and asked to illustrate graphically the common factors or attributes of two different selections of literature or two different periods of history, as well as to list major differences. Another visual for the outcome would be for the teacher to create a chart on which students are asked to list major points made in today's lesson; state points of agreement, disagreements and/or "not sure"; and formulate any conclusions or summary statements reached at this stage of the lesson.

If students are expected to synthesize from various sources and to create new information, they will need more time and possibly greater direction from the teacher. An example might be a social studies lecture on the aging population in the United States, with an emphasis on how changing demographics are not only affecting social issues in the country, such as social security and health care, but also offering new career choices for today's students. A synthesis task might be to have students work in pairs or small groups to identify at least five possible career choices they may want to prepare for, considering our changing population and increasing life expectancy, and state reasons for their choices. Students might come up with numerous jobs in the field of health services. They may also note how needs for medical specialties have changed and how financial planning and estate planning have become more important.

DESIGNING A STAFF DEVELOPMENT PLAN

If a school or school district can provide only 5 days of staff development for the purpose of developing alternative instructional strategies for teachers who will be working in one of the block schedules described in this book, we suggest the following curriculum for those 5 days:

DAY ONE

If possible, we recommend that teachers receive training by peers who already have demonstrated subject-area excellence in a block-scheduled instructional situation. Our observation has been, that while teachers may benefit greatly from training in generic nonsubject-specific instructional strategies, what they really want, and find credible, is to work with someone who is succeeding in the trenches in *their subject*. Thus, we suggest that the person in charge of planning staff development amass a group of teachers from different disciplines, preferably from different schools, to create such a program.

DAYS TWO AND THREE

After time spent with subject specialists, we recommend 2 days of training to provide an introduction to the process of creating a collaborative classroom and strategies, such as those suggested by Kagan (1990) and Strebe (1996). We strongly suggest that during these 2 days, teachers *not* be engaged in complicated cooperative learning strategies, such as STAD (Slavin, 1990); early in the training, highly detailed strategies will turn teachers off. We suggest that teachers understand and practice such strategies as Listen/Think/Pair/Share, and then add Make Notes/Check Notes. Other strategies might include Pairs Check, Paired Questioning, Inside-Outside Circles, and pairing students to complete visual organizers. To help teachers make their lectures more interactive, we suggest that all teachers include in their repertoire of skills strategies such as Numbered Heads Together, Team Huddle, Roundtable, Recall Y'all, Send a Problem, and Value Lines (Kagan, 1990; Lanzoni, 1997).

DAYS FOUR AND FIVE

We believe that many teachers also would benefit from 2 days of training in the Paideia or Socratic approach to seminars. In lieu of the Paideia seminar training, math teachers might benefit from 2 days examining appropriate computer software.

DAYS SIX TO TEN

If staff development preparation efforts can be extended to 10 days, we suggest adding a second day with subject-specific facilitators; teachers could create pacing guides and design units and individual lessons. Two days of training in several of the models of teaching, such as concept development, synectics, and inquiry, also would be beneficial. Because of the many possibilities created through block scheduling, we suggest 2 days of instruction regarding the design of interdisciplinary units. If time permits, we suggest that a day be spent examining and trying various visual organizers (Hyerle, 1996).

We also believe that follow-up training is crucial for success, especially during the first several years. Regular team meetings and occasional department meetings should be devoted to sharing instructional strategies that work and to discussing common problems. Follow-up in-service in a variety of areas is also important. As new faculty are added, they too should receive training.

CONCLUSION

We believe that the success or failure of the block scheduling movement is determined largely by the ability of teachers and administrators to work together to improve instruction. Regardless of a school's time schedule, what happens between individual teachers and students in classrooms is still most important, and *simply altering the manner in which we schedule schools will not ensure better instruction by teachers or increased learning by students.* We strongly believe, however, that a well-designed school schedule *can be* a catalyst for instructional changes in middle schools across America. Educators must not ignore the window of opportunity that has been opened through the hope, energy, and enthusiasm of teachers, administrators, parents, and students. We must support their efforts with intelligence, patience, and resources.

REFERENCES

Adler, M. (1982). *The Paideia Proposal.* New York: MacMillan.

Alexander, W. M. (1987). Toward schools in the middle: Progress and problems. *Journal of Curriculum and Supervision, 2*(4), 314–329.

Alexander, W. M. & George, P. S. (1981). *The Exemplary Middle School.* New York: Holt, Rinehart & Winston.

Allen, H. A., Splittgerber, F. L. & Manning, M. L. (1993). *Teaching and Learning in the Middle School.* New York: Macmillan.

Alspaugh, J. W. (1998). Achievement loss associated with transition to middle school and high school. *Journal of Educational Research, 92*(1), 20–25.

Angola High School (1997). *Statistical Report.* Angola, IN: Author. 219-665-2186.

Ball, W. H., & Brewer, P. F. (2000). *Using Socratic Seminars in a Block Schedule.* Larchmont, NY: Eye On Education.

Ball, W. H., & Brewer, P. F. (1996). Socratic seminars (Chapter 2) in Canady, R. L., & Rettig, M. D. (Eds.) (1996). *Teaching in the Block: Strategies for Engaging Active Learners.* Larchmont, NY: Eye On Education.

Beane, J. A. (1999). Middle schools under siege: Responding to the attack. *Middle School Journal, 30*(5), 3–6.

Blaz, D. (1998). *Teaching Foreign Languages in the Block.* Larchmont, NY: Eye On Education.

Bloom, B. S. (Ed.) (1956). *Taxonomy of Educational Objectives: Handbook I: Cognitive Domain.* New York: David McCay Co.

Braddock, H. J. II (1990). Tracking the middle grades: National patterns for grouping of instruction. *Phi Delta Kappan, 71*(6), 445–449.

Bradley, A. (1998, April 15). Muddle in the middle. *Education Week, 17*(31), 38–42.

Brandenburg, A. C. (1995). *An Analysis of Block Scheduling Models and Their Impact on a Positive School Climate.* Unpublished doctoral dissertation, Pepperdine University, Malibu, CA.

Bryant, R. H. (1995). *A Comparative Study of Teaching Strategies Used in Block and Traditionally Scheduled High Schools in the State of Wyoming.* Unpublished doctoral dissertation, University of Wyoming, Laramie.

Canady, R. L. (1988). A cure for fragmented schedules in elementary schools. *Educational Leadership, 46*(2), 65–67.

Canady, R. L. (1990). Parallel block scheduling: A better way to organize a school. *Principal, 69*(3), 34–36.

Canady, R. L., & Fogliani, E. (1989). Cut class size in half without hiring more teachers. *The Executive Educator, 11*(8), 22–23.

Canady, R. L., & Hotchkiss, P. R. (1984). School improvement without additional cost. *Phi Delta Kappan, 66*(3), 183–184.

Canady, R. L., & Hotchkiss, P.R.. (1989, September). It's a good score! Just a bad grade. *Phi Delta Kappan,* 68–71.

Canady, R. L., & Reina, J. M. (1993). Parallel block scheduling: An alternative structure. *Principal, 72*(3), 26–29.

Canady, R. L., & Rettig, M. D. (1992). Restructuring middle school schedules. *Schools in the Middle, 1*(4), 20–26.

Canady, R. L., & Rettig, M. D. (1995a, November). The power of innovative scheduling. *Educational Leadership,* 4–10.

Canady, R. L., & Rettig, M. D. (1995b). *Block Scheduling, A Catalyst for Change in High Schools.* Larchmont, NY: Eye On Education.

Canady, R. L., & Rettig, M. D. (Eds.) (1996). *Teaching in the Block: Strategies for Engaging Active Learners.* Larchmont, NY: Eye On Education.

Carnegie Council on Adolescent Development. (1989, 1990). *Turning Points: Preparing American Youth for the 21st Century* (Publication of the Task Force On Education of Young Adolescents). New York: Carnegie Corporation of New York.

Carnegie Council on Adolescent Development. (March, 1996). *Great Transitions: Preparing Adolescents for a New Century.* New York: Carnegie Corporation of New York.

Carroll, J. M. (1994a). *The Copernican Plan Evaluated: The Evolution of a Revolution.* Topsfield, MA: Copernican Associates.

Carroll, J. M. (1994b, October) The Copernican plan evaluated. *Phi Delta Kappan,* 105–113.

Carter, T. L. (1995). Continuous improvement at Skyview Junior High. *Teaching and Change, 2*(3), 245–262.

Cashin, W. E. (1985). *Improving Lectures.* (Idea paper No. 14). Manhattan, KS: Kansas State University. (ERIC Document Reproduction Service No. ED 267 721)

Cawelti, G. (1997). *Effects of High School Restructuring: Ten Schools at Work.* Arlington, VA: Educational Research Service.

Cohen, P. (1995, Winter). Changing history: The past remains a battleground for schools. *Curriculum Update.* (Association for Supervision and Curriculum Development: Alexandria, VA)

Conner, S. R. (1997). *The Influences of Block Scheduling in Secondary Agriculture Science Programs in East Texas.* Unpublished doctoral dissertation, Stephen F. Austin University, Stevensville, TX.

Conti-D'Antonio, M., Bertrando, R., & Eisenberger, J. (1998). *Supporting Students with Learning Needs in the Block.* Larchmont, NY: Eye On Education.

Craig, J. S. (1995). Quality through site-based scheduling. *Middle School Journal, 27*(2), 17–22.

Cruickshank, D. R. (1980, Winter). Classroom games and simulations. *Theory into Practice,* 75–80.

Cunningham, D. J. (1997). *Implementation of an Alternate-Day Block Schedule: A Case Study.* Unpublished doctoral dissertation, Virginia Polytechnic Institute and State University, Blacksburg, VA.

Davis, J. E., Ross, J., Ducharme, D. J., & French, W. (1977). *The Impact of Semestering on Selected Secondary Schools in Ontario. Semestering in Secondary Schools.* Toronto, Canada: Ontario Ministry of Education.

Doda, N. M., & George, P. S. (1999). Building whole school communities: Closing the gap between exploratory and core. *Middle School Journal, 30*(5), 32–39.

Dossey, John A. (1989). Transforming mathematics education. *Educational Leadership, 47*(3), 22–24.

Eineder, D. (1996). *The Effects of Block Scheduling in a High School.* Unpublished doctoral dissertation, Appalachian State University, Boone, NC. (704-262-2214)

Eisner, E. W. (1988). Ecology of school improvement. *Educational Leadership, 45*(5), 24–29.

Ellington, H. (1984). *Some Hints on How to Be an Effective Lecturer.* Aberdeen, Scotland: Scottish Central Institutions Committee for Educational Development. (ERIC Document Reproduction Service No. ED 289 489)

Epsein, J., & MacIvor, D. (1996). *Education in the Middle Grades: National Trends and Practices,* Columbus, OH: National Middle School Association.

Felner, R. D., Jackson, A. W., Kasak, D., Mulhall, P., Brand, S., & Flowers, N. (1997). The impact of school reform for the middle years. *Phi Delta Kappan, 78*(7), 528–532, 541–550.

Fleck, L. M. (1996). *Block Scheduling: A Descriptive Study of its Effect on Student Distress.* Unpublished doctoral dissertation, Memphis State University, Memphis, TN.

Fogliani, E. (1990). *A Case Study of Parallel Block Scheduling: An Instructional Management Strategy.* Unpublished dissertation, University of Virginia, Charlottesville, VA.

Freeman, C. J. (1996). *Block Scheduling: A Vehicle for School Change.* Unpublished doctoral dissertation. University of Minnesota, Minneapolis, MN.

Gallagher, J. (1999, February). Teaching in the block. *Middle Ground: The Magazine of Middle Level Education,* 10–15.

George, P. S., & Alexander, W. M. (1993). *The Exemplary Middle School* (2nd ed.). Fort Worth, TX: Harcourt Brace Jovanovich College Publishers.

George, P. S., Stevenson, C., Thomason, J., & Beane, J. (1992). *The Middle School—and Beyond.* Alexandria, VA: Association for Curriculum Development and Supervision.

Gilkey, S. N., & Hunt, C. H. (1998). *Teaching Mathematics in the Block.* Larchmont, NY: Eye On Education.

Gunter, M. A., Estes, T., & Schwab J. (1990). *Instruction: A Models Approach.* Boston: Allyn and Bacon.

Guralnik, D. B. (Ed.) (1974). *Webster's New World Dictionary of the American Language.* Cleveland & New York: William Collins & World Publishing Co. Inc.

Guskey, T., & Kifer, E. (1994). *Program Evaluation: Block Scheduling at Governor Thomas Johnson High School, Second Year Report.* College of Education, University of Kentucky, Lexington. Unpublished manuscript.

Haberman, M. (1992). The pedagogy of poverty versus good teaching. *Phi Delta Kappan, 73*(4), 290–294.

Hopkins, H. J., & Canady, R. L. (1997, March). Integrating the curriculum with parallel block scheduling. *Principal,* 28–31.

Hotchkiss, P. R. (1996). Chart included in Chapter 1 of Canady, R. L., & Rettig, M. D. (Eds.) (1996). *Teaching in the Block: Strategies for Emerging Active Learners.* Larchmont, NY: Eye On Education.

Hundley, W. W. (1996). *A Comparative Study of Classroom Environments in Traditional and Block Scheduled Classes.* Ph.D. dissertation, Seattle Pacific University, Seattle.

Hunter, M. C. (1976). *Improved Instruction.* El Sequndo, CA: TIP Publications.

Hunter, M. C. (1982). *Mastery Teaching.* El Sequndo, CA: TIP Publications.

Hyerle, D. (1996). *Visual Tools for Constructing Knowledge.* Alexandria, VA: Association for Supervision and Curriculum Development.

Irvine, T. H. (1995). *An Evaluation of Flexible Scheduling in an Urban High School.* Unpublished doctoral dissertation, Northern Arizona University, Flagstaff, AZ.

Johnson, D. W., & Johnson, R. T. (1987). *Learning Together and Alone: Cooperative, Competitive, and Individualistic* (2nd ed.). Englewood Cliffs, NJ: Prentice-Hall.

Johnson, D. W., Johnson, R. T., & Holubec, E. J. (1990). *Circles of Learning: Cooperation in the Classroom* (3rd ed.). Edina, MN: Interaction Book.

Jones, B. (1997). *A Status Report of Block Scheduling in Nine High Schools.* Office of High School Instruction and K–12 Curriculum Service, Fairfax County Public Schools, 7423 Camp Alger Avenue, Falls Church, VA. 22077.

Joyce, B. (1992). *Models of Teaching.* Boston: Allyn and Bacon.

Kagan, S. (1990). *Cooperative Learning: Resources for Teachers.* San Juan Capistrano, CA: Resources for Teachers.

King, A. J. C., Clements, J. L., Enns, J. G., Lockerbie, J. W., & Warren, W. K. (1975). *Semesterizing the Secondary School.* Toronto, Ontario: Ontario Institute for Studies in Education.

King, B. B. (1996). *The Effects of Block Scheduling on Learning Environment, Instructional Strategies, and Academic Achievement.* Unpublished doctoral dissertation, University of Central Florida, Orlando, FL.

Klein, K. (1985). Practical applications of research: The research on class size. *Phi Delta Kappan, 66*(8), 578–580.

Knapp, M. S., & Shields, P. M. (1990). Reconceiving academic instruction for children of poverty. *Phi Delta Kappan, 71*(10), 754, 756.

Knapp, M. S., Turnbull, B. J., & Shields, P. M. (1990). New directions for educating the children of poverty. *Educational Leadership, 48*(1), 7.

Kohn, A. (1991, February). Group grade grubbing versus cooperative learning. *Educational Leadership,* 83–87.

Kramer, S. L. (1997a, February). What we know about block scheduling and its effects on math instruction, Part I. *NASSP Bulletin,* 18–42.

Kramer, S. L. (1997b, March). What we know about block scheduling and its effects on math instruction, Part II. *NASSP Bulletin,* 69–82.

Kramer, S. L. (1996). Block scheduling and high school mathematics instruction. *The Mathematics Teacher, 89*(9) 758–767.

Lanzoni, M. (1997). *A Middle School Teacher's Guide to Cooperative Learning.* Topsfield, MA: New England League of Middle Schools.

Lawton, E. (1993). *The Effective Middle School Teacher.* Reston, VA: National Association of Secondary School Principals.

Lehr, J. B., & Martin, C. (1994). *Schools Without Fear: Group Activities for Building Community.* Minneapolis, MN: Resources for Teachers, Inc.

Lipsitz, J. (1984). *Successful Schools for Young Adolescents.* New Brunswick, NJ: Transaction Books.

Marsh, D. D. (Ed.) (1999). *ASCD 1999 Year Book: Preparing Our Schools for the 21st Century.* Alexandria, VA: Association for Supervision and Curriculum Development.

Mayes, L. M. (1997). *Relationship of Instructional Changes in High Schools with Intensive Scheduling Models.* Unpublished doctoral dissertation, Widener University, Chester, PA.

McEwin, C. K., Dickinson, T. S., & Jenkins, D. M. (1996). *America's Middle Schools: Practices and Progress—A 25 Year Prospective.* Columbus, OH: National Middle School Association.

Mistretta, G. M., & Polansky, H. B. (1997, December). Prisoners of time: Implementing a block schedule in the high school. *NASSP Bulletin,* 23–31.

National Center for Educational Statistics (1995). *Digest of Education Statistics.* Washington, DC: U.S. Government Printing Office.

National Council of Teachers of Mathematics (1989). *Curriculum and Evaluation Standards for School Mathematics.* VA: Author.

National Education Association (1966). *Innovations for Time to Teach: Time to Teach Project.* Washington, DC: Author.

National Middle School Association (1995). *This We Believe.* Columbus, OH: Author.

National Middle School Association (1997). *A 21st Century Research Agenda. Issues, Topics & Questions Guiding Inquiry into Middle Level Theory & Practice.* Columbus, OH: Author.

North Carolina Department of Public Instruction (1998). *Block Scheduling in North Carolina: Critical Issues* (research report). Raleigh, NC: North Carolina Department of Public Instruction.

Oakes, J. (1985). *Keeping Track: How Schools Structure Inequality.* New Haven, CT: Yale University Press.

Oakes, J. (1986). Keeping track, part 1: The policy and practice of curriculum inequality. *Phi Delta Kappan, 68*(1), 16.

O'Neil, J. (1995). Finding time. *Educational Leadership, 53*(3), 11–15.

Phelps, C. R. (1996). *An Examination of 8-Block Scheduling: A Case Study of Three Selected Illinois Schools.* Unpublished doctoral dissertation, Southern Illinois University, Carbondale, IL.

Pisapia, J., & Westfall, A. L. (1996). *Alternative High School Scheduling: Student Achievement and Behavior.* Richmond, VA: Metropolitan Educational Research Consortium (804-828-0478).

Pulaski County High School (1994). *Survey Report: Four-four Block Schedule.* Dublin, VA: Author (540-674-4357).

Quinn, K. M. (1997). *The Effects of Intensified Scheduling on Instructional Methodologies.* Unpublished doctoral dissertation, Immaculata College, PA.

Rafferty, C. D., Leinenbach, M., Helms, L. A. (1999). Leveling the playing field through active engagement. *Middle School Journal, 30*(4), 51–56.

Rettig, M. D., & Canady, R. L. (1998). High failure rates in required mathematics courses: Can a modified block schedule be part of the cure? *NASSP Bulletin,82*(596), 56–55.

Rettig, M. D., & Canady, R. L. (1995, December). When can I have your kids? Scheduling elementary specialists. *Here's How.* Alexandria, VA: National Association of Elementary School Principals.

Sabo, D. J. (1995, Spring). The organizational climate of middle schools and the quality of student life. *Journal of Research and Development in Education, 28,* 150–160.

Salvaterra, M., & Adams, D. (1995). Departing from tradition: Two schools' stories. *Educational Leadership, 53*(3), 32–36.

Scales, P. C. (1999). Increasing service-learning's impact on middle school students. *Middle School Journal, 30*(5), 40–44.

Schoenstein, R. (1995). The new school on the block schedule. *The Executive Educator, 17*(8), 18–21.

Sessoms, J. C. (1995). *Teachers' Perceptions of Three Models of High School Block Scheduling.* Unpublished doctoral dissertation, University of Virginia, Charlottesville (804-694-1412).

Shaverson, R. J. (1983). Review of research on teachers' pedagogical judgements, plans, and decisions. *Elementary School Journal, 83,* 392–414.

Shaw, V. (1992). *Community Building in the Classroom.* San Juan Capistrano, CA: Kagan Cooperative Learning.

Slavin, R. E. (1980). Cooperative learning. *Review of Educational Research, 50,* 315–342.

Slavin, R. E. (1987). Ability grouping and student achievement in elementary school: A best-evidence synthesis. *Review of Educational Research, 57,* 328.

Slavin, R. E. (1988). Cooperative learning and student achievement. *Educational Leadership, 50*(2), 31–33.

Slavin, R. E. (1990). *Cooperative Learning: Theory, Research, and Practice.* Englewood Cliffs, NJ: Prentice-Hall.

Smith, D. G., Pitkin, N., & Rettig, M. D. (1998). Flexing the middle school block schedule by adding non-traditional core subjects and teachers to the interdisciplinary team. *Middle School Journal, 29*(5), 22–27.

Smith, S. G. (1998). *A Multi-case Study of Flexible Block Scheduling in Three Middle Level Schools: Perceptions of Administrators and Counselors.* Unpublished doctoral dissertation, University of Virginia, Charlottesville.

Snyder, D. (1997, October). *4-Block Scheduling: A Case Study of Data Analysis of One High School after Two Years.* Presented at the annual meeting of the Midwest Educational Research Association, Chicago, IL.

Southern Regional Education Board (March, 1998). *Education's Weak Link: Student Performance in the Middle Grades.* Atlanta: Author.

Staunton, J. T. (1997a). *A Study of Teacher Beliefs on the Efficacy of Block Scheduling.* Unpublished doctoral dissertation, University of Southern California, Los Angeles.

Staunton, J. T. (1997b, December). A study of teacher beliefs on the efficacy of block scheduling. *NASSP Bulletin,* 73–80.

Strebe, (1996). The collaborative classroom. In Canady, R. L., & Rettig, M. D. (Eds.) (1996). *Teaching in the Block: Strategies for Engaging Active Learners* (pp. 65–107). Larchmont, NY: Eye On Education.

Strzepek, J. E., Newton, J., & Walker, L. D. (2000). *Teaching English in the Block.* Larchmont, NY: Eye On Education.

Sweet, A. P. (1993, November). *State of the Art: Transforming Ideas for Teaching and Learning to Read.* Washington: U.S. Department of Education, Office of Research, 1–17.

Vawter, D. H. (1998). *Changes Associated with the Implementation of Block Scheduling in American Secondary Schools.* Unpublished doctoral dissertation, University of Virginia, Charlottesville.

Viadero, D. (1996, May 29). Middle school gains over 25 years chronicled. *Education Week,* p. 1.

Virginia Department of Education (1996). *1995-96 Superintendent's Annual Report for Virginia.* Richmond, VA: Author.

Watts, J., & Castle, S. (1993, December). The time dilemma in school re-structuring. *Phi Delta Kappan,75,* 306–310.

Wiles, J., & Bondi, J. (Eds.) (1993). *The Essential Middle School* (2nd ed.). New York: Macmillan.

Wormeli, R. (1999, February). One teacher to another: Block classes change instructional practice—Carpe Diem! *Middle Ground: The Magazine of Middle Level Education,* 17–19.